CONSERVATIVE BAPTIST
THEOLOGICAL SEMINARY

3401 S. University Blvd.
Englewood, Colorado

# A HISTORY OF PSYCHOLOGY

# A HISTORY OF PSYCHOLOGY

BY

OTTO KLEMM

EXTRAORDINARY PROFESSOR OF PHILOSOPHY IN THE UNIVERSITY OF LEIPZIG

AUTHORIZED TRANSLATION WITH ANNOTATIONS

BY

EMIL CARL WILM, Ph.D., LL.D.

PROFESSOR OF PHILOSOPHY IN WELLS COLLEGE AND LECTURER IN PHILOSOPHY AT BRYN MAWR COLLEGE FOR 1914-15

AND

RUDOLF PINTNER, Ph.D.

ASSISTANT PROFESSOR OF PSYCHOLOGY IN THE OHIO STATE UNIVERSITY

CHARLES SCRIBNER'S SONS

NEW YORK    CHICAGO    BOSTON

COPYRIGHT, 1914, BY
CHARLES SCRIBNER'S SONS

# PREFACE FOR THE ENGLISH EDITION

THE following work is a translation of Professor Klemm's *Geschichte der Psychologie*, which constitutes Volume VIII of the now widely known series "Science and Hypothesis." As a searching study of an enormously wide and difficult field the original German work has already won for itself an established place in the recent literature of the subject, and it is confidently believed that the qualities which have given the original work its deserved popularity, the author's equally firm grasp of the most widely separated psychological epochs and tendencies, his admirable attention to both the speculative and the scientific aspects of psychology, and, finally, the relative prominence given to recent and experimental psychology, will at once commend the work to the large number of workers in modern psychology to whom English works of just this type have heretofore not been available.

The work of translation has been about equally divided between the two translators, Chapters I–VI, inclusive, having been executed by myself, and Chapters VII–XII, inclusive, by Doctor Pintner, and each translator is solely responsible for the final form in which his own part of the work appears.

I wish to express my cordial acknowledgments to Professor Münsterberg, to whose friendly suggestion the plan for this translation owed its first inception, and to Professor Titchener for a number of valued suggestions on terminology.

E. C. WILM.

BRYN MAWR COLLEGE,
    BRYN MAWR, PA., October, 1914.

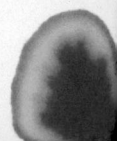

# AUTHOR'S PREFACE FOR THE ENGLISH EDITION

IN the autumn of 1911 I received a letter from Doctor Wilm informing me that at the suggestion of Professor Münsterberg he was maturing plans for an English translation of my *History of Psychology*, and requesting my coöperation. I very gladly granted him permission for such an undertaking, and I have since then had much pleasure, as different parts of the translation have come to me, in seeing how completely he and his excellent collaborator, Doctor Pintner, have overcome one after another the manifold difficulties which such a translation presents.

The present English edition is making its appearance under quite different circumstances from those which prevailed when the original German edition went into print. I make reference in the course of the book to the irregular development of psychology. The history of psychology seems to be undergoing a development of a similar sort. Although the triumphant advance of the experimental method has for some time obscured the connection of modern developments with the earlier epochs of our science, there has recently appeared a whole series of comprehensive works on the history of psychology to which the valuable additions to my own bibliography made by the English editor bear testimony. The history of psychology has thus itself become a problem. With the varied treatment, however, which such a wealth of material permits, one of these works is not likely to crowd out another, but rather to supplement and enhance it. No one, in any case, is more clearly aware than I that my own selection and arrangement of the material are partly determined by the present position of psychology in my own country. I do not, indeed, see how it could be otherwise in the case of a historical presentation which itself extends directly into the present.

May I hope, then, that my little book will also find readers beyond the sea who will follow in it the fortunes of psychology among its sister sciences in western Europe, and that Doctor Wilm will thus find himself repaid for the trouble and care for which I am myself permanently indebted to him!

OTTO KLEMM.

LEIPZIG, June, 1914.

# CONTENTS

## INTRODUCTION

|   | PAGE |
|---|---|
| 1. General Characteristics of the History of Psychology | 1 |
| 2. Plan of the Present Work | 2 |
| 3. Modern and Ancient Elements in Psychology | 6 |
| 4. Literature | 8 |
| Translators' Note on English Literature | 10 |

## PART I

## GENERAL TENDENCIES OF PSYCHOLOGY

### I. METAPHYSICAL PSYCHOLOGY

#### Chapter I. Dualism in Psychology

| 1. Relation of Metaphysical and Empirical Tendencies | 12 |
|---|---|
| 2. Dualistic Psychology | 14 |

#### Chapter II. Monism in Psychology

| 1. Spiritualism | 26 |
|---|---|
| 2. Materialism in Psychology | 32 |
|     (a) Atomistic Materialism | 33 |
|     (b) Mechanistic Materialism | 36 |
|     (c) Psychophysical Materialism | 38 |

## II. EMPIRICAL PSYCHOLOGY

### Chapter III. Descriptive Psychology

1. Period of Pre-Scientific Concepts: The Doctrine of Mental Faculties . . . . . . . . . . . . . . 44
    (a) The Doctrine of the Parts of the Soul . . . . . . . 46
    (b) The Beginnings of Empirical Psychology in Scholasticism 50
    (c) The Psychology of the Renaissance . . . . . . . 56
    (d) The Newer Faculty Psychology . . . . . . . . . . 58
2. The Psychology of the Inner Sense . . . . . . . . 69
    (a) The Older Doctrine of the Inner Sense . . . . . . 72
    (b) The Inner Sense as an Independent Source of Experience 76
    (c) The Relation of Inner Sense to Epistemological Problems 82

### Chapter IV. Explanatory Psychology

1. Association Psychology . . . . . . . . . . . . . 87
    (a) The Early Beginnings of Association Psychology . . . 88
    (b) The Dominance of the Concept of Association . . . . 92
2. Psychology as a Mechanics of Ideas . . . . . . . 103
3. Comparative Psychology . . . . . . . . . . . . 111
    (a) Ethnic Psychology . . . . . . . . . . . . . . 111
    (b) Animal Psychology . . . . . . . . . . . . . . 113
    (c) Influence of Darwinism . . . . . . . . . . . . 115
    (d) Individual Psychology . . . . . . . . . . . . 117
4. Influences of Natural Science . . . . . . . . . 119
    (a) The Newer Phrenology . . . . . . . . . . . . 119
    (b) The Influence of Sense Physiology . . . . . . . . 123
    (c) Experimental Psychology . . . . . . . . . . . 127

# PART II

# DEVELOPMENT OF THE FUNDAMENTAL CONCEPTS OF PSYCHOLOGY

### Chapter V. The Idea of Psychology as a Science

|  | PAGE |
|---|---|
| 1. Older Conceptual Formulations of Psychology | 147 |
| 2. The Problem of a Science of Psychology | 150 |
| 3. The Modern Concept of Psychology | 155 |
|    (a) Psychology and Philosophy: Psychologism and Its Opponents | 156 |
|    (b) Psychology and Natural Science: Differentiation of Physical and Psychical Phenomena | 159 |

### Chapter VI. The Subject-Matter of Psychology: Consciousness

| | |
|---|---|
| 1. The History of the Concept of Consciousness | 166 |
|    (a) Early Developments of the Concept | 166 |
|    (b) Development of the Modern Concept of Consciousness | 169 |
| 2. The Concept of the Unconscious | 172 |
|    (a) Representatives and Opponents of the Notion of the Unconscious | 172 |
|    (b) Arguments for and against the Unconscious | 175 |
| 3. The Range of Consciousness | 181 |
| 4. The Graduation of Consciousness: Attention | 184 |

### Chapter VII. Classification of the Contents of Consciousness

| | |
|---|---|
| 1. Survey of the Most Important Principles of Classification | 191 |
|    (a) The Rise of Psychological Classification | 192 |
|    (b) The Principle of Non-Derivability | 194 |
|    (c) The Principle of Intentional Relationship | 200 |
|    (d) The Principle of Analysis | 202 |

## CONTENTS

| | PAGE |
|---|---|
| 2. Modern Forms of Classification | 205 |
| 3. The Concept of the Psychical Element | 210 |

### Chapter VIII. Psychological Methods

1. Observation and Introspection . . . . . . . . . . . 212
2. Physiology the Basis of Psychology . . . . . . . . 215
3. The Development of the Methods of Psychical Measurement . . . . . . . . . . . . . . . . . 218
    - (a) The Older Forms of the Methods . . . . . . . . 220
    - (b) The Influence of the Theory of Error . . . . . . . 222
    - (c) Connection with the Expression Methods . . . . . 229

### Chapter IX. Psychical Measurement

1. Early History of Psychical Measurement . . . . . 232
    - (a) The Earliest Suggestions of Psychical Measurement . . 233
    - (b) Weber's Law and Its Preliminary History . . . . . 235
2. The Founding of Psychical Measurement by Fechner . 242
3. Discussions Arising out of Fechner's Psychophysics . 245
    - (a) Objections and Attacks . . . . . . . . . . . . 245
    - (b) Fechner's Reply . . . . . . . . . . . . . . . 252
    - (c) Some Philosophical Opponents . . . . . . . . . 254
4. The New Foundation of Psychical Measurement . . 257
    - (a) G. E. Müller's Foundation of Psychophysics . . . . 257
    - (b) The Psychological Interpretation of Weber's Law . . . 262

# CONTENTS

## PART III

## A HISTORY OF THE MOST IMPORTANT PSYCHOLOGICAL THEORIES

### Chapter X. Theories of Sensation

|  | PAGE |
|---|---|
| 1. General Theories of Sensation | 271 |
|    (a) The Older Theories | 273 |
|    (b) The Theory of Specific Energy of the Nerves | 275 |
| 2. Theories of Vision | 279 |
|    (a) Ancient Theories of Light | 279 |
|    (b) Separation of Physical and Physiological Optics | 283 |
|    (c) Modern Color Theories | 287 |
|         (1) The Three-Color Theory | 290 |
|         (2) The Four-Color Theory: Opposition and Development | 292 |
| 3. Theories of Audition | 297 |
|    (a) Preliminary History of the Resonance Theory | 297 |
|    (b) The Theory of Resonance | 299 |
|    (c) Further Development of the Resonance Hypothesis | 304 |
|    (d) Consonance Theories | 308 |

### Chapter XI. Theories of Spatial Perception

| 1. The Natural Scientists of the Middle Ages | 317 |
|---|---|
| 2. Some Special Problems | 322 |
| 3. Nativism | 326 |
|    (a) The Founding of the Theory by Johannes Müller | 326 |
|    (b) Its Transference to the Sense of Touch | 327 |
|    (c) The Later Nativistic Theories | 330 |

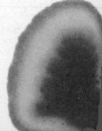

## CONTENTS

|  | PAGE |
|---|---|
| 4. EMPIRICISM | 333 |
|    (a) The Origin of Empirical Theories of Space | 334 |
|    (b) Helmholtz's Theory of Space | 335 |
| 5. THE GENETIC THEORIES | 337 |
|    (a) Herbart's Fusion Theory | 337 |
|    (b) Purely Psychological Theories | 338 |
|    (c) The Local Sign Theories | 340 |
|       (1) Lotze's Theory | 340 |
|       (2) Its Physiological Development | 342 |
|       (3) Its Psychological Development | 343 |

### CHAPTER XII. THEORIES OF FEELING AND VOLITION

| | |
|---|---|
| 1. THEORIES OF FEELING | 346 |
|    (a) Phenomenological Presuppositions | 347 |
|    (b) Intellectualistic Theories of Feeling | 350 |
|    (c) Psychomechanical Theories of Feeling | 352 |
|    (d) Physiological Theories of Feeling | 355 |
|    (e) Psychophysical Theories of Feeling | 358 |
| 2. THEORIES OF VOLITION | 359 |
|    (a) Intellectualistic Theories of Volition | 361 |
|       (1) The Ancient Concept of Freedom | 361 |
|       (2) The Primacy of Will or Intellect | 362 |
|       (3) The Classical Period of the Problem of the Freedom of the Will | 364 |
|    (b) The Absolute Theory of the Will | 366 |
|    (c) Heterogenetic Theories of the Will | 368 |
|    (d) The Emotional Theory of the Will | 370 |
| INDEX OF NAMES | 373 |
| INDEX OF SUBJECTS | 379 |

# A HISTORY OF PSYCHOLOGY

# A HISTORY OF PSYCHOLOGY

## INTRODUCTION

### 1. General Characteristics of the History of Psychology

A contemporary psychologist has said that psychology has had a long past but a brief history. Scattered reflections on psychological questions indeed abound throughout the entire history of science, but the continuity of psychological investigation has often been interrupted, while a really fruitful development of psychology belongs to very recent times.

With this the extreme complexity of mental processes, a complexity which seems only to increase the more intimately we come to know them, has had no little to do. There is something in the very nature of mental processes, even in their simpler forms, which resists the attempt to subject them to scientific treatment. In the first place, they do not constitute a special group of facts which can be unambiguously distinguished from other groups of facts, and which perhaps have to be discovered. They are constantly with us; indeed, every fact is in part, or on one of its sides, a mental fact. Moreover, the facts of consciousness are not data which are discovered like a rare mineral or which can be observed like an unfamiliar phenomenon in nature. Long before these facts are subjected to scientific analysis they have been subjected to innumerable influences of social life. Language, for example, to mention only the most important of these influences, has already appropriated them, has described them, and has interpreted them according to the needs of practical life. There is a further peculiarity of the material of psychology which makes the scientific investigation of it especially difficult. In all scientific investigation a certain emotional detachment would seem to be absolutely necessary for the success of the scientific enterprise. But in psychology the feelings and emotions become themselves objects of investigation, and the most central questions of psychology are intimately related to the important interests of our common life. It is true that even in the physical sciences the methods of investigation have only gradually been freed from the subjective interference of feeling. It is told of no less an observer than Galileo that he was so irritated by the inexplicable changes in the form of Saturn, due to the position of its rings, which were at the time still unknown to him, that he refused to observe this planet at all. How much more difficult must it be for psychology to fulfil the demands of purely objective observation when its fundamental problems are so deeply interwoven with man's deepest interests, hopes, and passions! It is only a consequence of these circumstances that psychology has undergone a different historical development from that of cognate sciences and that the historical account of its development must follow its own more or less unique methods.[1]

## 2. Plan of the Present Work

One of the most notable differences between the development of psychology and that of the other empirical sciences, particularly the natural sciences, lies in the relation between the two stages of development which we may call the prac-

[1] *Cf.* Ebbinghaus, "Psychologie," in *Kultur der Gegenwart*, I, 6², 1908, pp. 173 *ff.*

tical and the purely observational or descriptive. Most of the sciences which we to-day class as descriptive sciences had as their original aim some sort of control over nature and fortune. Man does not at first observe the processes of nature in the midst of which he lives merely for their own sake; he rather observes them in order that he may himself influence and control them in the interests of his own needs and purposes. Thus astrology, which sought to afford guidance in conduct through the prognostication of events, became astronomy; alchemy, which had as its object the artificial production of precious metals, became chemistry, and so on. Following up this analogy, one would be led to look for the antecedents of modern psychology in chiromancy, in mnemotechnics, and in witchcraft, which plays such an important rôle even with so thoroughgoing an empiricist as Bacon. These occult sciences, however, which are obviously the antecedents of modern spiritism, have borne little or no relation to the scientific analysis of mental life. It is true that we find in modern times many attempts to give explanations of spiritistic phenomena which lay claim to scientific status. Count Gasparin, for example, attempts to explain spiritistic phenomena by reference to a fluid, called "psychode" by Thury, which is subject to voluntary control. And between the wholly transcendental explanation of the astronomer Porro, with his hypothesis of a divided personality, and the pseudo-empirical view of Maxwell that spiritistic phenomena are to be explained by the collective consciousness of the participants in the psychic experiment, there is a whole series of more or less fantastic attempts to extend the concepts and categories of modern psychology to the realm in question.[1] But the transition from the practical to the purely observa-

[1] The more important of these attempts at explanation have been compiled by Camille Flammarion in *Unbekannte Naturkräfte;* German translation by Michalski, 1908, p. 343.

tional stage, so characteristic of the natural sciences, evidently does not repeat itself here.

It is due to the very nature of the contents of consciousness that their scientific study has profited but little from contact with the species of practical psychology referred to above, and that such study could prosper only within the bounds of a world view in which theoretical motives predominate or in which, at any rate, practical motives are moderated by contact with ethical or religious needs and interests. Thus the meagre practical application of psychology which the history of this science reveals would also find its explanation. While, then, on the one hand, scientific psychology owes little to the doubtful successes of the occult sciences, based upon an alleged knowledge of mental life, scientific psychology has, on the other hand, rather persistently declined to take any interest in the practical problems of the occult. The alliance which has for a considerable period been established between psychology and pedagogy seems, indeed, to promise well for the future. If psychology is ever to become a practical science it will become such by entering the fields of pedagogy, law, and medicine, fields which have, indeed, already been opened to modern psychology. And when one compares the success of psychology in these fields with the success of the natural sciences in their various applications, the comparative recency of psychology as a theoretical science must not be lost sight of.[1] From these changes in the point of view adopted by psychology result a number of general psychological tendencies which we shall seek to review in the first chapter of this book.

The development of opinion regarding principial questions in psychology, as exhibited in certain fundamental psychological concepts, has a certain historical continuity of its own.

[1] *Cf.* Wundt,"Über reine und angewandte Psychologie," *Psychologische Studien*, V, pp. 1 *ff.*

In this respect, too, psychology differs characteristically from the natural sciences. Theories regarding the connections of external phenomena appear comparatively early in the history of civilization. The antithesis between the teleological and the mechanical views of nature, for example, is already clearly presented in the writings of Aristotle and Democritus, and the antithesis has persisted throughout the whole subsequent history of science. Principles of a similar nature appear much later in the history of psychology. The inner life of man was not only not an immediate object of theoretical investigation, but it was from the outset subjected to the influence of ethical and religious ideas. While the task of natural science was merely to subject recognized phenomena to scientific treatment and interpretation, psychology was first obliged to bring the phenomena with which it dealt into conscious existence. The act of willing, for example, which appeared in the first place as either good or bad, had to be viewed as a pure experience, without reference, that is, to its ethical or social significance; or the features which are common to a sensation, as a cognitive process and, say, a feeling of pleasantness had to be determined, etc. It is such efforts as these that we shall seek to follow in our second chapter, which deals with the fundamental concepts of psychology.

Finally, there have arisen in connection with a number of psychological problems, such as sense-perception, volition, etc., certain theories which cannot always be readily fitted into the framework of a systematic psychology, but which can be treated historically, since it is the same problems which persist throughout all the metamorphoses which their explanations undergo. We shall, of course, understand by the phrase "psychological theories" only such concepts and principles as are able to meet the demand which every scientific theory must meet, viz., that it shall connect phenomena with their causes in accordance with natural laws. The older doctrine of mind-stuff, for example, is not a psychological theory but a metaphysical interpretation of mental phenomena. The history of the most important of these psychological theories will be dealt with in the final chapter.

Since the development of psychology is but a phase of intellectual development in general, it would doubtless be possible to identify in psychology the same general stages through which the history of intellectual culture has passed. The attempt, however, to deduce from the latter the laws for the historical development of psychology would be fruitful only for special tendencies or problems of psychology or else it would lose itself in unprofitable generalities. As an example of the latter we might cite the three organic laws for the development of psychology enumerated by Maurice de Wulf,[1] which, however, tell us nothing more than that psychology passes from a dogmatic through a critical stage in order to complete its development when the human spirit itself reaches its maturity. It has seemed to us a more interesting and attractive task simply to follow the movement of history and to separate out from the broad stream of tradition those ideas which appeared significant and which are sometimes so much in advance of their time that we feel a sense of kinship with bygone thinkers as if they belonged to our own time.

### 3. MODERN AND ANCIENT ELEMENTS IN PSYCHOLOGY

The principal aim of the present treatise is to trace modern psychology back to its historical antecedents. Anticipations of modern psychology are, of course, to be found at all stages of the history of the science; in fact, the order of ancient and

[1] "Les lois organiques de l'histoire de la psychologie," *Archiv f. Gesch. d. Phil.*, X, 1897, pp. 393 *ff*.

modern is not seldom curiously reversed. Who, for example, does not find in Alhacen's *Optics*, published in 1269, a mode of thinking more akin to our own than that contained in many of the speculations of the school of Schelling concerning the alleged analogies between sense qualities and the mode of appearance of physical forces? And if we go back still further we shall find a form of mental mechanics in Aristotle which, as an anticipation of modern explanatory psychology, ranks far above the Wolffian faculty psychology of the eighteenth century.

It is difficult, accordingly, to assign with much confidence a date at which modern psychology may properly be said to begin. There is hardly a division point in the history of philosophy which may not also, from some point of view, be regarded as the beginning of modern psychology. If one is thinking of psychology as an exact, experimental science, developing in close relation to physiology, then modern psychology may be said to date from the middle of the nineteenth century. Frequently the empirical psychology of the eighteenth century, in which individual psychology and psychiatry were closely connected interests, is pointed out as a mode of thinking which is related to our own. John Locke, the founder of the so-called psychology of the inner sense, is usually named as the founder of modern empirical psychology, thus placing the beginning of modern psychology near the end of the seventeenth century. Again, the significance which Descartes' definition of consciousness assumed for psychology has been thought sufficient to make the Cartesian system the dividing point between ancient and modern psychology. Still further back do we find empirical psychology explicitly contrasted with the traditional metaphysical psychology, as by Ludovicus Vives, who has himself been called the father of modern psychology, thus placing the beginning of the science in the first half of the sixteenth century. Siebeck's researches, finally, have detected the fruitful beginnings of empirical psychology in Scholasticism. Observations on certain striking color phenomena are utilized for illustrative purposes in the theological tractates of the followers of Eckhart, which exact psychology has been very tardy in taking into account. Although these beginnings of empirical psychology consist mainly in a departure from the Aristotelian tradition, it must not be forgotten that the Aristotelian writings contain anticipations which extend into the most modern times.

Although, therefore, our task takes us back into the remotest antiquity, the history of psychology, perhaps more than the history of any other science, falls into periods and epochs in which scattered ideas of real significance stand out in clear relief against a colorless mass of traditional learning. A proper historical appreciation of such phenomena is often made difficult by the exaggerated estimate of some single thinker, like Aristotle, for example, who is often said to have had only predecessors and imitators. Some such remark might, indeed, apply to certain ideas in the history of science, particularly in the history of psychology of which it can truly be said that they have had only anticipations and developments.

## 4. LITERATURE

The first attempt to write the history of psychology was made by Aristotle (*De Anima*, I, 2). But it is not until the historical sense is awakened by Romanticism that the study of the history of psychology begins. The most notable work which has come down to us from this period, a book which is still instructive on many points, is F. A. Carus's *Geschichte der Psychologie*, published in 1808.

If we confine ourselves to the one most important modern

work for the discussion of any given period, the most exhaustive work on the history of ancient psychology down to Thomas Aquinas is H. Siebeck's *Geschichte der Psychologie* (1880–4), which is supplemented by a series of articles on scholastic psychology, published in *Archiv für die Geschichte der Philosophie*, I–III (1888–90). No work of similar scope and value exists for the period of the Renaissance and for the metaphysical systems of the sixteenth century. In fact, there is no other period in which scientific psychology breaks up into so many scattered observations and unrelated points of view. The most complete account of the period from Leibniz to Kant is contained in Dessoir's *Geschichte der neueren deutschen Psychologie*, part I (2d ed., 1902). The main problems of the history of psychology in the nineteenth century are treated, very unevenly, to be sure, by Eduard von Hartmann, in his *Die moderne Psychologie*, 1901 (*Werke*, XIII). A circumstantial account of the more modern tendencies of psychology is to be found in Ribot's *Psychologie anglaise contemporaine* (2d ed., 1875), and *Psychologie allemande contemporaine* (2d ed., 1885). The points of view, finally, which have dominated the developments of experimental psychology have been briefly summarized by Wundt in his article "Psychologie," contained in the Kuno Fischer *Festschrift*, *Die Philosophie im Beginn des* 20. *Jahrhunderts* (2d ed., 1906). Among the works on systematic psychology Volkmann's *Lehrbuch der Psychologie* (4th ed., 1894–5) contains a wealth of historical references and excursions which is worthy of admiration even to-day.

With neither of these works, each of which is based upon an extensive literature in the form of monographs and special investigations, does the present book wish to enter into competition. It rather presupposes them, as it does the study of the sources, and it should be supplemented by references to them. Siebeck's and Dessoir's books, particularly, are utilized extensively in the treatment of ancient psychology and the psychology of the Enlightenment, respectively. But the writer does hope that the treatment of psychology in its historical development will exhibit the problems of contemporary psychology in their genesis and will thus prepare the way for their independent study and treatment. At a time when psychology is taking her place as an independent empirical science among her sister sciences such a treatment will, perhaps, help to obviate certain misunderstandings such as are illustrated in profusion in the attempt of a brilliant contemporary writer to prove that psychology is quite without prospects. In thus tracing the development of psychological reflection, certain border problems occupy attention perhaps somewhat more than their importance may seem to warrant at a time when psychology is taking her place among the other sciences as a special empirical science. In the history of psychology, however, the border lines between science and hypothesis have always been obscure. It is the hypothetical element in psychology, in fact, which has invested psychological problems with peculiar interest and vitality. One is reminded here of the statement of Poincaré that the growth of a science occurs along its borders.

## Translators' Note on English Literature

The reader may also be referred to the following works on the history of psychology which have appeared in English either as original works or as translations:

Baldwin, J. M., *History of Psychology*, New York and London, 1913.

Brett, G. S., *A History of Psychology*, London, 1912.

Dessoir, M., *Outlines of the History of Psychology*, tr. of *Abriss einer Geschichte der Psychologie*, by Donald Fisher, New York, 1912.

Ribot, Th., *English Psychology*, tr. of the work cited above, by J. M. Baldwin, New York, 1897.

Ribot, Th., *German Psychology of To-Day*, tr. of the work cited above, by J. M. Baldwin, New York, 1899.

# PART I
# GENERAL TENDENCIES OF PSYCHOLOGY
## I. METAPHYSICAL PSYCHOLOGY
### CHAPTER I
#### DUALISM IN PSYCHOLOGY

**1. Relation of Metaphysical and Empirical Tendencies**

Although psychical phenomena are of all data the most accessible, the history of psychology bears witness to the extreme difficulty of gaining the proper point of view for the study of the phenomena in question. Psychology, indeed, appears surprisingly early as one among the other sciences, but for centuries psychology does little more than reflect the presuppositions and conclusions of philosophy. When the points of view of a metaphysical world view are transferred to the realm of conscious phenomena, the latter appear as manifestations or modes of activity of a soul, an entity usually thought of as substantial. The particular phenomena of consciousness are deduced from the conceptual definition of the soul. Side by side with metaphysical psychology appears empirical psychology which makes psychical phenomena objects of introspection, and seeks to exhibit their scientific connection. The metaphysical and the empirical tendencies are by no means mutually exclusive. Empirical materials are to some extent utilized in every type of metaphysical psychology, and empirical psychology, on the other hand, gives rise to problems which properly belong to metaphysics. In this respect psychology does not differ from the rest of the factual sciences. And if metaphysical problems arise more inevitably in psychology than in some of the other sciences, it is doubtless due to the close affinity between the subjective mode of viewing the contents of consciousness and the reflection upon the movements of the inner life which so naturally carries one forward to a metaphysical view of existence.

The various tendencies within metaphysical psychology exhibit a close resemblance in the manner in which psychical phenomena are deduced from the concept of the soul, the difference appearing in the definition of the soul itself. The empirical tendencies start with the same method, that of introspection; they differ from each other mainly in the principles employed in the interpretation of the data which introspection reveals.[1]

The oldest forms of metaphysical psychology were dominated by categories developed within the domain of natural science, from which they were transferred to the realm of the inner life. The soul, accordingly, appears as an entity, a substance, corresponding to substances and things in the external world. There occurs thus a complete reversal of the more familiar anthropomorphic modes of thinking: psychical facts, in order that they may be thought real at all, are brought under concepts originally derived from the domain of external nature.

The contrasts between spirit and matter familiar in metaphysical systems thus reappear in psychology in the speculations concerning the nature of the soul. The most natural conception here is dualism, which opposes material substance and soul substance. Attempts to transcend this antithesis lead

[1] These and a number of subsequent distinctions are drawn from Wundt's *Grundriss der Psychologie*, 1909. [English tr. by C. H. Judd, *Outlines of Psychology*, 2d ed., Leipzig, 1902. Trs.]

to spiritualistic psychology, in which physical processes are held to be essentially identical with psychical processes, and materialistic psychology, in which psychical processes are held to be merely a mode or a manifestation of matter.

## 2. Dualistic Psychology

Dualism results from the introduction of prescientific ideas into the whole of a world view in which the phenomena of reality have been subjected to little or no interpretation. For primitive thought, man, like everything else in the world, is a composite of body and soul. As knowledge increases, many objects are bereft of soul life, so that eventually only living beings remain endowed with psychical qualities. These conceptions of primitive peoples form the subject-matter of folk psychology. They are of interest to the history of psychology, since they have been made the objects of conscious reflection and have been raised to the dignity of psychological theories. From the earliest representatives of Oriental philosophy to the time of Plato we find a primitive dualism which teaches that the soul leads only a shadowy existence after its separation from the body.

The first attempt to give a connected account of mental phenomena within the framework of a metaphysical world view is made by Heraclitus of Ephesus. The system of Heraclitus, like that of his predecessors, is monistic in the primitive sense of the term. All things, including the soul, originate from fire, the soul appearing at that stage of the evolution of the universal element where the latter breaks up into earth and fiery vapor. In the human organism the body represents the earthy, the soul the fiery element. Through the breath it partakes of the warm air and thus of the same rationality as fire is supposed to possess. Its origination and destruction are merely phases of the general rhythmic movement of existence: "It is death to souls to become water, and death to water to become earth. But water comes from earth; and from water, soul." The experienced difference between body and soul Heraclitus explains by the hypothesis that they represent two stages in the development of fire. The knowledge of the soul accordingly presupposes a knowledge of reality as a whole. Like the universe, it is unfathomable, as the well-known saying testifies: "You will not find the boundaries of soul by travelling in any direction."[1]

It is not until we come to Empedocles of Agrigentum that Ionic hylozoism becomes consistently dualistic. It is true that Empedocles reduces all becoming to relationships of matter and force. Matter is composed of four elements, while force manifests itself in the interplay of attraction and repulsion, figuratively called love and hate. The soul, however, is not affected by these physical theories. The hypotheses of the philosophy of nature that the soul, like everything else, consists of the various elements combined in the proper proportions become mingled with religious ideas according to which the individual soul is merely a part of the world soul. The elements themselves are now transformed into divinities; the soul is capable of an existence separate from matter, and the doctrine of metempsychosis clearly indicates contact with Pythagorean ideas. Pythagorean psychology, from all we are able to ascertain concerning the matter, was also dualistic in character. The saying that the soul is a harmony, or possesses harmony, was already within the Pythagorean school a statement of equivocal significance. It is beyond question, however, that the dualism of body and soul was for the Pythagoreans merely a repetition of the familiar antithesis between the unlimited and the limited, between matter and force.

[1] [Burnet, *Early Greek Philosophy*, p. 138. Trs.]

A new form of dualism, in which the priority of spirit over matter first received recognition, is represented by Anaxagoras. To the indistinguishable mixture of all things, which represents the material world, is opposed a homogeneous and independent principle which furnishes the condition of motion. This principle of movement is at the same time a principle of order and intelligence (νοῦς). In the description of the νοῦς a tendency toward pure spiritualism makes itself felt. It is unmixed, unitary, and free from suffering. It is self-governing; it possesses all knowledge and very great power. On the other hand, we find the idea persisting in Anaxagoras that the spirit is but a part or a fragment of matter. He calls it "the finest and purest of all things," and the soul becomes again a part of that spiritual essence which pervades things, "now increasing, now diminishing."

Although theoretical speculation often advanced to the doctrine of the purely spiritual existence of the soul, it did not develop, unaided, the conception which has been a mainstay of dualism, the conception of immortality. Neither could the belief in immortality develop from the soul cult of Greek popular religion. It rather originates in mysticism, which had its bands of votaries among the Greeks and existed side by side with the popular religion, little heeded by the latter. In the Orphic and Eleusinian mysteries are heard the echoes of the worldly wisdom of ancient India according to which the body is the sepulchre of the soul (σῶμα σῆμα ψυχῆς). The idea of immortality found fruitful soil in the cult of Dionysos in which the experience of ecstasy furnished materials sufficiently striking for spiritualistic hypotheses. The convulsive movements and visions in the moment of divine madness must have suggested a realm quite removed from the ordinary realities of every-day life. The belief in the separate existence of the soul which the experiences of dreams and swoons made natural was thus confirmed by the experiences during ecstasy. It was an easy step from this point to the doctrine of the dual existence of body and soul. The descent from the heights of emotional ecstasy, to which the soul had been raised upon its temporary release from the body, to the realities of the bodily life came to be felt as a passage from one world into another.[1]

The inclusion of these conceptions within a theoretical world view brought psychological dualism to its highest point of development, a point reached in the philosophy of Plato. In Plato's theory of ideas the soul is assigned a sort of intermediate position between the world of ideas and the world of matter, since the soul knows ideas, but is itself bound to the body. The fundamental contradiction between experience and the conceptual world, which runs throughout the entire Platonic system, is nowhere revealed more strikingly than in the relation between body and soul. They do not constitute an organic unity; the body rather appears as an obstacle hindering the soul in the attainment of knowledge and of its true life. The complete contrast between the body and the soul is, indeed, made the condition of the latter's immortality. This pronounced dualism reappears in the empirical constitution of the soul, which contains two elements, a natural and a supranatural. The contrast between the spiritual and the natural assumes a more striking form in Plato than in Anaxagoras. Although the connection between body and soul becomes thus an insoluble riddle, the soul becomes thereby an object of supreme interest for speculation. While the knowledge of the empirical world is for Heraclitus a precondition of the knowledge of the soul, as we have seen, the relation here is completely reversed: the knowledge of the soul forms the only avenue to the knowledge of the world. Plato thus drew the pregnant consequences involved in the positions of the Sophists and

[1] *Cf.* Rhode, *Psyche*, II, 1898, pp. 32 *ff.*

Socrates, and the existence of psychology as an independent science is demanded, even if not actually assured. It was impossible to carry dualism to a higher point of development than it had attained in Plato. It is not until the beginning of the modern era in philosophical speculation that we find a dualism equally consistent and thoroughgoing, though it is now based upon a different conceptual formulation.

A number of dualistic features appear also in the psychology of Aristotle, whose metaphysical presuppositions lead him to make the distinction between the active and the passive reason. The active reason is of divine lineage; separated from the organic development of human mental life, it enters this life from without ($\theta \acute{v} \rho a \theta \epsilon \nu$). Such an obvious contradiction Aristotle, master that he was of the art of conceptual manipulation, could not allow to remain unrelieved. His metaphysical theory that every movement presupposed three conditions, something moved, something at once mover and moved, and, finally, an unmoved mover, suggested the solution: reason in the human soul discharges the same function as the divine being in the universe as a whole, that, namely, of an unmoved mover. Like the divine being, it represents the capstone of organic evolution.

A source of dualistic ideas similar to that of the Dionysian cults is to be found in the Hebrew representations of the soul. The fusion of Hebrew and Greek conceptions in Alexandrian-Judaic psychology is illustrated in the system of Philo, an older contemporary of Jesus, according to whom the human body is composed of earthy elements, while the soul, which traces its lineage to the divine $\pi \nu \epsilon \hat{v} \mu a$, is composed of ether. Platonic dualism is here seen to approach again the Orphic-Pythagorean conceptions, thus giving way to a supranaturalistic theory of soul life which for a long period dominates philosophical speculation.

It is here, too, that a differentiation is effected between two factors which had been united in the traditional notion of the soul, a physiological factor, vital force, and a psychological one, consciousness. The distinction indeed already existed in germ in Aristotle. Stoicism, too, had prepared the way for the separation of these elements by their distinction between the ἡγεμονικὸν and the πνεῦμα, thus creating, by a partial interpretation of the Aristotelian "*quinta essentia*," the conception of "animal spirits," *spiritus animales*, a conception destined to a long-lived existence in the history of psychophysical speculation. This higher part of the soul, which had hitherto been regarded as merely a general principle of rationality, is now designated as a principle of individuality as well. The threefold division of the personality into spirit, soul, and body dominates anthropology from this time on. While this triadic theory obviously represents an attempt to connect psychology with religious ideas and interests, it also suggests misgivings on the part of those who held the theory that the complex variety of psychical phenomena may, after all, not be capable of derivation from a single unitary principle. An exhaustive exposition and proof of the triadic theory is undertaken by Origen (185–254), who ascribes to the soul the powers of movement, representation, and desire, the spirit being endowed with the power of judgment.[1]

The exposition contained in the metaphysical system of Plotinus is of a very similar character. Separate independent and substantial souls owe their existence to the world soul. The incarnation of the soul within the body is to be explained by the fall of the soul from a previous state of blessedness. The relation of the soul to the body is compared with that between light and air. It is said to be "everywhere present without surrendering its identity, penetrating everything without mixing with it."

[1] *De princ.*, III, 1–5.

The influence upon psychology of the religious mysticism of the Neo-Platonists after Plotinus becomes more pronounced as time goes on. The Neo-Platonic definition of the soul given by Porphyry, οὐσία ἀμεγέθης αὐλὸς ἄφθαρτος ἐν ζωῇ παρ' ἑαυτῆς ἐχούσῃ τὸ ζῆν κεκτημένη τὸ εἶναι, is widely followed by the Greek Church Fathers. Prominent among the amalgamations of Christian and Neo-Platonic ideas are the teachings, based upon the system of Plato, of Gregory of Nyssa (331–394). He considers the soul as an incorporeal, independent substance which permeates the body. The latter phrase, however, is not to be taken in a spatial sense; the relation between soul and body is much like that between light and air.

More convincing proofs of the incorporeal nature of the soul are offered by Augustine (354–430). The idea that the knowledge of a thing implies an ontological affinity between the knower and the thing known, and that, consequently, that which knows the incorporeal must itself be incorporeal, is reminiscent of Plato. More important is the purely psychological argument that the soul, since it is the experiencing subject, cannot be itself an object of observation and cannot, therefore, have material properties. The soul has an immediate knowledge of itself in self-consciousness. The problem of the relation between soul and body Augustine seeks to make intelligible in a manner characteristic of his time. The reigning dogma of soul substance prevents him from advancing to a monistic position and leads him to assert that the combination in man of body and soul results in a third substance, the exact nature of the relation between these substances, however, remaining unfathomable. A clear expression of the tendencies of later Patristic psychology is found in the teachings of Nemesius, bishop of Emesa in Phœnicia, who wrote between 400 and 450. Taking his stand against both materialism and the Aristotelian doctrine of the soul as the entelechy of the body, he defends an outspoken dualism of body and soul, contenting himself with the definition of the latter as an incorporeal, independently existing substance.

The psychology of Scholasticism, too, is largely dominated by dualistic conceptions. The early Scholastics, Alcuin, Isaac of Stella, and Hugo of Saint Victor, base their ideas upon the Augustinian-Platonic system. With the rehabilitation of Aristotelianism in the thirteenth century this development is for a time interrupted, but the fundamental idea of spiritualism soon succumbs again to dualism, which received powerful support from its affiliation with current religious convictions. The Arabian philosophers also assisted the cause of dualism by making the necessary reinterpretations of the distinction between the active and the passive reason. The authority of Aristotle served also to protect partly the pneuma doctrine which, originally growing out of hylozoistic ideas, was now employed to explain the connection between soul and body. Pneuma became a sort of intermediate agent, so that the main outlines of the triadic philosophy, with its division of spirit, soul, and body, were again restored.

A naturalistic interpretation of Aristotelian doctrines occasionally bordering upon pantheism was given by Averroës (1126–98).[1] The soul is distinguished both from the body and from the impersonal intellect. The aim of intellectual knowledge as it develops is the comprehension by the universal intellect of its own activity and life within the individual, a process which Averroës describes as the attainment by the intellect of abstract ideas.[2] And since forms emerge from matter of necessity, in virtue of the principle of movement inherent in matter from eternity, the development of

[1] *Cf.* Siebeck, *Archiv f. Gesch. d. Phil.*, II, pp. 516 *ff.*
[2] "Ascendit ille intellectus in actu ad assimilationem rerum abstractarum et intelleget suum esse, quod est actu intellectus." *De an. beat.*, 66 A.

the spiritual principle is a process which is both natural and necessary.

It is true that Thomas Aquinas (1224–75), standing at the very summit of Scholasticism, turned away from Platonic dualism and accepted the Aristotelian conception of the soul. The dogma of the church, however, demanded an adaptation of the Aristotelian distinctions so as to bring them into harmony with the reigning system of theological dualism. He accordingly made the distinction between subsistent and inherent forms and attributed to the former an existence independent of matter. The comment often made upon the philosophy of this period, namely, that it is no more and no less scientific than the literary sources upon which it drew, applies, on the whole, to psychology as well, whose affiliation with philosophy was at this period constant and intimate.

In the period immediately preceding modern philosophy dualistic theories underwent few modifications. This applies, for instance, to the Marburg school, known to us through the *Psychologia* of Rudolf Gockel, published in 1590.[1] Modern dualism originates with Descartes (1596–1650) where it is based upon new conceptual presuppositions. Descartes did not, indeed, succeed in liberating himself completely from the scholastic tradition. Still, his thinking was dominated by the new scientific spirit of the time, with the result that the distinction between matter and spirit, which had hitherto been regarded as merely one of degree, completed itself in his philosophy in the entire separation of the two spheres in question. Descartes thus for the first time assigned to the physical and the mental sciences their distinct subject-matter: to the former extended substance, to the latter conscious substance.

There is probably no other distinction in the history of

[1] Casmann defines man as "genuinæ naturæ mundanæ: spiritualis et corporea in unum hyphistamenon unitæ participes essentiæ."

metaphysical psychology which has been as momentous as this. The conceptions and categories of the older systems of philosophy are often so ambiguous in character that it is impossible to say whether they are physical or psychological. They seem to fall somewhere between. Even where the antithesis between the two realms is made explicit, as in Plato, it tends to pass over into the antithesis between the good and the bad or between the true and the false. The transformation which occurred is well-nigh impossible of vital apprehension to-day, for the Cartesian distinction still coincides with the concepts in accordance with which naïve thought interprets the whole of our experience. With the Cartesian substitution of a pure dualism of substances for the Platonic dualism of values the problem of the relation of mind and body was raised into greater prominence than ever before. The attempts to solve this problem were of first-rate influence in carrying psychology beyond the dualistic hypothesis. To be sure, dualistic ideas come into prominence again with the return to the great metaphysical systems of the seventeenth century, especially in the popular philosophy of the Enlightenment. Indeed, the Cartesian dualism became the generally accepted view-point of popular thought. As a metaphysical tendency, however, it henceforth assumes a subordinate rank. And although we find writers even in the nineteenth century who espouse dualism, like Krause, for example,[1] they do not do so without exhibiting monistic tendencies.

With the exception of the innovation of Descartes which influenced every subsequent psychological tendency,[2] the development of dualism was fairly consistent and uniform. In this respect it resembles the earlier forms of empirical psychology, to be described later, especially faculty psy-

[1] *Vorlesungen über die psychische Anthropologie*, 1836.
[2] *Cf.* below, Chapter VI, 1 (*b*).

chology. The reason for this lies in the fact that dualism never undertakes any genuine interpretation of the phenomena of experience. It is only with the progress of sophistication that the wealth of contrasts shown by monistic tendencies becomes possible.

## CHAPTER II

### MONISM IN PSYCHOLOGY

Monism in psychology can either grow out of the problems raised by dualism or it can from the outset treat psychical and bodily phenomena as equivalent. In the former case, the point of departure is the problem of the mutual relation of body and mind; in the latter, the common characteristics of bodily and mental phenomena become the starting-point. Speaking generally, the effort to identify the soul, taken as an independent reality, with the body, leads to the primacy of the former and thus to spiritualistic psychology. On the other hand, the identification of bodily and psychical processes tends to make the physical world appear as the real world, and the result is materialistic psychology. It happens, accordingly, that in the history of psychology spiritualistic tendencies follow in the wake of a pronounced dualism, while materialistic psychology grows out of natural science when carried on independently of metaphysical presuppositions and influences. But the relation is sometimes reversed, with the result that one finds very diverse tendencies combined in a given form of spiritualistic or materialistic psychology.

Between these two types stands pure monism, such as one finds in Spinoza, for example, which co-ordinates completely the physical and the psychical aspects of reality. Since this theory, however, fails to take account of the empirical connections existing among the contents of consciousness, it can hardly be said to constitute a separate branch of metaphysical psychology, although it bears close relations to efforts to rid a given system of empirical psychology of contradictions and thus to bring it to a definitive conclusion. Within the science of psychology itself the principle of so-called psychophysical parallelism has been reduced to a heuristic principle, a process which has been repeated in the case of metaphysical principles of a number of other sciences, the principle of finalism, for example, in biology.

## 1. Spiritualism

Spiritualism in psychology is the result of the gradual development of the concept of spirit and of the sharpening of the contrast between spirit and matter. A number of spiritualistic features are found as early in the history of psychology as Anaxagoras, who describes spirit as something simple and unmixed; but his definitions are not free from materialistic implications.[1] It is not until Aristotle (384–322), the thinker who might be said to have originated psychology as an independent science with definitely fixed boundaries, that the magic word expressing the really inexpressible nature of the soul was spoken. The soul is to the body what form is to matter; it is that which makes of the body a living being, and which through its activity completes the body, by leading it to its true goal. This is the meaning of that noteworthy definition of the soul as the entelechy of the living body: ἔστιν οὖν ψυχὴ ἐντελέχεια ἡ πρώτη σώματος φυσικοῦ ζωὴν ἔχοντος δυνάμει. In this conception of the soul are contained the initial suggestions which psychology has not availed itself of until the most recent times. In Aristotle's psychology the soul is no longer a substance, but an activity, a formative principle. The most important conception of spiritualistic psychology comes here to its fullest expression, although Aristotle, influenced by his meta-

[1] *Cf.* above, p. 16.

## MONISM IN PSYCHOLOGY

physics, again lapses into dualism.[1] In spite of repeated attempts on the part of Neo-Platonism to construct a monistic psychology, spiritualism remains a subordinate type for a considerable period. It is revived again in the metaphysical systems of modern philosophy, reaching its highest development in Leibniz (1646-1716), the Aristotle, as he has been called, of modern times.

The psychology of Leibniz is based upon the doctrine of monads, a wholly metaphysical conception. Inasmuch as the soul is the only part of reality which we immediately know, we must interpret the rest of reality in analogy with it. All reality is, therefore, psychical in character. It is composed of monads of varying degrees of development arranged in a hierarchy whose order is determined by the particular grade of development reached by the monads composing it. On the lowest plane are found simple monads, whose psychical condition resembles our own in a state of drowsiness or swoon. Animal souls are endowed with memory. The human soul, finally, participates in the highest forms of experience through its knowledge of necessary truths. Since all the grades of consciousness are represented in the monad constituting the human soul, the metaphysical conception in question, although confining itself to cognitive experiences, was not without significance for the interpretation of the empirical data of consciousness.[2]

The purest form of spiritualism ever achieved, that of Berkeley (1685-1753), arose out of different antecedents. The starting-point of Berkeley's system, it is true, was the empirical psychology of Locke, since he characterized all experiences as forms of self-observation. But his interpretation of sense-perception as the lowest form of self-observation already carries him beyond the bounds of experience.

---

[1] *Cf.* above, p. 18.
[2] *Cf.* below, Chapter VI, 2 (*a*).

Once thoroughly launched upon metaphysics, Berkeley finds nothing but souls and their experiences. The soul is a simple, indivisible, active being which, in its capacity to perceive ideas, is called intelligence; in its capacity to produce them, will. The peculiarity of the subject of inner experience is suggested by the observation that we can form only a concept, not an idea, of spirit; nevertheless, the definition of spirit here proposed carries us far beyond the bounds of science into metaphysics.

The spiritualistic psychology which nourished itself on the Leibnizian ideas tended always to lapse into vulgar dualism. After Kant had dealt the death-blow to this species of psychologizing, as well as to the more traditional type of rationalism, psychology passed under the sway of the Romantic philosophy. A related form of spiritualism is found in France after the Revolution. Cabanis (1757–1808) had, indeed, sought to explain the relations between physiological and psychological processes in his principal work, *Les rapports du physique et du moral de l'homme* (1798–9 and, separately, 1802), but he assumed with Leibniz a number of subordinate minds in addition to the central mind, eventually adopting a form of pantheism not unlike that of ancient Stoicism.

A complete contrast to sensualism of the type found in Condillac is encountered in Maine de Biran (1766–1824), who has done much for the revival of psychology in France. In his *Essai sur les fondements de la Psychologie* he opposes equally the point of view of the metaphysicians who treat the soul as an absolute being and that of pure empiricists who recognize in the mental life only sensations and connections among sensations. Reflection on our inner life forces us to recognize conation or wilful effort as the primary fact of consciousness. Will and resistance are inseparable experiences: it is through resistance that the self becomes aware that it is limited. Other deductions of Maine de Biran remind one of the interpretations of consciousness in German Romanticism. A characteristic doctrine is that of inner space. This is the immediate seat of the ego and is formed by the various points of resistance which the will encounters in the various organs.

The Leibnizian tradition is continued by Herbart (1776–1831), who himself acknowledged Leibniz as his precursor. Herbart, too, is not exempt from the influence of the dialectic of Romanticism in so far as the problem of psychology arises only as a result of the contradictions contained within the concept of spirit. In the fact of self-consciousness is contained, according to Herbart, the identity of being and knowledge, of the subject and object of consciousness, without being differentiated within it, however, by thought. Thus psychology confronts a metaphysical problem at the very outset and it emerges from its attempts to solve this problem as a mechanics of ideas. On account of the contradictions among the empirical concepts to which experience gives rise, the latter does not even furnish us with phenomena from which the nature of reality might be inferred. It gives us nothing but semblance, and this semblance it is the business of metaphysics to dissipate. With this object in mind, Herbart resorts to the Leibnizian monadology. He defines even more sharply the concept of the individual, simple being of "the real." Out of the disturbances and the tendencies to self-preservation or persistence of these reals he deduced both the phenomena of the outer world and the processes of consciousness. The latter consist entirely in the movements of ideas. The whole of reality is thus dissolved, as if by an act of force, into reals. The physical and psychical represent merely different stages in the competitive action, the disturbance and self-preservation, of simple elements.

Aside from this main line of the development of spiritualism which has persisted in its Herbartian form up to very recent times, other spiritualistic motives have made themselves felt in the nineteenth century, especially in connection with the school of Schelling. The Aristotelian definition of the soul reappears in the *Vorlesungen über Psychologie* (1831) by C. G. Carus, who again defines it as the principle of life. Fantastic analogies between body and soul, between organs and their functions, are met with in a number of psychologists representing similar tendencies, Schubert, Fischer, Burdach, and Heinroth, whose names have now passed into oblivion. This form of spiritualism received its most exhaustive treatment at the hands of J. H. Fichte (1797–1879), who combined a strong theological tendency with the most fanciful psychological hypotheses.

Much more congenial is the mature form of spiritualism which serves as the background of the empirical psychology of one of the most important psychologists of the nineteenth century, Hermann Lotze (1817–81), the successor of Herbart at the University of Göttingen. Lotze's thought is firmly based upon natural science, and he recognizes fully the dependence of mental states upon bodily condition. Nevertheless, the ultimate ground of reality is for him spiritual. "Thus we are led back," he writes, "to a psychophysical mechanism within which all interactions occur among homogeneous elements. This does not mean that we reduce mind to terms of matter, as is done by materialism, but rather that we interpret matter in terms of mind, or of some substance essentially akin to mind." [1]

Within the movement of spiritualism itself several sharply contrasted tendencies have lately made themselves felt. In contradiction to the fundamental metaphysical principle that the soul is a spiritual substance and the empirical principle

[1] *Medicinische Psychologie*, 1852, p. 80.

that the intellectual processes furnish the foundation for all other mental processes, the claims are advanced, first, that the immediately experienced actualities of the mental life are themselves the ultimate reality of that life, and, second, that the phenomena of volition represent the fundamental traits of mental life as a whole. Thus arises the distinction between substantialism and actualism, on the one hand, and between intellectualism and voluntarism, on the other, these constituting the metaphysical border problems of contemporary psychology. Anticipated by Hume and Kant, who had subjected the notion of spiritual substance to a vigorous criticism, actualism is represented at the present day mainly by Wundt and Paulsen, who also champion a pronounced voluntarism as against various forms of intellectualism. The controversy between substantialism and actualism turned mainly upon the metaphysical question whether the relation between the substantial bearer of qualities and the qualities or phenomena themselves was thinkable. As was to be expected, the influence of these considerations upon empirical psychology has not been very great, as can be seen by comparing the theories, say, of Lipps and Wundt, the former of whom showed on the whole a tendency toward substantialism.

Of more empirical significance is the controversy between intellectualism and voluntarism. The latter has antecedents in the history of psychology in various theories of the will which go back to Duns Scotus, or to the end of the twelfth century.[1] A distinction, must, of course, be made between metaphysical voluntarism, such as we associate with the name of Schopenhauer, and psychological voluntarism, which regards the empirical process of volition, with its affective, sensational, and ideational constituents, as the type of consciousness in general. It is just in the composite

[1] *Cf.* Chapter XII, 2, below.

character of the volitional process that its typical significance lies.[1] This principle, however, which was originally meant to be merely a methodological principle, tends very readily to become transformed into the dogma of the metaphysical priority of volition.

If we review from this point the development of spiritualistic psychology we shall recognize the tendency to shift the problem of spiritualism to the realm of the border problems of psychology. The various tendencies of spiritualism, in so far as they have relevance for psychology, meanwhile exhibit a noticeable similarity for a considerable period, since, while extending the boundaries of the psychical, they do not resort to heterogeneous principles of explanation, as materialism so often does.

## 2. Materialism in Psychology

Materialistic psychology divides into three main forms according to the relation asserted to exist between mental and physical processes. In the most naïve form of this doctrine the soul is treated as a special kind of substance which penetrates the body, or else it is outrightly identified with some part of the body, usually the brain. Since this form resolves the soul into atoms similar to the atoms of physics, it may be called atomistic materialism. The growing knowledge of brain processes combined with epistemological considerations rendered atomistic materialism unsatisfactory and led to the interpretation of mental processes as the effect of brain processes. Thus arose mechanistic materialism, a form which developed concomitantly with the mechanistic conception of nature. The third most general form is psychophysical materialism, according to which mental processes are functions of specific bodily processes. While atomistic

[1] *Cf.* Wundt, *Grundriss der Psychologie*, § 2, 10*a*.

materialism shows affiliations with substantialism in psychology, psychophysical materialism resembles actualism, since the soul here consists simply in the combination of elementary psychical processes, while mechanistic materialism seems again to represent an intermediate conception. The three forms enumerated also represent roughly the historical sequence which obtains among them. In any event, the earliest form of materialism to appear in the history of psychology is atomistic materialism.

### (a) Atomistic Materialism [1]

The antitheses of spiritualistic and materialistic metaphysics developed out of the hylozoism of the ancient Ionians, in which the concepts of soul and body were still undifferentiated. The first sketch of materialistic metaphysics was drawn in outline, and with bold strokes, by Democritus. The atomistic materialism of Democritus dispenses entirely with a spiritual ground of becoming. The soul is composed of a particular group of atoms, of tenuous structure, smooth and round, like those of fire. These atoms are the most mobile of all, they penetrate the entire body and impart to it the principle of life. The life of the soul depends upon the breath, $i.\ e.$, upon the unrestricted supply of soul atoms. The reason the soul is invisible, Democritus quite consistently adds, is that the atoms composing it are too small to be seen. From these general presuppositions Democritus deduces, with admirable attention to logical sequence, the various empirical phenomena of mental life.

Although the system of Diogenes of Apollonia does not correspond to the atomism of Democritus in detail, it is,

[1] For the material which follows the writer is in part indebted to F. A. Lange's *Geschichte des Materialismus*, which is still the most instructive treatment of the problems of materialistic psychology that we have. [English translation by E. C. Thomas, London, 1878–81. Trs.]

nevertheless, materialistic in character. The eternal and unlimited element is air, through the condensation and rarefaction of which originate cold and warmth, the dry and the moist. The soul itself is only a special form of air. A decided tendency toward materialism manifests itself in various branches of the Peripatetic school. As early as Dicæarchus of Messene we find a repetition of the old formula that the soul is a harmony, *i. e.*, a proper proportion of the four elements composing the body. A thoroughgoing materialistic psychology was developed within the Peripatetic school by Strato, the physicist, who asserted that all mental processes were modes of motion. Ignoring the subtle conceptual discriminations of his master, he adopted the principle of pneuma, already domesticated in the medical psychology of his day, as a special principle of explanation. Although pneuma was described as warm air, which penetrates the body in respiration, the close relation of air to mental life could not be lost sight of so long as the principle of pneuma served as a connecting link between soul and body. The conception of pneuma played a leading rôle in the psychology of the Stoics. The less, however, they felt it as a difficulty that the fiery vapor of which pneuma was composed could be at once mental and material, the more they departed from the fundamental ideas underlying the atomism of Democritus.

The sublime materialism of Epicurus (341-270 B. C.) represents the highest development to which atomistic materialism attained. According to him, too, the soul consists of round and smooth atoms whose substance, however, is more tenuous than that of the odor of a flower or of ointment. The soul represents the union of four elements, fire, air, a vaporous substance, and a fourth unnamed element, the most tenuous and mobile of all. These physical distinctions are paralleled by certain psychological distinctions in accordance with which spirit emerges in an analogous manner from among the other parts of the soul. So long as it remains intact other parts of the soul substance can perish without jeopardy to life.

The materialism of Epicurus and the Stoics passed over into the psychological systems of Roman writers. The pneuma doctrine exhibited a peculiar vitality in this process, surviving up to the period of Patristic philosophy, where we meet with it quite frequently. Tertullian (160–222), from whose unmeasured polemic against Greek philosophy the work *De Anima* originated, adopted the materialism of Stoicism in its crassest form. The soul is literally the breath of God (*flatus dei*); it has the same form as the body and is composed of a bright, vapory substance of great tenuity. Pneuma is no longer a special kind of substance, different from the soul: it is the soul itself, which emanates from the paternal seed at the time of birth. It has organs which it uses in thought, in dreams, and after death. It is even visible to the eye of one in a state of ecstatic excitement. The same combination of religious dogmatism and extreme materialism is found in Arnobius of Sicca, who finds no difficulty in uniting the ideas of the corporeality of the soul and its immortality. The materialism of Tertullian, sanctioned, as it was, by authoritative belief, survives in a number of Church Fathers in the self-contradictory definition of the soul given by Methodius of Tyre as a spiritually discernible body ($\sigma\hat{\omega}\mu\alpha$ $\nu o\epsilon\rho\acute{o}\nu$), and as late as 350 A. D. Hilary of Poitiers unhesitatingly taught the doctrine of the soul's corporeality. Materialism disappears in the Scholastic philosophy, only to be revived in the seventeenth century under the influence of natural science and of a sensualistic theory of knowledge. The physician David Sennert (1572–1637), who rehabilitated physical atomism in Germany, thought it possible that the soul could exist in the atoms composing living bodies, and held that seeds were atoms endowed with latent consciousness. It is upon a similar idea of animated atoms that Fortuninus Licetus (1577–1657) is said to have based his theory of spontaneous generation. The tendency of atomistic materialism, however, was to pass over into one of the other types already mentioned: mechanistic materialism or psychophysical materialism.

### (b) *Mechanistic Materialism*

The philosophy of the Renaissance broke with the tradition of Scholasticism without developing any marked tendency toward materialism. The nearest approach to materialism among the leading thinkers in the early period of modern philosophy is perhaps made by Bacon. Bacon's psychological views were extensively influenced by the conception of animal spirits (*spiritus animales*), the presence or absence of which distinguishes, according to him, living from inanimate bodies. Bacon goes so far as to surmise that sensation itself consists in nothing but the movement of animal spirits. The doctrine of animal spirits is the common element among many otherwise diverging tendencies in the psychology of this period. Descartes, too, utilized the hypothesis for the explanation of the manner in which external impressions can affect the soul. His belief was that animal spirits existed in the shape of highly mobile blood particles which, after being thinned by the warmth of the heart, flow to the brain in order there to form the mediating link between brain impressions and the pineal gland.[1]

The real founders of modern materialism are Gassendi and Hobbes. It is the lasting merit of Gassendi (1592–1655) that he revived the most finished system of materialism of antiquity, that of Epicurus. Preoccupied as he was,

[1] *Les passions de l'âme*, I, 10.

however, with the external world, he purposely abandoned the problems of psychology with the confession that it was impossible to explain how sensation can arise out of mechanical antecedents.[1] The hypothesis that germ particles endowed with the principle of life have existed from eternity seems to him to offer a way of escape from the difficulty. While he attributes sensation to the material soul, which is composed of atoms, he reserves thought for the rational, immaterial soul, which is created separately for each individual by the Creator. Thus Gassendi abandons that consistency of form which made the system of Democritus so admirable a theoretic structure.

Modern mechanistic materialism was founded by Hobbes (1588–1671), who took up the very problem which Gassendi had given up as hopeless. Even in the face of this problem Hobbes is not willing to abandon the fundamental principle that movement is the sole reality. The movements of corporeal substances are transmitted to the senses, whence they pass to the brain and from there to the heart. Here the movement is reflected, and the counter-movement, proceeding from the heart to the brain and thence to the peripheral organs, is the sensation. All the other psychical phenomena develop out of the movement of sensation by mechanical processes of a similar sort. The soul is thus no longer a particular kind of matter as in ancient materialism; it has become an effect of mechanical processes. Moreover, Hobbes does not start with the concept of the soul but with the elements of mental life. Here, too, the first influence of empiricism makes itself felt. England, henceforth, remains the home of materialism. One of the best-known literary documents of the psychological materialism associated with the free-thought movement are Toland's *Letters to Serena*,

[1] *Opera*, Florence, 1725, II (2) 8, sect. III, t. VI, c. 3: "Qui sensibile gigni ex insensibilibus possit."

Sophia Charlotte, Queen of Prussia (1704), in which thought is described as an accompaniment of the material processes in the brain.

The type of materialism under consideration is enriched by the founders of associational psychology, Hartley and Priestley. Hartley (1704–57) is the originator of the vibration hypothesis according to which mental processes have as their physical counterparts specific vibrations of brain fibres. He did not, however, draw the materialistic consequences of this hypothesis, but confessed that the analysis of psychical processes must always yield psychical constituents, and that a sensation which is not capable of further analysis cannot be explained by movement. Priestley (1733–1804) developed these new materialistic presuppositions into a rounded system of psychology. He sees a proof for the identity of brain and mind in that uniform coordination in consequence of which all psychical phenomena, among which the associations of ideas form the most important rôle, are determined by brain vibrations.

Without contributing to psychology any original points of view, mechanistic materialism, together with all it implied, passed over into the systems of Lamettrie and Holbach. At the same time we encounter here the transition to our final form of materialism, psychophysical materialism.

### (c) *Psychophysical Materialism*

This form of materialism was introduced into psychology by Diderot, who held that some material process was involved in every act of sensation. It is true that in expressing this thought he was not without forerunners, and there were other writers of his own period who agreed with him. The general background is furnished by the metaphysics of Spinoza, whose principles have influenced psychology in very diverse ways. Maupertuis, too, had written of sentient atoms in an anonymous piece published in 1761, and in his *Buch von der Natur*, published in the same year, he applied the principle of psychophysical parallelism throughout in connection with the discussion of voluntary movement. While his fantastic system permitted of only an occasional application of this principle, Diderot developed the psychological principles involved in parallelism with much clearness. Thus he accounted for the unity of consciousness by the supposition that the sentient particles of matter come into immediate contact with each other. From the spatial continuity of atoms follows the unity of the mental elements associated with them.

The form of materialism under discussion has also influenced the most recent psychological movement in Germany, where we find indications of materialistic ways of thinking as early as the beginning of the eighteenth century. A much-discussed anonymous piece, *Briefwechsel über die Seele* (1713), which apparently originated under the influence of the English Enlightenment, defended the view that all sensations and ideas originate from movements of brain fibres (*fibris cerebri*). In the eighteenth century, the century of the Enlightenment, a period so memorable for the history of our science, materialistic psychology was widely influenced by the presuppositions, borrowed from association psychology, of the dependence of psychical processes upon brain processes.[1] A deeper comprehension of the principle of psychophysical parallelism is revealed in many utterances of Kant, which point to a pure monism. His criticism of rational psychology indeed involved a demand for a purely empirical psychology, but he admitted the possibility, at the same time, of a solution of the fundamental metaphysical problem of psychology. If matter were a thing in itself, it

[1] *Cf.* Chapter IV, 2, below.

would, as a composite reality, be absolutely different from the soul, which is simple. But since it is merely an external phenomenon, it is possible to suppose that what appears to the physical senses as extended substance is endowed with thought which can be consciously apprehended by its own inner sense. That which in one relation is called corporeal would in another relation be conscious.[1]

A new era in the history of materialistic psychology begins as a reaction to the philosophy of Romanticism, and develops hand in hand with the progress of natural science. The most influential representatives of this tendency in the latter half of the nineteenth century were Moleschott and Büchner. Moleschott's view approaches equative materialism, which identifies brain and mind, while Büchner contents himself with asserting the indissoluble connection between spirit and matter. Just how physical movement is transformed into consciousness is for him an irrelevant question. With all the emphasis which one finds here upon experience, there is a curious absence of any genuine psychological analysis. With a *naïveté* which is nothing less than archaic, all conscious processes are classified under the common head of "thought." Empirical psychology can, of course, not be built upon such foundations. Even the most profound thinker among these materialists, Czolbe (1819–73), who made the exclusion of the supersensible the fundamental principle of his system, abandoned all pretence of empirical investigation, losing himself in a maze of hypotheses concerning the sentiency of atoms, and arriving at a sort of world soul composed of vibrating atoms endowed with consciousness. It is only in the human organism that they consolidate sufficiently to make individualized psychical life possible.

The controversy over materialism in Germany differed

[1] Kant, *Kritik der reinen Vernunft*, ed. Rosenkranz, p. 288.

from earlier controversies mainly in the influence of Darwinism. On the whole, psychology profited but little from this controversy. In the far-ranging discussion regarding the nature of the soul between Carl Vogt and Rudolph Wagner, Virchow also took part.[1] The energy of soul substance or of psychical ether, he insisted, must ultimately be susceptible of physical measurement. The controversy reached its climax in the association of natural scientists which convened in Munich in 1877, where Haeckel asserted that the cell was the basis of all psychical life. We must assume the existence of soul life in the cell, and, in order to carry the matter to a logical conclusion, attribute consciousness to atoms. This "Plastidulseele," as it was humorously called, was criticised with unsparing irony by Virchow.

Thus psychological materialism in this final form either dropped back into the ways of thinking of older metaphysical systems, or else it recognized the principle of psychophysical parallelism and became a border problem of empirical psychology, as in Bastian, for example, in Germany, or in Herbert Spencer, in England.

Materialistic presuppositions also occasionally developed into specifically modern ideas. A peculiar form of materialistic psychology was worked out by Jäger,[2] a Darwinian zoologist of the old school, according to whom psychic vapors radiate from the body which affect the olfactory sense, and thus give rise to love, family and race solidarity, etc., in the percipient.[3] Jäger's ideas won some recognition, especially among the Darwinians, who hailed Jäger's efforts as the beginnings of a chemistry of the soul, but they were also subjected to much ridicule. Jäger's theories met with some favor outside of the exact sciences. Mantegazza, for ex-

---

[1] *Ges. Abh. z. wiss. Med.*, 1856, p. 17.
[2] Jäger, G., *Die Entdeckung der Seele*, III, 2d ed., 1880.
[3] *Cf.* Rádl, *Geschichte der biologischen Theorien*, II, 1909, p. 435.

ample, utilized them in his notorious work, *Physiology of Love*. They have to some extent been revived by J. Loeb, who attempted to construct a comparative psychology upon chemistry, and who saw in his theory of tropism the key to the elementary phenomena of life.[1] The discussion, however, as will be seen, has now shifted completely from the field of metaphysics to that of physiology.

A comparison of the various forms of materialistic psychology shows that they have developed in connection with different influences. In dualistic psychology, for example, we find a combination of popular ideas and religious demands; spiritualistic psychology has been very closely associated with the great philosophical systems; while, finally, materialistic psychology has always appeared concomitantly with natural science. These general influences have always dominated psychological reflection; we shall meet with them again as we seek to trace the various tendencies of empirical psychology.

[1] *Dynamics of Living Matter*, 1906.

## II. EMPIRICAL PSYCHOLOGY

### CHAPTER III

#### DESCRIPTIVE PSYCHOLOGY

Empirical psychology can be divided according to different points of view. Although its various tendencies agree among themselves as regards the proper point of departure for psychological investigation, namely, the testimony of introspection, they differ from each other partly as regards the principles to be employed in the analysis and combination of psychical facts, partly as regards the exact scientific goal which empirical psychology should set for itself. The latter difference divides empirical psychology into two leading types, descriptive psychology and explanatory psychology. To be sure, descriptive and explanatory psychology do not represent contradictory but supplementary points of view. Nevertheless, the preponderance of the one or the other method of procedure is usually sufficiently distinct to keep the tendencies separate. The conceptual separation of these two points of view has, of course, not taken place until comparatively recently. Some psychologists—Lipps, for example—have taken an extreme view of this relation and have declared the problem of explanatory as distinguished from descriptive psychology to be the establishment of causal connection within reality, thus gaining a basis or substructure for the empirical data of consciousness.[1] The sharp opposition of the two tendencies seen here has de-

[1] *Leitfaden der Psychologie*, 3d ed., 1909, p. 43.

veloped out of an earlier status, where the contrast was not nearly so marked and where the descriptive type of psychology was on the whole the predominant one. Meanwhile there are various points of contact between the two forms of psychology under consideration. Thus what is called intellectualism in psychology has often operated against an unbiassed study of the mental life. The tendency to intellectualize the mental processes, to force them into a conceptual system dominated by intellectual categories, has characterized descriptive and explanatory psychology throughout.[1] Supported, on the one hand, by the ideas current in popular psychology and, on the other, by certain metaphysical presuppositions, intellectualism has made itself felt both in faculty psychology and in association psychology.

Descriptive psychology was for a long period dominated by prescientific conceptions. This period coincides in the main with that of faculty psychology. Reflection upon the question as to how psychical facts are known led to the psychology of the inner sense, which forms the starting-point for a number of tendencies in the modern phenomenology of consciousness.

## 1. Period of Prescientific Concepts: The Doctrine of Mental Faculties

Perhaps more than any other science, psychology has had to face and settle accounts with prescientific conceptions, such as one encounters at the threshold of every science. The terms of every-day speech which are used to designate certain experiences are adopted uncritically both for purposes of description and of explanation. But explanation must

---

[1] *Cf.* Wundt, "Logik u. Psychologie," *Zeitschrift für pädagogische Psychologie u. Hygiene*, 1910, pp. 1 *ff*.

always remain primitive and inadequate so long as the hasty descriptions of common usage are substituted for the genuine analysis of the phenomena concerned. Prior to every form of scientific psychology the terms soul, reason, will, and the like are already in common use. They serve the purposes of classification about in the same way that the terms light, sound, etc., serve to classify physical phenomena. Such rude classifications are indispensable for purposes of general orientation, and even scientific usage must begin with them. While, however, popular physical classifications have corresponded fairly well to the classifications which have resulted from a more exact analysis of physical phenomena, the needs which have been of influence in shaping the distinctions of popular psychology have not been quite the same as those which influence scientific psychology, so that a considerable discrepancy between the popular and the scientific classifications was bound to result.

Most of the concepts in question show a considerable degree of generality, while appropriate designations for the more specific groups of mental phenomena, like certain kinds of simple feelings, are wanting altogether. It was the salient differences in complex experiences which first forced themselves upon the introspective attention. The generality of the concepts thus originating favored the tendency to substantialize them, a tendency which is traceable to the earliest nature mythologies, from which the concepts in question passed over into metaphysical psychology. The traces are also revealed in the empirical applications which these concepts have received. The need for a rational comprehension of psychical facts prompted the appropriation of these class designations and transformed them into powers or faculties which are supposed to produce the psychical facts to be explained. The notion of power is meanwhile still mythological in its significance. If human volition constituted the origin of the idea of power, and if power thus manifests itself in things as the human will manifests itself in actions, then the transformation into faculties, together with the personification implied in that, must find its justification in the caprice with which psychical phenomena manifest themselves. Thus arose the concept of mental faculty, which, self-contradictory as it appears, was well adapted to account for psychical experiences as these presented themselves to the primitive mind.

Faculty psychology originally stood in intimate relation with the metaphysical doctrine of the parts of the soul. Notable beginnings of empirical psychology were made in the faculty psychology of Scholasticism. The psychology of the Renaissance, developing, as it does, in many directions, represents a transition to the faculty theories of modern psychology. The various forms of faculty psychology are meanwhile principally distinguishable on the basis of historical epochs, a matter which is readily understood since the development of any new point of view would of itself lead psychology beyond prescientific conceptions and hence also beyond the point of view of faculty psychology.

### (a) *The Doctrine of the Parts of the Soul*

In its earliest form the doctrine of mental faculties is difficult to distinguish from the doctrine of the parts of the soul. The only thing possible for metaphysical psychology was to divide the soul in accordance with existing verbal distinctions. Such a partition of the soul could either take place upon the basis of empirical differences found among different psychical processes or else a gradation of these processes could be undertaken. The first principle of division depends, from our modern point of view, upon the fact that certain mental contents can be classed together in virtue of the possibility of passing from one to another of the contents within a group by intermediate gradations, whereas such a transition is impossible between members of one group and those of another. Thus one can pass from one feeling to another through intermediate feelings, but one could by no possibility pass from, say, a feeling of unpleasantness to the sensation of blue. The second principle of division depends upon the observed fact that within a given group of more or less complex processes, as, for example, cognitive processes, a number of different steps or stages can be distinguished. Other classes of processes can be marked off on the basis of their objects or of their relation to other mental processes.[1]

The first-mentioned and most commonly accepted ground of division was the one which forced itself first upon the attention. We meet it in the Pythagorean doctrine of the parts of the soul. It was here that Aresas of Croton invented the terminology later adopted by Plato. The well-known tripartite division of the soul into reason (τὸ λογιστικόν), will (τὸ θυμοειδές), and desire (τὸ ἐπιθυμητικόν) were in Plato, of course, still derived from the idea of the mixture of the soul with the body in the sense of his metaphysical psychology. The Platonic division, however, is an anticipation of the later classification of psychological processes into those of cognition, feeling, and desire.

To these psychological distinctions corresponds a spatial separation of the various parts of the soul, with the νοῦς located in the head, the θυμός in the breast, and the ἐπιθυμητικόν in the lower part of the body. This localization of the parts of the soul was widely accepted in the psychology of antiquity. Even Democritus, whose scientific attainments far exceeded those of his contemporaries, agrees in this respect with the traditional views, locating

[1] For further particulars concerning principles of classification see Chapter VII, below.

reflection in the brain, anger in the heart, and desire in the liver.

Plato apparently drew a further distinction within each of the parts of the three divisions of the soul. Each of the parts is characterized by a particular form of desire, the highest by Eros, the characteristic of the φιλόσοφος. Each, too, is characterized by a particular kind of pleasure whose grade is determined by the value of the particular part of the soul to which it belongs. There are also suggestions of a relation between sense-perception and desire (ἐπιθυμητικόν), and between opinion (δόξα) and θυμοειδές. Here the second principle of division makes itself felt in so far as different grades are assumed within the departments of cognition, feeling, and desire. Side by side with these distinctions is also found the distinction— a direct outgrowth of metaphysical dualism—between the higher and the lower parts of the soul, a division plainly based upon the various grades of conscious processes and brought into harmony with the former by the fact that the lower part of the soul as sensibility comprehends both desire and feeling.

The doctrine of the parts of the soul is in Aristotle transformed into the doctrine of mental faculties. Aristotle located the soul in the heart, as the centre of the body, an idea which for a long time competed successfully with the scientific doctrine that the brain was the seat of psychical phenomena. The latter doctrine, already held by the physicians of ancient Egypt, was eventually recovered by Herophilus of Alexandria and Galen. The older spatial separation gave way in Aristotle to conceptual distinctions which are based upon the successive stages of biological development. Experience reveals four such stages: (1) growth and nutrition (τὸ θρεπτικόν), (2) sensation and imagination (αἰσθητικόν and φανταστικόν), (3) conation and locomotion (ὀρεκτικόν and κινητικὸν κατὰ τὸν τόπον), and (4) thought (διανοητικόν). Conation, however, which occasionally is divided into desire (ἐπιθυμία), feeling (θυμός), and will (βούλησις), and locomotion are in the main subordinated to sensation as impulse and to thought as will, so that the scheme reduces to a tripartite division, the nutritive, sensitive, and rational soul. The plant possesses only the first, the animal the first and the second, while man possesses all three. The Platonic bipartite division here reasserts itself, since the two lower faculties present a common antithesis to reason (διανοητικόν).

Although the Aristotelian system offers no new distinctions, it nevertheless possesses two advantages. In the first place, the idea of the unity of the soul is asserted, since neither of the faculties mentioned is capable of operating in independence of the rest. Secondly, there is a clear suggestion of the evolutionary point of view. The rough distinctions proposed do not, of course, completely solve the problem of classification; but with the contention that the higher faculties presuppose the lower is combined the thought that the human soul stands in the same relation to the animal soul as the higher faculties stand to the lower, so that here, too, the unifying idea of evolution tends to bridge over the dualism which would otherwise exist.

It is the latter idea especially which was followed out in Patristic philosophy. Dicæarchus even refused to recognize any longer the distinction between the rational soul and the sensory functions. Diodorus of Tyre supported him in this, but associated both functions with an identical substance, ether. The Stoics, indeed, possessed in pneuma the physical principle of unity of the soul life, but they did not hesitate to grant the existence, at the same time, of an increasing number of mental faculties. The Stoics were, perhaps, the first to recognize the five senses as parts or faculties of the soul, *i. e.*, of the pneuma. Adding to these the power of reproduction, of speech, and of reason, there resulted a total of eight faculties, with the ruling faculty, reason (ἡγεμονικόν), at the head. In later Stoicism and in the earlier developments of Neo-Platonism, psychology merely repeats the Platonic and Aristotelian distinctions. The doubtful comparison of the soul and its faculties to a house and its inmates originated with Philo.

Patristic philosophy, whose metaphysical psychology unavoidably involved the doctrine of the unity of the soul, appears to have been only slightly influenced by the faculty psychology. Tertullian opposed the Platonic division of the soul into parts, pointing out convincingly that the difference between the higher and the lower faculties of knowledge rested upon the nature of the objects of knowledge, the cognitive soul being equally active in all cases, and he compared the distribution of the soul throughout the body to the division of a column of air as it passes into the different pipes of an organ. To be sure, the tripartite division of Aristotle reappears in Gregory of Nyssa, the parts of the soul being expressly designated as mental faculties. On the other side, however, is the great authority of Augustine, who insists upon the strict unity of the soul. It is not until the period of Scholasticism that the Aristotelian doctrine of mental faculties is again revived; here, however, it is combined with sundry efforts at purely empirical investigation, a fact which differentiates the faculty psychology of Scholasticism from all previous types.

### (b) *The Beginnings of Empirical Psychology in Scholasticism*

Scholasticism seems often at first sight to be merely a synonym for useless dialectical controversies. Nothing is more improbable, however, than the belief that men's desire for empirical knowledge should have remained latent for a period of history of the extent of Scholasticism. In the absence of an interest in external nature, the knowledge of which, at least during the Platonic period of Scholasticism, was largely dependent upon the fantastic nature philosophy of Timæus, men's interest in empirical knowledge turned the more exclusively to the phenomena of the inner life. This led to the beginnings of an empirical psychology whose justification is recognized in the oft-repeated statement that the knowledge of reality divides into two branches, *physica corporis* and *physica animæ*. Empirical psychology was, of course, developed in the manner of the time. Psychology, among other things, is not content to describe and classify mental processes but seeks to view them teleologically as well. It is the history of the soul which is to be expounded, and the Scholastic writers accordingly appear not as cautious scientists but as pious souls yearning to comprehend the divine mysteries and thus to share in the divine favor.

The first beginnings of psychological reflection from an empirical point of view are to be found in the older nominalism.[1] The author of the conceptualistic treatise *De Intellectibus* teaches the close connection between sense-perception and thought (*sensus* and *intellectus*).[2] Between these stands the sensuous imagination (*imaginatio*), whose contents, like those of sense-perception itself, are said to be indistinct (*confusa animæ perceptio*). One calls to mind here the rôle which the alleged indistinctness of sense-perception played in the theory of knowledge subsequent to Descartes and the reflex influence it exerted upon physiological psychology. Already in the tenth century the three higher cognitive faculties (*intellectus, ratio, mens*) are described as *sensus animi* by a nominalistic glossarist; the fac-

---

[1] *Cf.* Siebeck, *op. cit.*, I, pp. 384 *ff.*
[2] See Cousin's edition of *Abélard*, II, p. 732.

ulties of the soul are localized in the three ventricles of the brain (*folliculi*), in which the *principalitas vitæ, sensus,* and *motus* have their seat.[1] Nevertheless, the traditional lore from which the Occident benefited before the introduction of Arabian philosophy was sufficiently meagre. The teaching of Damascenus concerning the mental faculties and their respective functions seems to have been held in peculiar esteem.[2] This writer contents himself, in the sketch referred to, with a meagre enumeration of the best-known psychical states; in the discussion of the will, for example, six leading concepts (*consilium, judicium, sententia, electio, impulsus, usus*) are dismissed with a few lines.

The influence of Arabian culture upon psychology was mediated through the translations and adaptations of Constantine of Carthage, who flourished in the second half of the eleventh century.[3] Constantine's view of the nature of the soul represents a superficial admixture of Aristotelian and Platonic conceptions.[4] The soul is treated as specifically different from the body. It is the primary cause of life, the secondary being pneuma, which acts by means of special physiological processes. The different manifestations of the function of cognition correspond to the anatomical divisions of the brain. The pneuma of the anterior ventricle yields sensation and perception, that of the posterior, movement and memory. In detail, his exposition resembles fairly closely that of Galen. Among those most immediately influenced by Constantine is William of Conches.[5] His definition of the soul as *spiritus corpori conjunctus* is, indeed, meagre enough. Of real importance, however, are the unmistakable beginnings of genetic psychology made by

[1] Barach, *Zur Geschichte d. Nominalismus von Roszellin*, 1866, pp. 9 ff.
[2] John Damascenus, *De orthod. fid.*, II, cap. 13 ff.
[3] Siebeck, *op. cit.*, I, pp. 527 ff.
[4] *De commun. medic. cogn. necess. loc.* (ed. Bas.), IV, 1.
[5] Siebeck, *op. cit.*, I, pp. 531 ff.

this writer. A number of faculties mediate between perception and understanding (*ratio*). The understanding, which knows physical causes, becomes intelligence when knowledge extends to the non-physical, and this development has actually taken place in the process of historical evolution.[1]

In John of Salisbury we meet a similar effort to connect genetic ideas with a fundamentally Platonic theory of the nature of the soul.[2] His attempt to exhibit the development of the various grades of mental functions from sense-perception is a partial anticipation of the type of genetic-sensualistic psychology destined later to become so familiar on British soil. The complete execution of this task was rendered impossible, of course, by the limited knowledge of the time. Sense-perception is called a combination of sensation and judgment.[3] A series of higher judgments leads up to conviction (*ratio*) which has its seat in the brain between imagination (*cella phantastica*) and memory. As *ratio* is superior to the senses, it is in turn subordinated to intellect, which, in spite of the divine enlightenment it receives, depends upon sense-perception. Empirical psychology did not pass beyond these beginnings until its contact with Arabian science.

Avicenna (980–1037), the celebrated teacher of philosophy and medicine at Ispahan, left behind him a body of empirical psychology which became the common heritage of the various branches of Scholasticism.[4] He separated philosophical psychology from medical psychology, although his empirical investigations do not carry him far beyond an elaborate system of classification. In his theory of sensation, for example, he distinguishes eight pairs of contrasting sense qualities,

---

[1] See Cousin, *Œuvr. inéd. d'Ab.*, pp. 671 *ff*.
[2] Siebeck, *op. cit.*, I, pp. 518 *ff*.
[3] *Primum judicium viget in sensu; Metalogicus*, 1159–60, IV, 11, p. 892.
[4] Siebeck, *op. cit.*, II, pp. 22 *ff*.

four for the sense of touch, and one for each of the remaining senses. The various parts of the soul are subdivided also, while each of the three kinds of *anima vegetativa* is in turn split up into smaller divisions. The relation of body and soul is conceived from a peculiar teleological point of view. Each soul, namely, belongs to that particular body for which it is best fitted. The attempt to construct a genetic conception is suggested by the doctrine that the principles of knowledge, although innate, can develop only in the wake of perception. To be sure, this reflection loses much of its force through the assumption that the senses are capable only of sensation, true knowledge being the exclusive product of the soul.

With the incorporation of the views of Avicenna into the theological system of Alexander of Hales (d. 1245)[1] we reach the point in mediæval psychology where the older Platonic characterizations yield before the influence of Aristotle. Alexander again distinguished mental faculties from vital functions, defining the soul as a thinking and active substance whose continuous activity constitutes life. The original active power of the soul is desire (*appetitus*), which has as its aim the unification of potentiality and actuality.

More closely related to the ancient models, the exposition of Thomas Aquinas adds to the Aristotelian system only an elaborate conceptual apparatus. The relation of the soul to the mental faculties is the same as that of substance and accident. The soul alone is the subject of reason and the rational will, while the organism as a whole serves as the basis of the vegetative and the sensitive functions. The contrast between the higher and the lower functions of the soul thus reappears in this rationalistic form.

The gradually awakening epistemological interest of the time finds expression in the psychological theories of Roger

[1] Siebeck, *op. cit.*, II, pp. 180 *ff.*

Bacon.[1] The lower and the higher faculties of cognition are for him two different stages of the same inner experience which arises partly out of sense-impressions and is partly of a transcendent origin. Neither are intellect and will two separate powers, but functions, rather, of one and the same fundamental psychical faculty, a doctrine which makes Bacon the immediate predecessor of a more influential writer, Duns Scotus. The most thoroughgoing efforts to arrive at a psychological theory of the process of knowledge, however, were made by Occam.[2] The external object, in virtue of its own peculiar quality, gives rise to a sense-impression which is perceived by the sensuous soul (*apparitio*). Through an act of abstraction, which is a function of the inner sense (*phantasticum*), the conscious perception becomes an inner image. Sense-perceptions and their reproductions are now elaborated by the intellect, which, through a process of abstraction, forms concepts and judgments, affirmative and negative judgments being formed through the co-operation of the will. This psycho-epistemological sketch serves to illustrate how far these ancient thinkers, although laboring under the limitations of the faculty psychology with its barren intellectualism, succeeded in analyzing an important process like that of cognition.

Whether we are to see in the psychology of Scholasticism as a whole the final phases of the tradition of antiquity or the beginnings of modern empirical psychology need not be decided here. In any case, the psychology of the Renaissance, to which we now turn, presents a different picture in both respects.

---

[1] Siebeck, *op. cit.*, III, pp. 177 *ff*.
[2] Siebeck, *op. cit.*, X, pp. 317 *ff*.

### (c) The Psychology of the Renaissance

One of the best evidences of the stimulating effect upon psychology produced by the vital participation in all phases of life so characteristic of the period of the Renaissance is the psychology of Ludovicus Vives (1492–1540). His principal work, *De Anima et Vita* (Bruges, 1538), which exerted a large influence upon the psychological theories of the sixteenth and seventeenth centuries, is characterized by a definitely empirical point of view. The task of psychology is to discover the manner of the soul's activity. Psychological description must be rigorously faithful to experience. Although the investigation still employs the tools and conceptions of faculty psychology, there are suggestions of a sort of physiological psychology which brings the concepts of soul and body into close relation. Vives, moreover, proves himself emancipated from the Aristotelian school by treating the brain as the seat of psychical processes.

The influence of the new knowledge upon the various tendencies and directions of ancient psychology is also clearly discernible. With the recrudescence of Platonic psychology the whole swarm of ancient psychological conceptions again became current, and in their mutual contradiction the scepticism of the period found a ready support. In the chapter On the Soul in his book, *De Incertitudine et Vanitate Scientiarum* (1527), a work characteristic of this tendency, Agrippa of Nettesheym makes a collection of these contradictions; but, while referring to the fiendish Aristotle and the divine Plato, he himself sceptically refrains from expressing any opinion of his own concerning the soul.

More definite opinions are expressed by certain philosophizing physicians of the time of Paracelsus, whose psychology represents a fusion of traditional conceptions with the new doctrine of Archeus. Paracelsus himself fantastically transformed many of the older teachings. He abandoned the time-honored doctrine of temperaments taught by Galen, substituting for the four elements the main principles of alchemy, sulphur, salt, and mercury. This tendency is also represented by the chemist Van Helmont, who distinguishes the sensitive soul (*anima sensitiva*), whose seat is the duumvirate, from spirit (*mens*), an imperishable substance, whose attributes are *intellectus, voluntas,* and *amor*.[1] The manner in which this part of the soul, which is subject to neither fatigue nor disease, can act upon the others is left undetermined.[2]

Connected only slightly with this questionable theoretical psychology, a secular Renaissance psychology is developed which we can recognize as a forerunner of the empirical psychology of the eighteenth century. The doctrines of temperaments, astrology, and physiognomy here stand in the service of a realistic characterology. Juan Huarte's *Examen de ingenios* (1575) thus teaches an individual psychology which seeks to bring the mental traits of the individual into relation with bodily constitution. With the French psychologists of this period, beginning with Michel de Montaigne (1580), this individual psychology tends more and more to become practical anthropology.[3]

More important than these fantastic or superstitious ideas and this secular psychology is the controversy between the traditional faculty psychology and the new conception of soul substance which was already preparing in the Marburg school. Casmann[4] does not, indeed, explain the relation be-

[1] *Cf.* Strunz, "Die Psychologie des Joh. Bapt. van Helmont in ihren Grundlagen," *Zeitschrift f. Phil. u. phil. Kritik*, CXXV, 1905, p. 2.
[2] Van Helmont, *Imago Mentis*, § 7, *Opera*, 1648.
[3] *Cf.* with this the pregnant discussion of M. Dessoir, *Gesch. d. n. d. Psychologie*, I, 2d ed., 1897, pp. 47 ff.
[4] *Psychologia anthropologica*, 1594.

tween a unitary soul and a plurality of faculties; nevertheless, he raises the objection that each faculty requires a second faculty for the explanation of its peculiar functions. Neither did the psychology of Descartes tolerate a multiplicity of separate faculties, for the soul has only a single faculty, that of thought; and the distinction of the various thought processes, which all rest upon the fundamental distinction between active and passive thought, does not in any way jeopardize the underlying unity. The popular distinction between a higher and a lower mental faculty Descartes, clinging closely to the metaphysical presuppositions of his psychology, explains by a supposed conflict between them in the pineal gland in which a movement set up by the animal spirits in the body meets another movement set up by the soul through the activity of the will. For the rest, the distinction between power and faculty does not as yet exist in the Cartesian psychology, while later the concepts of psychical powers and psychical faculties are used interchangeably, a convincing illustration of the fact that in the history of psychology distinctions of terminology and of fact are difficult to keep separated.[1]

### (d) The Newer Faculty Psychology

It was John Locke who, writing from the standpoint of empirical psychology, was the first to urge emphatically against faculty psychology those objections which have become commonplaces in modern psychology. In the discussion of the freedom of the will he pointed out the futility of the attempt to explain freedom by reference to a faculty of volition; as well call in a vocal faculty to explain singing, or a faculty of dancing to explain dancing. Psychology

---

[1] See the following from the Cartesian Clauberg: "Vis facultas potentia quæ nihil aliud quam non repugnantia ad agendum."

gained little, however, through Locke's substitution of powers for faculties. This is evidenced in Locke himself by his curious oversight of the mutual interaction of mental processes. The separate powers no more influence one another than the power to sing, for example, influences the power to dance. In the enumeration of mental powers, moreover, Locke was hardly less generous than faculty psychology. Leibniz transformed the concept of faculty into that of actual tendency, and he was able to dispense with the swarm of faculties the more easily inasmuch as his doctrine of the persistence of *petites perceptions* permitted him to refer what were apparently novel phenomena to their temporal antecedents.

In Christian Wolff (1679–1754), who first employed the term mental faculty, the Leibnizian tendency was directly continued.[1] In his rational psychology he designates the power of representation (*vis repræsentativa*) as the fundamental power of the soul. This is the sufficient reason for every mental phenomenon, in so far as it transforms the possibilities of psychical processes, *i. e.*, the faculties, into actualities. On the ground of the conceptual discriminations attempted by Leibniz, therefore, power and faculty are kept distinct, thus resulting in a distinction which goes back directly to the Aristotelian δύναμις and ἐνέργεια. But Wolff does not remain long upon these heights of abstraction. The faculties, which in the beginning are mere possibilities of mental processes, now become attributes of the soul; at first mere *nudæ agendi possibilitates*, they now turn into the more substantial forms of natural dispositions, so much so that their relation to the mind can be compared with the relation of bodily organs to the body. The classification of these faculties is based upon the overlapping oppo-

---

[1] Wolff, *Psychologia rationalis*, 1734; *Psychologia empirica*, 1732. The difference between the two treatises is less than the titles would suggest.

sites of cognition—desire, and of sense—reason. In the first pair of faculties the Leibnizian distinction between cognition and appetition as attributes of the monad, a distinction to which Wolff always adhered, is clearly discernible. While cognition and desire (the latter term also includes feeling) are here juxtaposed without any difference of valuation, the second principal division yields a lower and a higher faculty of cognition, as also a lower and a higher faculty of desire. In the subdivisions of these four principal faculties, meanwhile, there is not the slightest attempt at system. Even the most complex mental faculties are "explained" by invoking the magic words mental faculty. In his attempt to explain the interaction of the various faculties each faculty functioned as a sort of intelligence or, at least, had enough in common with the faculty of intelligence to render intelligent co-operation among the faculties possible. The various grades of intelligence, furthermore, could readily be represented on the analogy of the Leibnizian distinction between clear and obscure perceptions.

There is not a writer in the history of faculty psychology after Aristotle who gives so much attention to mental faculties as Wolff. With Descartes the contrast between the active and passive mental processes had received the prime emphasis; Locke had designated sensation and reflection as distinct sources of knowledge; in Leibniz, finally, the principle of psychological explanation of primary importance was the power of representation. It must, of course, be remembered that Wolff passed into only a part of the Aristotelian heritage, which had been the common possession of scientific thought for so many centuries. He was incapable of the painstaking and ingenious methods of investigation characteristic of Aristotle. His empirical psychology, in fact, is little more than a questionable determination of the number and the character of mental faculties.

In the Wolffian school the doctrines of faculty psychology were extended to the cognate sciences, like ethics, in the rational utilitarianism of which it readily struck root, and æsthetics, which contented itself for a long period with calling the creative imagination a lower order of the faculty of cognition. In spite of the arbitrary manner in which they were deduced, the Wolffian distinctions long maintained their influence. When we come to examine in detail the faculty psychology of the eighteenth century emanating from Wolff we find it to be an achievement of doubtful value. It must not be forgotten, however, that the real aim was to construct an empirical psychology which should discover introspectively the contents of consciousness and then discover the elementary powers of which they are the manifestations. The methods of description and classification employed here were, as in many other branches of psychology, modelled after the methods of the natural sciences. It will be remembered that the eighteenth century was the century of those descriptive sciences in which Linné and Buffon were masters. To be sure, attempts at explanation in the field of psychology could not but have meagre results. The following is a typical example: If the power of imagination combines with the understanding, the creative faculty results; if it combines with reason, we get the power of anticipation, etc. The attempt to explain, to reduce the complex to the simple, is sufficiently commendable; but the actual explanation is undertaken with methods wholly insufficient for the purpose.

Even the opposition to the Wolffian psychology did not succeed in freeing itself from the domination of the conceptions of the school psychology. Crusius attacked the doctrine of mental faculties in his work, *Entwurf der notwendigen Vernunftwahrheiten* (1745), asserting that they were merely so many arbitrarily abstracted powers which made a purely causal explanation impossible. To meet the latter demand, he assumed actual powers in the soul substance which itself remained simple. There are mental powers of first order, like consciousness and sensation; of the second order, like imagination and the capacity for incomplete ideas. In spite of the strong emphasis upon causal explanation, these determinations are still distinctly reminiscent of the point of view of the faculty psychology. The psychological disciples of Bonnet, men like Irwing, Lossius, and Hissmann, schooled as they were in the methods of physiology, passed a more effective criticism upon the old doctrine of mental faculties. They were themselves, however, not free from the inclination to explain the various conscious processes by reference to some single fundamental power. As a rule, sensation, which was thought of as a reaction of the soul to the excitation of nerve fibres, figured as such a fundamental power. Tetens (1736–1805) criticised this view on the ground that perception and judgment were thus treated as belonging on the same plane as sensation, while he himself held that sensation, perception, and thought were distinguished only in the degree of self-activity which the soul displayed.

Tetens, meanwhile, made an important contribution to the school psychology.[1] He effected a breach in the Wolffian scheme by the addition of a new faculty, that of feeling, to those sanctioned by the Wolffian tradition. Tetens proposed a new pair of fundamental mental activities. In his attempt to "reduce the various capacities to the simplest faculties, and to penetrate to the primary origins of these faculties in some fundamental power," he comes upon the opposites of receptivity and activity. The first is feeling, the second embraces the various activities of will, the inner activities of idea and thought as well as the outer. Thus originated the tripartite division of feeling, cognition, and will, which was destined to dominate psychology for a long time to come.

[1] *Versuche über die menschliche Natur*, 1776–7, pp. 4, 7.

The rationalistic origin of the scheme is evident from the description of feeling, ideation, and thought as phases or subdivisions of the general faculty of cognition.

Both of the above classifications meet us again in Kant. Sense and understanding, the receptive and the spontaneous sides of mental life, appear as lower and higher faculties of cognition. Cognition, feeling, and desire, on the other side, appear as three fundamental faculties, separate and irreducible. The Leibnizian distinction between faculty and power, on the other hand, disappears.[1] Furthermore, Kant proposes, as correlatives of concept, judgment, and conclusion in logic, the trichotomy of the higher faculty of cognition into understanding, reason, and judgment. For the relation of these three phases of the higher faculty of cognition to the principal faculties of the mind mentioned above, the relation of reason to the faculty of desire appears to have been normative. Reason, as the faculty of ideas, could have a constitutive significance only in the sphere of practical conduct. Since the understanding coincided with the faculty of cognition, feeling naturally came under the faculty of judgment. In so far as this schematization took into account only the higher manifestations of the faculties concerned, it exercised an unfavorable influence upon the psychological treatment of the three fundamental faculties. Furthermore, the sharp separation of the fundamental faculties obscured the fact of their essential unity and the fruitless interaction of faculties everywhere took the place of the actual phenomena of the mental life. Fortunately, Kant did not adhere to the schematism of the three *Critiques* in his principal psychological work, *Anthropologie*, but presented instead a body of practical psychology which he had inherited from the Enlightenment and which is still worthy of study to-day.

The Kantian faculty psychology was continued by his

[1] *Cf., e. g.*, Krug, *Philosophisches Lexikon* (1827–34), article "Kraft."

school. K. L. Reinhold sought to explain the several varieties of the faculty of cognition by reference to the faculty of ideation or representation. Representation without a faculty of representation is to him unthinkable. He even believed himself to be acting in particular sympathy with the spirit of Kant when he substituted the investigation of mental faculties for the investigation of the mind itself. For the same reason he keeps in strict separation the representing subject from the faculty of representation. The former determines the attributes of the faculty of representation merely in a logical, not in a real sense. J. F. Fries (1773-1843) insisted upon a sharp separation of philosophical anthropology and empirical psychology. The latter is an experimental physics of the inner life, whereas the former is a theory of this life, bearing about the same relation to empirical psychology as the philosophy of nature holds to physics. Fries grants to the usual conceptual determinations of mental faculties only a descriptive significance and demands their proof by philosophical anthropology. These faculties must, furthermore, be subordinated to general laws.[1] All causal relations of inner experience must be ascribed to a faculty as cause, not to an activity as its manifestation. So long as the activity of a faculty consists only in modifying other faculties in respect to their manifestations, as will, *e. g.*, acts upon attention, they are intermediate faculties. But they themselves have as their ground the primary faculties which manifest themselves on their own account and act according to a law of their own activity, as, *e. g.*, thought and cognition. Nevertheless, mental faculties are not susceptible of classification as are, for example, plants and animals, for all the fundamental dispositions are active in every vital function, only in different degrees. The difficulty growing out of this conception Fries attempts to meet with

[1] *Neue Kritik der Vernunft*, 1807, §§ 5-8.

his doctrine of the stages of mental development. There are distinguishable in each of the three fundamental faculties three stages, sense, habit, and understanding. If we add to these the two fundamental opposites of spontaneity and receptivity, which repeat themselves at every stage of development, we see how prolix the faculty psychology again becomes in the hands of a man who had come to understand the inadequacy of it in its traditional form.

The theory of faculties is so natural as an explanatory hypothesis that we can trace its influence even in tendencies of modern psychology not directly dependent upon the traditional sources. The so-called psychological school in France, for example, bears the impress of the faculty psychology during the first third of the nineteenth century. It is true that Jouffroy demanded the separation of psychology both from philosophy and from physiology. His own psychological observation, however, offers little that is new, and his assumption of six original mental faculties differs from the customary classification only in the systematic character of his own scheme. The case is similar with the celebrated physicist and student of the classification of the sciences, Ampère, although he does, of course, make an attempt to explain the connection of psychical processes by his theory of "concretions," the theory that sensations spontaneously combine with remembered previous impressions to form groups or "concretions."

The decisive step in the history of faculty psychology was destined to be taken in Germany. Faculty psychology had already come in for its share of criticism in the reaction to the Kantian system, as in the case of Schulze-Ænesidemus, who characterized the faculty theory as a mythological treatment of psychology. The real turning-point, however, in the history of the faculty theory was signalized by Herbart's memorable criticism. There are two principal objections which remove the foundations from the faculty theory. The first is that the mental faculties are mere class concepts which are derived from experience by a process of provisional abstraction and cannot rightly be raised to the dignity of fundamental powers. In the second place, mental faculties are nothing more than possibilities, which are not found among the facts of inner experience. For it is only the particular idea, not a faculty of ideation, the particular feeling, not a faculty of feeling, which forms the content of our actual experience. But from the mere possibility the real happening can never be derived. The first of these objections applies primarily to the doctrine of the plurality of separate faculties. There is a certain relationship, indeed, between the psychological class concept and other classifications, such as have been formed, for example, in the history of the life sciences. How rich, for example, was the physiology of Romanticism in organ-building powers! In this respect psychology only shares the fate of all the other sciences. But, whereas the expanding knowledge of facts leads to a reduction of such superfluous notions of power in the natural sciences, faculty psychology demands their indefinite multiplication. The faculty of memory, for example, divides into a whole series of special memories, such as verbal memory, memories for numbers, persons, etc., which eventually turn out to be as different from one another as the faculty of memory is different from that of imagination. The second objection attacks the notion of faculty directly. Herbart proposes to substitute for it the notion of power, which differs from faculty in the respect that it arises as a necessary result of the appropriate conditions. We thus arrive at the most important point of view in which explanatory psychology goes beyond a merely descriptive psychology. In the faculty psychology mental faculties have free play, but when the notion of faculties has once fallen to the ground the question as to the conditions under which given kinds of mental processes regularly run their course can arise.

One last phase of the faculty psychology remains to be mentioned. F. E. Beneke (1798–1854) made the singular attempt to bring about the dissolution of faculty psychology by giving the tendency to unlimited specialization of faculties unrestricted play. The idea that every new mental process meant the development of another specific faculty modified the whole conception of mental faculties in a peculiar way. Faculties are for Beneke no longer mere empty possibilities. They rather stand for an undetermined psychical occurrence within the sphere of the unconscious, which occasionally enters consciousness. They are also described as tendencies which seek realization through sensation. Thus Beneke, although in his method more nearly allied to the psychology of the inner sense, approaches Herbart, whose ideas are often merely couched in a different terminology. In this singular manner two tendencies so opposite as the faculty psychology and psychical mechanics meet each other. Beneke's primitive faculties are, taken fundamentally, Herbart's simple representations. Corresponding to the fusions and complications in Herbart, we have, in Beneke, the flowing together and the flowing through each other, in opposite directions, of the mobile elements of the soul. The power of the primitive faculty to cause itself to be filled and filled to overflowing, about like an empty vessel, is, of course, an idea peculiar to Beneke.

There is little that is pleasing in the influence exerted upon the faculty psychology by the philosophical systems of Schelling and Hegel. If one takes up, for example, the *Vorlesungen über Psychologie* of C. G. Carus (1831), one, indeed, finds the author renouncing the "polytheism" of mental faculties and extolling the genetic method, but the latter is little more than an enumeration of the various psychological phenomena which run their course in the history of the individual's life. The apparent derivations are in reality nothing more than naïve descriptions, and the analogies which are drawn between the mind and processes in nature, such as plant growth, are still more superficial. G. H. von Schubert also, in his *Geschichte der Seele*, contents himself with an exposition, aided by analogies with the animal organism, of the fundamental tendencies of mental activity, unconcerned to make a single psychological analysis.

It was a characteristic assertion of Hegel's that the psychological works of Aristotle continued to be the most important, if not the only, work of speculative interest on the subject.[1] The only contribution of his own was to render fluid the Aristotelian faculties by the melting process of his own dialectic. The Hegelian psychology, as this was developed in the spirit of Hegel by Rosenkranz, Michelet, and Erdmann, was sharply criticised by F. Exner,[2] who charged that this mechanical system meant a relapse of psychology even beyond Wolff himself. It is in this criticism that we see scientific thought making a determined stand against the speculative thought of the past.

With this the faculty psychology may be said to have come to a definite end. Its long reign illustrates how tardily exact thought turned its attention to the actual psychical facts embedded in prescientific conceptions. Faculty psychology ignored the fact, particularly, that through the fusion of simple processes combinations which are qualitatively novel can arise. It acknowledged only the innate faculties and the empirical contents of the mind with which they work. Thus almost the whole psychology of Greek antiquity started with the assumption that mental contents

---

[1] *Enzyklopädie*, 1817, § 378.
[2] *Die Psychologie der Hegelschen Schule, beurteilt von Dr. F. Exner*, 1842.

either originate in sense-perception or that they are an innate possession of the soul. The most significant testimony of this is Plato's theory of ideas, that mystical recollection by the soul of contents which could, according to their definition, not have originated in experience. Although this alternative was probably primarily of an epistemological origin, it dominated psychology for a long period. To overcome it required a methodological apparatus which was impossible until the advent of analytic psychology. Faculty psychology, meanwhile, has the lasting merit of having anticipated, in a general way, the aims of descriptive psychology and, furthermore, of having occupied itself with a problem with which every system of psychology must deal, that of the classification of mental processes. It was faculty psychology that drew the principal distinctions out of which the classifications of analytical psychology were to grow.

## 2. The Psychology of the Inner Sense

Opposed to faculty psychology are all systems of psychology which employ in common some form of analysis. For it is through the analysis of phenomena that prescientific concepts become scientific concepts. Psychological analysis, however, has a uniqueness which sets it off from other forms. The data of psychology, namely, have the peculiarity which we designate by calling them experiences, without being able to give a more definite description of them. With the attempt to lay hold upon these data the fundamental distinction between physical and psychical phenomena became apparent. Introspection was found to be a wholly different process from the observation of external phenomena, so that the attempt to analyze mental experiences led to a sharp separation between outer and inner experience. The first demand of psychological description was thus satisfied. But the particular form which the efforts of descriptive psychology took, and in which it superseded the older faculty psychology, depended upon a still more general aspect of thought of a more scientific sort. For to the stage of the classification of phenomena there corresponds some consideration as to methods of observation. Thus, for example, the philosophy of nature of antiquity, which, in contrast with the mythological interpretation of nature, already undertook a derivation of complex phenomena from more simple ones, early occupied itself with theories, primitive enough, to be sure, of sense-perception. In a similar manner, analysis within the sphere of the psychical is preceded by reflections upon the peculiar nature of inner perception. In analogy to the outer senses the term "inner sense" became domesticated as a term for this species of perception. Now, if the inner sense is to be directed toward specific objects, as the analogy to the outer sense suggested, it is cognitive processes which lend themselves most readily to introspective observation. A psychology whose analyses depend upon the peculiarites of such an inner sense naturally developed from the very outset a tendency toward intellectualism. When such an intellectualistic psychology combined with faculty psychology, logical reflections would take the place of psychological processes and psychology relapse into a prescientific stage, or else become dominated by a metaphysical conception of the soul, as it was, for instance, in the case of the rational psychology of the eighteenth century.

There is a second reason why cognitive processes, particularly perception or ideation, should become the special subject-matter of the psychology of the inner sense. It is in connection with these that the fact is most distinctly observable that, while ideation is always directed toward an object, the process of ideation can itself become the object of introspective observation. In the case of a feeling, this change in the method of observation would be less easily observable.

The exclusive employment of the inner sense as a source of experience led eventually to a purely introspective psychology, a form which has in most recent times developed in close connection with the problems of explanatory psychology.

A common distinction made by the psychology of the inner sense is that between outer and inner experience, with the demand that the methods of investigation in the two spheres should be correspondingly different. Modern psychology tends, however, to emphasize the unity of experience, the difference between mediate and immediate depending mainly upon the point of view adopted.[1] The history of psychology did not, however, start with these contrasts. The point of departure consisted rather in a phase of the problem of inner perception, the problem, namely, how it is possible to have a consciousness of one's own perceptual activities. It is not the difference among the phenomena, like feelings, emotions, decisions, etc., on the one side, and colors, tones, etc., on the other, but the fact that in the perception of colors, tones, etc., we have also a consciousness of these perceptions that led to the assumption of a special inner sense. The inner perception, in the pregnant sense of the term, whose object is itself an ordinary perceptual process, appears to us as a special form of inner experience, as a turning inward (to remain within the same circle of ideas) of the inner sense itself. But, as happens so often in the history of psychology, it was the most striking phenomenon, which need not by any means be the simplest, which became a starting-point for psychological investigation.

A second point of view originated in the older doctrine of inner sense from the mistaken distinction between sense-

[1] *Cf.* Chapter V, 3 (*b*).

perception and its reproductions, reproductions which were called memory if they recurred in their original connections, and imagination if they were fantastically combined. It was the outer sense which was active in sense-perception, the inner, in memory and imagination. This external point of view became prominent particularly in connection with faculty psychology.

A second and higher stage of psychological reflection than that of the older psychology of inner sense arose when the totality of mental phenomena was conceived as a closed system of experience accessible only to the inner sense, and when the latter was regarded as an independent source of experience. The merit of having taken this step belongs to John Locke. The connection of psychology with epistemological questions finally led, in the second half of the century, to a branch of psychology which in a peculiar manner formed the basis of a descriptive or phenomenological psychology of the inner sense.

The expression "inner sense" is one of the oldest of German philosophical terms. As old a writer as Notker (d. 1022), who, following the version of Boethius, was the first to translate the writings of Aristotle into German, translated *sensus* by "uzero sin" and *imaginatio, ratio,* and *intelligentia* by "innero sin." The term inner experience (*innere Erfahrung*) is of much later origin, occurring as *Erfahrenheit* in the works of the mystic Weigel in the sixteenth century.

## (a) The Older Doctrine of the Inner Sense

Scattered observations on the peculiar nature of inner perception are found early in the history of psychological reflection. Plato referred to a cognition of cognition, a knowledge of knowledge. He also held that for true pleasure the δοξα ἀληθής of it was necessary. But he did not continue this addition of one psychical act to another, because it led, as he thought, to an infinite regress. It was Aristotle who recognized the true nature of the problem of inner perception and who had the good fortune, in dealing with the problem, to make his beginning at a much more tangible point. After discussing the activity of outer perception he raises the question by what activity we become aware of the act of perception itself as distinguished from the objects perceived. There can be no special sense for the perception of the act of perception, according to Aristotle, as that would necessitate another sense for the perception of the first. Accordingly, all the senses must have in common the power to perceive themselves, a power which Aristotle calls the πρῶτον αἰσθήριον. Since this power also perceives the common attributes of the different sensory contents, it is also called the common sense (Gemeinsinn, κοινὴ αἴσθησις). It is noteworthy that Aristotle does not make the distinction between inner and outer sense at all. He rather avoids the assumption of an inner sense co-ordinate with the outer and adheres to the purely conceptual distinction according to which a common faculty of sensation merely shows differing modes of activity. The concept of consciousness, which we see Aristotle approaching here, is not actually developed by him in the present connection. He does not approach it until later, in his description of the attributes of the Supreme Being, in the Metaphysics.[1]

Within the Peripatetic school Strato saw in the consciousness of the contents of sense-perception a result of an activity which was from the outset separated from perception. In a peculiar way Alexander of Aphrodisias returned from this to the older conception, employing the term συναίσθησις for the consciousness of perception, a notion which was destined to remain of central importance in the Neo-Platonic

[1] *Cf.* Chapter VI, 1 (*a*), below.

psychology. The Aristotelian doctrine of a common sense, however, shared the fate of many of the other conceptual distinctions of Aristotle, and was interpreted pictorially as an inner sense, *sensus interior*, which was soon split up, as in the case of the faculty psychology. Galen, for example, distinguished three kinds of inner sense, corresponding to the main groups of phenomena which are its objects, namely, imagination, thought, and memory (τὸ φανταστικόν, τὸ διανοητικόν, τὸ μνημονικόν), thus illustrating the second point of view referred to above.[1]

For many centuries hereafter the inner sense is reckoned among the other mental faculties, losing its own distinctive significance more and more in the process. In keeping with the terminology of Neo-Platonism and with the *sensus interioris hominis*, as Augustine called it, Scotus Erigena in the Scholastic period contrasted the inner to the whole group of outer senses. Its analogy to the five external senses is emphasized still more by Avicenna, who has five inner senses —*sensus communis, vis imaginativa, vis œstimativa, memoria*, and *phantasia*—which are, like their external counterparts, variously localized.

The opposition between outer and inner senses recurs in Thomas Aquinas. The senses themselves cannot become aware of their own activities. The activities of the outer senses are rather perceived by a sense different from them, an inner sense, the *sensus communis*. This sense, too, is, like its corresponding object, physical. It can, accordingly, not perceive its own activity, and we thus have left one unconscious mental activity within the sphere of sense. The doctrine of the inner sense assumes a peculiar relation, moreover, to that of "intentional" or "mental" existence. The notion of psychical immanence (*Einwohnung*) is found as early as Aristotle in the doctrine that the perceived object

[1] See pp. 71-2.

exists as such in the perceiver and that the object thought of exists in the reflective intelligence. The history of philosophy records this confusion between mental existence and actual existence. Philo's theory of ideas is founded on the notion, while Saint Anselm developed it into his proof for the existence of God. Thomas Aquinas teaches that the thing thought of is "intentional" in the thought. Consciousness of this thought is rendered possible on account of the incorporeal character of the understanding, through the reflection of the activities upon themselves. Meanwhile, Saint Thomas denies to the understanding a plurality of simultaneous thoughts, holding that such plurality is possible only as temporal succession. The perception of thought, therefore, follows the thought itself in point of time. Thomas Aquinas thus exposes some of the difficulties in the accepted doctrine of inner perception, difficulties which have reappeared in modern psychology. That the introspection of a mental process immediately follows the latter is a view of inner perception held by many modern psychologists.

This central problem of inner perception was subsequently lost sight of again. The treatments of the number and classification of the inner senses in the psychological systems of the Reformation period are far removed from the actual facts of consciousness. Here again the inner sense plays its part mainly in connection with the reproductive processes. Imagination and memory play the leading rôles. Associated with them, occasionally, is the old common sense. Distinct from these attempts at classification is the view of Amerbach who interprets the inner sense in Aristotelian fashion as the common sense, treating it as a necessary presupposition to the activity of the outer senses. The physiological interests of the time reflect themselves in the attempts to explain the activity of the inner sense by reference to the movements of "nerve spirits" in the brain, as, for example, in Casmann, who well characterized inner perception as *actus reflectus* or as *iterata cognitio*. The Cartesian definition of the soul as a thinking substance represented inner perception as belonging to the essence of the soul. The solution of the problem thus suggested was, however, not turned to account by Descartes for the advance of empirical psychology. He rather placed the outer and the inner senses side by side, thus preparing the way for the sensualistic psychology of a later day, in the sense, for example, of Hobbes, who called the discrimination of sensations itself a sensation.

(b) *The Inner Sense as an Independent Source of Experience*

The classical expression of the doctrine of the inner sense is found in John Locke. Locke based his *Essay Concerning Human Understanding* upon the simple fact that all our ideas originate either in sense-perception or in reflection, by which the soul becomes aware of its own activities. Thus introspection is recognized by the side of sense-perception as an independent source of knowledge. The traditional analogy between the outer and inner senses is thus strictly subordinated. It is true that reflection always presupposes sense-perception; at the same time Locke, supported by Cartesian metaphysics, asserts the independence of inner experience.

The epistemological consequences of this doctrine were drawn by the English sensualists Berkeley and Hume, in both of whom the Lockian antithesis continued. Berkeley found the object of reflection, of "inward feeling," as he called it, in one's own existence, without, however, admitting the idea of spirit or self. The subject of the various psychical activities enumerated—willing, ideation, etc.—cannot be grasped by reflection, although the latter can direct itself upon these activities themselves. The result is a considerable restriction of the scope of inner perception, which, for the rest, corresponds with Berkeley's conception of the soul.[1] Over against Locke's distinction between sense and reflection Hume placed his own antithesis of impressions and ideas. We now have impressions of introspection standing parallel to impressions of sense-perception. The latter originate within the soul, from unknown causes, whereas the former originate for the most part from our ideas. Thus the intellectualism which is the usual accompaniment of the psychology of inner perception asserts itself in Hume's psychology also.

Locke's distinction between sensation and reflection persisted in English psychology. It received a variety of interpretations in French sensualism. Condillac disputed the validity of reflection as an independent source of knowledge. It originates, rather, in the specific direction of the attention toward ourselves, which, of course, presupposes imagination and memory. This significant reference to the power of attention is meanwhile weakened by invoking another kind of consciousness, in addition to reflection, which is directed upon separate ideas. Neither can we attach much importance to the physiological explanation of the inner sense offered by Bonnet, who ascribed it to the power of the soul to set soul fibres in motion spontaneously.

Locke's doctrine of the inner sense received its most important transformation through Leibniz's celebrated distinction between perception and apperception. In perception the soul merely contains ideas, in apperception it becomes conscious of them. As a knowledge of the soul of its inner states, the Leibnizian apperception bears a fairly close resemblance to Locke's reflection. Leibniz's distinction derives a greater significance, however, for the development of the concept of consciousness in so far as it was later to

[1] *Cf.* p. 27.

become identified with the distinction between unconscious and conscious states of the soul.[1]

While Wolff repeats the Leibnizian distinctions with undiminished emphasis in the later phases of the period of Enlightenment, the traditional doctrine of the inner sense reappears, as in Baumgarten, who gives a complicated account of external and inner sensibility. Among the eclectic representatives of the "Popular Psychology," Meiners bases his doctrine of the inner sense upon the methodological principle that the number of separate organs must be determined upon the basis of the diversity of inner experience. The most interesting development of the doctrine of inner sense in this period is due to Tetens. Since psychical processes are perceived through the inner sense in the same manner as physical are perceived through the outer senses, he opines that we perceive nothing but phenomena in both cases. The two arguments for the objectivity of the external world prevalent in the theory of knowledge dominant at the time, namely, (1) that sensation, as confused perception, does not reproduce the simplicity of the outer world, and (2) that perception depends upon the condition of the sense-organ, are extended by Tetens to inner perception also. Every psychical process may be composed of heterogeneous elements, which have the appearance of simplicity only for our apprehension, and for inner observation the brain is the organ upon which it depends. For this reason mere introspection can never reach the elements of psychical life. These can be reached only by thought, which operates by analysis similar to that employed by natural science in the study of white light, which to observation appears simple in character. These consequences follow with a certain necessity when the doctrine of inner sense is really taken seriously, but they stand in sharp contradiction to psychological experience in

[1] *Cf.* Chapter VI, 2.

which, in contradiction to physical, the elements are given concretely.[1]

The inner sense assumed a many-sided significance through the psychology of Kant. Kant distinguished the inner sense from apperception. The experiences of the inner sense run their course in time, and yield phenomena, as do the outer senses. Apperception, on the other hand, relates to the pure ego, the subject of all thought activities. As object, meanwhile, of inner experience, the ego knows itself only as it appears. This view of the activity of the inner sense, which grows out of Kant's theory of knowledge, continues in Kant's empirical psychology, as set forth in his *Anthropologie*, in a close parallelism between the inner sense and the outer senses. Kant further distinguishes between the inner sense (*sensus internus*), as a mere cognitive faculty, and the inward sense (*inwendiger Sinn, sensus interior*), the feeling of pleasantness and unpleasantness, thus denying the original relation of the inner sense to the totality of inner experience.[2] A more exact definition limits the inner sense to passive psychical states. It is not pure apperception, as this belongs only to the faculty of thought; it is a consciousness of that which affects it in so far as it is affected by its own play of thought. As perception it is in this sense also subject to illusions, as when one, for example, mistakes perceptions of the inner sense for external phenomena. Here we obviously have a reappearance of the older idea that the objects of the inner sense are the processes of memory and imagination. The heart of the Kantian doctrine consists in the idea that the inner sense substitutes for the pure or transcendental ego the empirical ego with its variety of conscious phenomena. This curious duplication of the ego recurs frequently in subsequent philosophy.

[1] On the concept of psychical element, see below, Chapter VII, 3.
[2] *Anthropologie in pragmatischer Hinsicht*, 1798, § 13.

The Kantian doctrine of the inner sense was severely criticised by Herbart, who urged that, as a faculty of introspection, the inner sense would require some superior faculty in its turn, and so forth, without end. Still, the positive explanation of Herbart's, according to which one mass of ideas observes another, is still more seriously burdened with inner impossibilities, if possible, than the theory which he criticises.

Schulze controverted the assumption of an inner sense with different arguments in his *Psychologische Anthropologie* (1819). The analogy between the outer senses and the inner sense is untenable for the reason that the knowledge of a perception as one's own implies a judgment which cannot be ascribed to the activity of sense. The interposition of a special faculty between the soul and perception in the form of an inner sense can be defended by no arguments whatsoever. If, in spite of this criticism, certain representatives of sensualistic psychology still occasionally maintain the strict analogy of the inner to the external senses, as is done by Biunde in his *Versuch einer systematischen Behandlung der Psychologie* (1831) and by Lelut in his *Physiologie de la pensée* (1862), we may treat these utterances as the echoes, merely, of a theory which at this time and in this form has long been obsolete.

The merging of the old problem of inner sense in the more general problem of consciousness occurred partly in connection with the description which the *Philosophy of Identity* gave of the dialectical development of consciousness. One of the most characteristic attempts to make this development of consciousness intelligible as a psychological process was made by Ulrici, who held that inner perception was identical with the beginning of consciousness, and derived both from the distinction, originally unconscious, between the self and sensation.

But it was not in these more or less speculative efforts that the doctrine of inner sense came into contact with the most modern tendencies of descriptive psychology. The question which came into the foreground was the more general question as to whether pure introspection, which had been transmitted historically in the form of the inner sense, could form the basis of an empirical psychology. At first these efforts of empirical psychology lagged decidedly in spite of the expositions, so opulent in impressions, of Beneke. Fortlage, in his *System der Psychologie als empirischer Wissenschaft aus der Beobachtung des inneren Sinnes* (1855), asserted that the observation of the inner sense was the fundamental source of experience in psychology. He held that the task of psychology was to construct an empirical science of the human mind founded upon observation within the realm of the inner sense, and to arrive, by induction, at the ultimate concepts of instinct and reason.[1] But in the actual construction of this science the realm of "observation" became a mere jostling place of arbitrary assertions. After laborious expositions of the functions of the inner sense, to which are mainly ascribed the attributes of the external senses, the author begins his "observations," a term which, however, is here merely a synonym for inventive imagination. As F. A. Lange aptly remarks, it would be difficult to find in the two stout volumes a single genuine observation.

The sterility of such observations by means of the inner sense demanded its criticism as a source of knowledge. Comte had already made a very searching and influential criticism of it, in which, however, he had identified observation with perception. In his *Cours de Philosophie positive* (1830–42), he declared every form of psychology claiming to discover the fundamental laws of the human mind to be illusory as long as it relied upon introspection. In spite of

[1] *System der Psychologie*, Vorrede, X.

the fact that J. S. Mill, in his account of Comte, undertook to defend perception of psychical phenomena by means of direct memory, it was in England where Comte's doctrine made the greatest advance. Maudsley, too, in his *Physiology and Pathology of Mind* (1867), rejects self-consciousness as a source of psychological knowledge. In Germany F. A. Lange was particularly aggressive in his criticism of inner perception, maintaining that there existed no clear line of demarcation between outer and inner perception. The experience of color in imagery, for example, is regarded as due to the observation of the inner sense. Nevertheless, there is no essential difference between that and the actual sight of color. Helpless as was the psychology of inner sense against such criticisms, no result was reached regarding the significance of introspection in psychology. In the most recent developments the question has been considered from other points of view, in connection with experimental investigation, where the controversy has centred around the competency of self-observation when regulated by experiment.[1]

The doctrine of inner sense underwent a new development through its connection with certain epistemological problems raised by the question of the epistemological significance of the facts of inner perception.

### (c) *The Relation of Inner Sense to Epistemological Problems*[2]

The connecting-link between the theory of knowledge and the doctrine of inner perception was the problem of "evident" or immediately certain perception. With the external, illusory perception was contrasted inner, evident perception. Überweg, in his *Logik* (1865), ascribed to inner

[1] *Cf.* below, pp. 136 *f.*
[2] *Cf.* with this Brentano, *Psychologie vom emp. Standpunkte*, p. 101.

perception the characteristic of material truth, and made this identity of being and knowledge the point of departure for his theory of knowledge. The psychological investigation of the difference between external and inner perception was thus demanded by the theory of perception. In addition to this, empirical psychology had an interest of its own in attempting to establish its right to be regarded as a special science, through the discovery of a realm of phenomena peculiar to it. Whether this standpoint is made necessary by the nature of psychical phenomena need not be decided here. In any case, the attempt is made solely on the basis of the facts of inner perception.

The close relation to epistemological problems is further shown by the fact that it was not regarded as feasible to employ a principle of division derived from epistemological presuppositions. For it was psychology which, as the fundamental philosophical discipline, was to lay the foundation for epistemological distinctions. The classification of perceptions introduced by Locke, which presupposed the contrast of mind and body as something given, was accordingly insufficient for the more rigid demands. In contrast with these epistemological determinations, there was a demand for a classification of perception on the basis of purely descriptive characteristics. The Cartesian doubt, which stands at the threshold of the critical theory of knowledge, promised to be fruitful for the solution of this task. Without any presupposition regarding the nature of psychical events, it illustrated the character of "evidence" or certainty attaching to any given experience. Inner perception is necessarily "evident," while many experiences derived from external perception render the ascription of this characteristic to external perception impossible. Sir William Hamilton utilized this insight for the determination of the sphere of psychical phenomena, characterizing consciousness as immediate or intuitive knowledge, and emphasizing as a peculiar feature of psychical phenomena that they can be received only in the inner consciousness. The significance of this definition, which appears at first sight as a reversal of the natural determination of the act in accordance with the object, lies just in this ascription to inner perception of the character of certainty or evidence.

An attempt to sharpen the distinction between inner and outer perception to the utmost was made by Franz Brentano.[1] Upon the descriptive distinction between inner and outer perception he based a similar distinction between the two corresponding classes of phenomena. Psychical phenomena are accordingly such as can be perceived only by introspection, while physical phenomena are accessible only through external perception. Brentano thus carried through the descriptive classification of all phenomena into physical and psychical, without having to depend upon transcendental conceptions.[2] The psychology of the inner sense had long employed the assumption that physical phenomena are due to the action of objects upon the mind, while psychical phenomena have their origin in the perception of the activities of the mind. Psychical objects are now defined as the sole objects of inner perception. Brentano names still another characteristic of psychical phenomena, their intentional or mental "in-existence." Every psychical phenomenon refers to an object. In presentation something is presented, in judgment something affirmed or denied, etc. We have a repetition here, in a greatly refined form, of the Scholastic doctrine of "intentional" acts.[3] Indeed, psychical phenomena are for Brentano identical with the acts. The resulting classification contradicts the delimitation of the psychical realm given in the treatment of sen-

---

[1] *Op. cit.*, pp. 131 ff.  [2] See Chapter V, 3 (b), below.
[3] See p. 74, above.

sation and idea. Brentano regards only the acts of sensation and ideation as psychical phenomena. The things sensed or represented—a color, odor, or figure—are physical phenomena. The psychology based upon this distinction has recently been called act psychology. According to Brentano, each of these acts is accompanied by a consciousness of itself. Every act, accordingly, has two objects. The primary one is the intentional content, the tone, for example, in audition; the secondary one is the act itself as a psychical phenomenon, in this case as the phenomenon of audition. Inner perception thus accompanies every act and is conscious of it in a threefold way: it ideates it, recognizes it, and feels it. These three kinds of inner perception also represent the most general classification of psychical phenomena.

The teachings of Brentano, which were understood by many to represent a species of Neo-Scholasticism in psychology, have been subject to much controversy. They have received their most adequate criticism at the hands of Husserl, who at the same time dealt most successfully with several of the problems of a purely phenomenological analysis.[1] Husserl maintains the epistemological identity of inner and outer perception. It is true that there exists the distinction between evident and non-evident perception, but this distinction does not coincide with the distinction between inner and outer perception. An example of the non-evident character of inner perception is the perception of the ego as the empirical personality. Neither can the majority of psychical states localized in the body be perceived as evident, according to Husserl. The source of Brentano's errors lies in the equivocal use of the term phenomenon. By the phenomenon Brentano sometimes means the objects and attributes which appear, sometimes the experiences consti-

[1] *Logische Untersuchungen*, vol. II, 1901, pp. 703 *ff.*

tuting the activity of appearing (occasionally contents in the shape of sensations), and, finally, all experiences as such. We thus have a cross classification of experiences, as, *e. g.*, activities and non-activities, and of phenomenological objects, as, *e. g.*, those which belong to self-consciousness and those which do not, that is, psychical and physical objects. He treats, that is, the latter as a classification of experiences into activities and non-activities, and furthermore identifies the contents sensed with the phenomenal characteristics of external objects, so that a general classification of phenomenological objects results. This criticism is directed toward one of the last offshoots of the doctrine of the inner sense, and illustrates the keenness of the purely phenomenological method of investigation which has been attained in present-day psychology.

# CHAPTER IV

## EXPLANATORY PSYCHOLOGY

If we were to arrange the tendencies of psychology which have grown up around the problems of explanatory psychology in the chronological order in which the characteristic tools of these tendencies became known, we should have to put in the first place the observations regarding the uniformities in the more elementary psychic processes. In sense-perceptions, in memory, in impulsive and instinctive activities uniformities were observed even before the day of experimental investigation, which must have suggested strongly the idea of the uniform connection among psychical phenomena. The most important notion available for explanatory purposes was that of association. Association psychology terminated in the conception of psychology as a mechanics of ideas. A second point of departure consisted in the extension of psychological investigation beyond the border of individual psychology. The resulting science of comparative psychology was helped forward especially by the notion of development or evolution. But, more than anything else, it was contact with the natural sciences, during the century just passed, which furnished explanatory psychology with new tools and opened new paths which led to the discovery of those psychic laws which are the goal of association psychology.

### 1. Association Psychology

Explanatory psychology has been said to supplement descriptive psychology in the respect that it investigates the dispositional characteristics of mental life in addition to its phenomenological aspect. Although the field of explanatory psychology does not coincide with the doctrine of psychical dispositions, still the reference to dispositions constitutes one of the main forms of explanatory psychology, particularly of association psychology. But before the doctrine of association developed into a definite psychological tendency, the concept of association was not only elaborated but the notion of a mechanics of ideas had already appeared. The fitful beginnings of association psychology illustrate how frequently the continuity of psychological investigation has been broken. For a long period only the processes of association connected with memory were taken into account. It was only gradually that the far broader field of psychical connections, in which the concept of association was so long to dominate, was opened.

### (a) *The Early Beginnings of Association Psychology*

The earliest attempts to give an account of the most easily observed memory functions are made by hylozoism.[1] Parmenides of Elea accounted for memory and obliviscence as he accounted for all the rest of the phenomena of nature, by the mixture of cold and heat. Every idea presupposes a certain combination of these qualities, the idea disappearing when the combination no longer obtains. With no less dependence upon the half-mythical, half-metaphysical psychology of the time, Diogenes of Apollonia asserts as the cause of forgetting the obstacle which the body offers to the distribution of air, a belief based upon the observation that one breathes more freely when recollection has been successful. Aside from these beginnings, which in any case take

---

[1] *Cf.* with the following: Bergemann, "Gedächtnistheoretische Untersuchungen und mnemotechnische Spielereien im Altertum," *Arch. f. Gesch. d. Phil.*, VIII, 1895, pp. 336 *ff*.

into account only the negative aspect of memory, namely obliviscence, the first attempt to construct a genuine theory of memory was made by Plato. Plato distinguishes the concepts ἀνάμνησις from μνήμη. The former signifies the act of reproduction of previous impressions, the latter the passive persistence of ideas due to sense-perception.[1]

Ἀνάμνησις is the higher faculty. It manifests itself only when the soul in the knowledge of its ideas remembers the impressions of a previous existence. Μνήμη, on the other hand, is the capacity of the soul associated with the body to retain impressions of sense-perception. It is said to resemble a piece of wax, varying in size according to the individuality of different persons, becoming harder and softer, pure or defiled, etc.[2]

Aristotle was still more successful in his treatment of the phenomena of memory, dreaming, and the processes of association and reproduction. He takes into consideration not only the actual contents but the dispositional as well. His *De Anima* treats the phenomenology of mental life, the remaining psychological treatises (the so-called *Parva Naturalia*) dealing with the dispositional basis. Memory (μνήμη), as the faculty of psychophysical retention, is distinguished from recall (ἀναμιμνήσκεσθαι), which is made possible through the association of ideas. As the inner movements which run their course in a series of perceptions repeat themselves, the corresponding memory picture is called up. The principle of association is either similarity, contrast, or temporal succession (ἀφ' ὁμοίου ἢ ἐναντίου ἢ τοῦ σύνεγγυς). These laws hold not only for single ideas, but for series of ideas as well, only in the latter case they sometimes lose their simple character.[3] For the derivation of these laws of association, which have since become so celebrated, Aris-

[1] *Phædo*, 73 B ff.; *Philebus*, 34 B.   [2] *Theætetus*, 191, C ff.
[3] *De Mem.*, 2.

totle falls back upon the supposed movements of memory pictures in the blood. These are partly identical or similar, partly simultaneous or immediately successive. Now, the soul has the power to originate, through the agency of the heart, a movement of the blood which can revive the traces of previous impressions in the sense-organ. In addition to this physiological mechanics of associative memory, we find the beginnings of a general mechanics of ideas, at least as far as sense-perceptions are concerned. The stronger movement overcomes the weaker. A number of simultaneous sensations from a single sense-organ are impossible, as such sensations coalesce. Sensations from different sense-organs, however, do not coalesce. The fusion depends upon the fact that the soul can in a single movement sense the similar more readily than the dissimilar. And since every kind of sensation implies a specific kind of movement in the central organ, the simultaneous perception of opposite qualities would necessitate simultaneous opposite movements. Hence the simultaneous occurrence of different sensations is manifestly impossible. All this is distinctly suggestive of the modern attempts to construct a mechanics of ideas, illustrating how Aristotle's anticipations extend into the most recent times. While English psychology has been dominated by his laws of association, Herbart revived his principles of psychical mechanics.[1]

Ancient psychology did not, indeed, develop the Aristotelian tradition. Incidentally, Maximus of Tyre[2] enumerates the different types of association. The following sentence is ascribed to him: "As a motion imparted to one end of a cord traverses the whole length of the cord, so the reason requires only a slight impulse in order to recall whole trains of ideas."[3]

[1] *Cf.* Siebeck, *Quæstiones duæ de phil. Græc.*, 1872.
[2] *Diss.*, 16, 7.     [3] Siebeck, *Gesch. d. Psychologie*, II, p. 310.

Plotinus, too, mentions the fundamental idea of immediate reproduction, but describes memory merely as a power of the soul. Sense-perception is received into the φανταστικόν, where the images are stored. The higher soul then selects from the memories thus stored up in the lower soul.

The literature on mnemotechnics, which is rich in content, is distinct testimony to the interest in the practical uses of memory characteristic of the time. When one remembers that up to the time of Augustus no public speaker would dare to appear in public with even the scantiest notes, the interest in mnemotechnical devices is easily intelligible. The beginnings of mnemotechnics, whose discovery is ascribed to the poet Simonides, are legendary, as is the case with similar arts. Most of the precepts along this line about the time of Cicero advise the use of visual pictures as aids to memory. In order to have at one's command large masses of ideas, they must be localized, say, in a given city, and within the city, in the different buildings, chambers, etc. The theoretical gains from this sort of thing for psychology were small, as might have been expected.

In Scholasticism the psychology of memory was reduced to the singular assumption that the species of things are preserved by the soul. It is in this sense that Avicenna defined *virtus conservativa et memorialis*. More important are the views of John Buridan, which form a connecting-link between the older forms of psychical mechanics and association psychology. Although still largely dominated by the conceptions of faculty psychology, he is convinced of the unity of mental life. The principle of psychical mechanics underlying his description of the freedom of the will has caused him to be called the Herbartian among the Scholastics.[1]

For a long time knowledge of associative connections was confined to the phenomenon of memory. The law of im-

[1] *Cf.* Chapter XII, 2 (*a*).

mediate reproduction alone was not lost to empirical psychology. As a rule, the formulation was that of Vives: "Quæ simul sunt a phantasia comprehensa, si alterutrum occurrat, solet secum alterum repræsentare." It was reserved for English psychology of the eighteenth century to place the facts of association in the foreground and to regard it as the fundamental form of psychical connections.

### (b)  The Dominance of the Concept of Association

The involuntary association of ideas already played an important rôle in the English psychologists of the seventeenth century, Thomas Hobbes and John Locke. It was Locke, indeed, who introduced the term association of ideas to designate the process in question. Malebranche, too, was acquainted with the facts of association, which he explained by the simultaneous occurrence of ideas in consciousness. Not until Hume and Hartley, however, in the middle of the eighteenth century, was the concept of association made the central concept of explanatory psychology.

In the *Treatise of Human Nature* (1739–40), Hume enumerates three factors which can give rise to association: similarity, immediate spatial and temporal connection, and cause and effect; and in his *Dissertation on the Passions* (1770) he defines association generally as the principle of facilitated transition from one idea to another. In accordance with the principles of combination of simple ideas arise those complex ideas "which are the common subjects of our thoughts and reasoning": relations, modes, and substances. While Hume based his theory of association upon psychological experience, he utilized it for his empirical theory of knowledge, one of the main features of which is his bold reduction of the consciousness of reality to associatively conditioned relations. As is well known, Hume explains the different kinds of belief, particularly the belief in the reality of the external world, by the force and vivacity of the corresponding idea. In consequence of the principle of association, the force and vivacity which belong to a given impression communicate themselves to those related to it. In addition to the reality of sense-perception, there is also the reality of ideas of memory, which are distinguished from ideas of fancy by the necessary connections existing among the different perceptions, and, finally, the reality of judgment.[1] Thus, in virtue of the principle of associative connections, the various kinds of consciousness of reality are reduced to the same ultimate fact of consciousness. The connection with the theory of knowledge has stimulated an interest in the psychological investigation of the consciousness of reality which has been uninterrupted, and the modern Neo-Humeanism, which finds an ally in psychologism, occasionally approaches again the Humean solution of the problem.

Falling in with the ideas of the time, Hartley connected the doctrine of association with the hypothesis of nerve vibration and attempted to establish a psychophysical theory of association. He even tried to represent brain changes pictorially, thus returning to the older point of view of the school of Malebranche, a representative of which, Theodore van Craanen, had made graphic representations of material ideas.[2] We are here reminded of the teachings of Descartes, who had described *ideæ rerum materialium* as brain impressions produced by movements within the body which are sensed by the soul in perception. Hartley also has capital analyses here and there of complex mental processes, which employ distinctly the fundamental principles of association psychology according to which complex phenomena are explained by the association of their component elements. In

---

[1] *Treatise of Human Nature*, bk. I, part III, sects. VIII and IX.
[2] *Tractatus de homine*, London, 1689.

this sense he analyzed the process of speech, for example, into four component parts: auditory impressions, movements of the vocal organs, visual impressions of the written characters, and, finally, movements of the hand in writing.[1]

The physiological hypotheses of Hartley were further utilized by Charles Bonnet,[2] who, in his efforts to exhibit the physiological conditions of mental life, abandoned himself wholly to the speculations of the "nerve-fibre psychology."[3] Testimony to the many-sided psychological interests of this writer is his fondness for the study of bee life, which has ever been a puzzling problem for psychology.[4] Bonnet's theory of association can be summed up as follows: Nerve-fibres excited simultaneously or in immediate succession, and those which are spatially contiguous, are connected in such a manner that a repeated motion of any fibre gives rise to a sympathetic movement in fibres connected with it. Even remembered ideas owe their origin to specific movements of fibres. The impression, however, made upon the soul by fibres excited for the first time is different from that produced by subsequent excitations. Hence the difference between imagery and sense-perception. Thus the old doctrine of material ideas, which has passed through a whole series of metamorphoses, reappears again. Traces of the doctrine are also seen in the recent assumption of memory cells in Meynert and Ziehen.

In Germany the influence of the doctrine of association is seen partly in the Wolffian school, partly in the recent attempts to treat psychological problems in relation to nerve physiology and the physiology of the senses. Like the nat-

[1] *Observations on Man, his Frame, his Duties, his Expectations*, 1749.
[2] *Essai analytique sur les facultés de l'âme*, 1760.
[3] *Cf.* Speck, "Bonnets Einwirkung auf die deutsche Psychologie des vorigen Jahrhunderts," *Archiv f. Gesch. d. Phil.*, X, 1897, pp. 504 *ff*.
[4] Bonnet, *Œuvres d'histoire naturelle*, 1779–83.

ural sciences, it found support in the growing interest in pathological phenomena. It shared with faculty psychology and the psychology of the inner sense the results of that peculiar species of introspection to which the psychological periodicals of the second half of the eighteenth century, now mostly forgotten, bear instructive testimony.

Once the thought was grasped that so important a mental process as association could be explained by the mechanism of the nervous system, it was an easy step to extend this method to the whole field of mental phenomena. The tendency found a response in the psychophysical materialism of the French Enlightenment. Thus arose a physiological psychology which sometimes tended to approach pure materialism, sometimes recognized the independence of the realm of inner sense, but sought to bring its phenomena into relation with physiological processes. M. Hissmann aided in the dissemination of this tendency through his translation of Hartley, published in his own periodical (1778 *ff.*). In his *Psychologische Versuche* he makes the dependence of mental phenomena upon the brain his starting-point. The nervous system and the brain are conscious, just as other bodies are electric or magnetic. It behooves the psychologist, therefore, to give attention to physiology, and especially to the anatomy of the brain. To the two general laws of association, the laws of coexistence and of similarity, he added the law of the physical relation of the inner organs. Certain groups of ideas are to be explained by the natural relations of their corresponding bodily organs. A significant application of these points of view to the theory of knowledge was made by J. C. Lossius,[1] who attempted to construct a mechanics of the thought processes. Thoughts are composed of sensations: they become truths by a process of comparison with other thoughts, which, in turn, depend upon brain

[1] *Physische Ursachen des Wahren*, 1775.

movements. Truth as distinguished from contradiction is, therefore, to be explained by harmonious vibrations of nerve-fibres. Lossius thus approaches the form of empirical theory of knowledge which developed in the nineteenth century under the name of psychologism. The law of contradiction, for example, would be explained by him as follows: "Our inability to conceive simultaneously a triangle and a quadrangle is due to the fact that the movements of different nerve-fibres inhibit each other." It is only necessary to substitute psychical thought processes for the hypothetical nerve vibrations with which Lossius operates in order to get a pretty close approximation to the point of view of psychologism, as developed since the time of John Stuart Mill.[1]

A mediating point of view was taken by K. F. von Irwing,[2] who maintained that the physiological basis of sensations and of their connections was to be found in the connections among nerve-fibres within the brain. The human mind is distinguished from the animal mind, which is wholly dependent upon this structural basis, by the possession of self-active understanding. Irwing is more original in his criticism of Bonnet's naïvely pictorial theory of memory, and he occasionally has good observations in his more purely descriptive passages, as in his comparison of previously experienced secondary ideas with present ones.

The most important psychologist of this group is E. Plattner,[3] whose treatment of sense-perception is particularly detailed. To the external impression of the peripheral nerve-endings is added an inner impression in the "nerve spirits" of the brain. It is not until attention is turned upon this that the understanding recognizes ideas. The preservation of ideas he originally conceived after the fashion of the persistence of material ideas, later attributing it to facilitation

[1] *Cf.* Chapter V, 3 (*a*), below.
[2] *Erfahrungen und Untersuchungen über den Menschen*, 1778.
[3] *Philosophische Aphorismen*, 1776–82.

of nervous action. The combinations of the ideas of imagination are accounted for by the participation of active thought, as well as of the laws of association.

Another tendency of the day sought to interpret the facts of association in a purely psychological manner. Marcus Herz, who was acquainted with Kant through correspondence, not only outlined[1] a theory of association but also suggested a general mechanics of ideas. True to the intellectualism of his time, he viewed the activity of the ego as a form of ideation. Each idea has a focal point of greatest vivacity. A definite interval always elapses between the complete apprehension of an idea and the direction of the attention to its successor. The length of the interval depends partly upon the structural content of the separate ideas, partly upon their mutual relation, *i. e.*, their identity or similarity, difference or contrast, etc. The law of association, however, is not a primary law. It rather depends upon the law that the repetition of an activity occurs with minimized effort and hence with a lessened interval. A matter deserving of special recognition is his vigorous denial of the doctrine of the uninterrupted presence of ideas. His concept of facilitation approximates to some extent the modern notion of psychical disposition.

It is true that J. D. Hoffbauer's *Grundriss der Erfahrungslehre* (1794) is still based upon the old principles of faculty psychology and the psychology of the inner sense. Nevertheless, all the objects of the inner sense are shown to be subject to the law of association by the fact that the reproducing and the reproduced ideas are already connected within a single total idea. Against such a unitary law of association and its derivation from the concept of imagination L. H. Jakob contended in his *Grundriss der Erfahrungsseelenlehre* (1791), a work distinguished for its clear,

[1] *Versuch über den Schwindel*, 1791.

methodical formulations. In spite of many interesting remarks on the conditions of sensation, its dependence upon the receptivity of the sense-organs, and the like, we find many concessions to the old faculty psychology.[1]

The one work of this period which has been most successful in escaping general oblivion is the *Versuch über die Einbildungskraft*, by G. E. Maass, who represents a transition between the empirical psychology of the eighteenth century and the idealistic psychology of Romanticism. The definition which he offers of imagination as that active faculty of the soul which compares the parts of a complex object shows the influence of the great thinker who dominated all his contemporaries. Imagination underlies the law of association both in its three well-known forms and in its fourth form, the law of revival, which states that among "a number of ideas the most prominent idea is revived." Prominence here is determined by clearness. Maass thus suggests the point of view, common to many of his contemporaries, of psychical mechanics, a form developed particularly during the nineteenth century.

In this versatile period of the Enlightenment we find also the first attempts to apply the law of association to æsthetics, attempts based upon the significance of association for the affective life, with which writers had long been acquainted. As a famous historical illustration of the recognition of the associative connections between sensations and feelings may be cited the curious edict issued in Paris forbidding the playing of the Alpine cowherd's melody so long as Swiss mercenaries served in the French army, on the ground that it produced homesickness.[2] The principle of association which

[1] *Cf.* the particularly happy description of these efforts in M. Dessoir, *op. cit.*, pp. 232 *ff.*
[2] Homesickness (*Heimweh*) is the translation of nostalgia. The physician J. J. Scheuchzer published a work, *De nostalgia Helvetiorum*, in 1731.

Fechner introduced into æsthetics is partly anticipated in Henry Home in the form of the law that the pleasantness of a given object tends to spread to other objects.[1] The traditional principle of unity within variety is also explained by association. The succession of ideas which must occur at a certain rate presupposes a corresponding interchange among the ideas, which is partly facilitated by association, partly restricted to a determinate set of relationships. The principal function of association thus consists in binding together the greatest possible number of ideas into the closest possible relationship. A similar theory of association is formed in Diderot. His definition of the beautiful, "Beau est tout ce qui reveille en nous l'idée des rapports," seems to have been formed with the principle of association in mind.

The fusion of both tendencies is seen in the æsthetics of Herder, in which association also plays an important rôle. The psychological formulation of æsthetic problems appears in clearer form in his older studies and sketches on *Plastik*, and in the torso of his fourth *Kritische Wäldchen*, than in his earlier and more polemical *Kalligone*. The variety of individual taste as well as the mutual influence of the experience gained from the various senses, seen most conspicuously in the senses of sight and touch, everywhere emphasizes the significance of association. It is true that the problem of the relation of form and content was derived from the rationalistic æsthetics of Baumgarten. Nevertheless, the harmony of form and content shown in the æsthetic object is for Herder a fact which has definite psychological conditions; it is a special result of association. Herder anticipates modern æsthetics in still another way. If the spirit of a work

---

[1] *Elements of Criticism*, 1762, p. 66. *Cf.* A. Tumarkin, "Das Associationsprinzip in der Geschichte der Ästhetik," *Arch. f. Gesch. d. Phil.*, XII, 1899, p. 257.

of art and of its forms is to make its appeal, it must be through an act of sympathy, an inner affinity, in virtue of which we can transport ourselves into these forms, and thus simulate their psychic life.[1] Elsewhere he writes that we can appreciate the human form because we ourselves live a bodily life, and can thus share the life of the spirit which the body reveals.[2] We have here an anticipation of Lotze's symbolic beauty, in so far as æsthetic products appear to us as symbols of psychic states experienced by ourselves. These reflections, finally, suggest the notion of empathy (*Einfühlung*), a conception derived from the philosophy of Romanticism, which has become a concept of fundamental importance in æsthetics through the discussions of Lipps.

Association psychology shared the fate of many other intellectual tendencies of the eighteenth century in being obscured by the philosophical movement originated by Kant and developing into the philosophy of Romanticism. By the side of the mighty problems which emerged in this movement, the problem of the theory of knowledge, the problem of development in nature and history, the attempts of the psychology of the Enlightenment to add to the store of human knowledge, often motived, as they were, by practical interests, must have lost their significance. Association psychology was perhaps more successful in surviving the attacks of the Critical Philosophy and the storm of Romanticism. The tradition was continued in England, the home of associationism, occasionally even throwing off the influence of intellectualism, as in the case of Brown,[3] who extended the processes of association to the realm of the feelings. Brown further sought to unify the laws of association, and his assumption that a principle of unity was to be

---

[1] *Plastik*, and the accompanying studies, VIII, pp. 56 *f.*, 91, 153 *f.*
[2] *Kalligone*, 1800, XXII, p. 173.
[3] *Lectures on the Philosophy of the Human Mind*, 1820.

found in the coexistence of ideas with a common feeling again shows the significance of the feelings for the processes of association. Among the Scottish philosophers Sir William Hamilton, although still under the influence of faculty psychology, gave a description of the association processes, which he treated as an illustration of the law of redintegration, the law that ideas which have formed parts of a system tend to recall each other. In closer connection with English empiricism of the eighteenth century, the fundamental outlines of associationism were drawn by James Mill (1773–1836), who ranks as one of the most important of the founders of the new association psychology. The only class of psychical facts recognized by Mill is sensation, the only law recognized is the law of association, of which association by contiguity is the most general form.

Associationism owes its traditional logical formulation to John Stuart Mill, who announced, in his *System of Logic* (1843), a psychological law which was to serve as a universal explanation of the connection among states of consciousness.[1] The main classes of states of consciousness are thoughts, feelings, will-acts, and sensations. The classification is indeed unsatisfactory enough. What is important is the claim that it is the laws according to which states of consciousness succeed each other which form the proper subject-matter of scientific psychology. The usual laws of association are cited as illustrations of the process in question, and they are given a fictitious significance by their suggested analogy to the law of gravitation. An example of such a general law is the law that any psychical impression, no matter what its cause, will reappear in a similar though weakened form when the original cause is no longer present. Mill thus calls attention for the first time to the so-called symbolic function of memory images, which has been treated

[1] Bk. VI, chap. IV.

by a number of modern psychologists, H. Cornelius, for example, as an ultimate and inexplicable fact of consciousness.

The attempt to unify the doctrine of association eventually left standing only two fundamental forms of the process: inner association, for which similarity and contrast are the two most important qualitative characteristics of the contents associated, and outer association, which results from the empirical connections of these contents within consciousness. The demand for unification was also met by Alexander Bain, from whose first important psychological work, *The Senses and the Intellect* (1855), dates an increasing interest in the association theory. He reduced the various forms of association to association by similarity and contiguity, a contrast which resembles that between inner and outer association. Aside from these simple forms of association, there are also complex forms, and, within the realm of imagination, so-called constructive associations. The rigid scheme of association is thus expanded so as to include all forms of psychical phenomena from the most simple mental connection to voluntary actions. If the law of self-preservation is added, you can take even a voluntary action and reduce it completely to associations between spontaneous actions and the chance agency of pleasure.

The tendency toward the unification of the associative processes has recently given rise to the singular controversy over the question whether in the last resort association by similarity or association by contiguity is to be regarded as the primary form. In the discussion between Höffding and Lehmann one of the most instructive examples was the association, Alexander the Great–Frederick the Great, which Höffding ascribed to similarity between the two generals, while Lehmann[1] regarded the case as one of association by contiguity due to the common predicate, "the great."

[1] Wundt, *Phil. Studien*, V, pp. 96 ff.; VII, pp. 169 ff.; VIII, pp. 86 ff.

The measure of truth in both positions well illustrates the futility of the whole question.

The whole theory of association was thought out to its ultimate consequences by Herbert Spencer. His elements of psychical life or "units of feeling" are psychical atoms constituting an unknowable spiritual substance. The connections among these simple contents of consciousness are formed in accordance with the fundamental laws of association that every "feeling" as well as every relation between "feelings" associates itself with its like in the past experience of the individual. There is evidently a close relation between this process and the physiological processes of habituation, and Spencer thus returns, in a sense, only in a greater measure, to the physiological point of view of Hartley. But Spencer belongs to a new epoch. His psychology is based upon the notion of development or evolution and thus connects itself with the more recent tendencies of psychology in Germany.

Psychology was not directly influenced by the ideas of Romanticism so much as were the other mental sciences. Its development rather occurred in connection with the thinker who, alone among his idealistic contemporaries, sought to found the science of psychology anew—I mean Herbart. In his hands psychology becomes a science, striving to express psychical uniformities by the aid of an exact scientific terminology. Going far beyond the facts and forms of association, he seeks to restate these in terms of a science of psychical mechanics.

## 2. Psychology as a Mechanics of Ideas

At the time of Herbart German psychology had lost itself in the ideas of Romanticism. The most important psychological idea of the time, if we abstract from the metaphysical background, was the construction of the history of consciousness out of the concept and the fundamental facts of consciousness.[1] Herbart himself is, perhaps, more representative of his time than he is often thought to be, since he based his psychology largely upon metaphysics. In his observations on the history of psychology he discussed the relation of his own point of view with those of a number of his predecessors and his contemporaries.[2] He defends the rational psychology of Leibniz against the attacks of Kant. He asserts his own point of departure to be the psychology of Fichte, whose merit it was to expose the contradictions involved in the concept of the ego. Among his contemporaries Fries had, according to Herbart, most conclusively proved the shortcoming of the Kantian psychology, while Weiss had based psychology upon a dynamic conception of nature. The metaphysical presuppositions upon which he founded his own psychology assigned him a position from which he never advanced. He is left standing at the beginning of the nineteenth century much as Leibniz was left standing at the beginning of the preceding one.[3] Nevertheless, it is the merit of Herbart to have introduced into explanatory psychology the concept of a mechanics of ideas based upon the valuable conception of psychical uniformity. The soul which, on account of the unity of consciousness, must be thought of as a simple, real being, contains, as forms of its self-preservation, presentations or ideas. Similar or disparate ideas fuse with one another; opposite or partially opposite ideas inhibit one another in proportion to their opposition. Inhibition has the effect of diminishing the intensity of ideas. The relations involved in the process of inhibition, moreover, are amenable to exact mathematical treatment. As a "statics of ideas" mathematical psy-

[1] *Cf.* p. 29.      [2] *Werke*, Hartenstein ed., V, pp. 251 *ff*.
[3] *Cf.* p. 27.

chology seeks to ascertain the terminal condition in which ideas are in equilibrium; as a mechanics of ideas it seeks to determine their intensities during their course.

A statics of ideas takes as its point of departure reflections such as the following: If we start with two opposite ideas of equal intensity, the intensity of each will, in consequence of the resulting inhibition, be diminished to one half of its original intensity. The inhibition sum is in this case equal to the total inhibition which distributes itself over the two ideas. In the case of the unequal intensity of the two ideas, $a$ and $b$ ($a > b$), it is sufficient that a quantity, $b$, be inhibited in both. Now an inhibition sum, $b$, will distribute itself over both ideas in such a manner that each will suffer inhibition the less, the greater the force which it possesses. The inhibition of $a$ will therefore be $\frac{b^2}{a+b}$; of $b$, $\frac{ab}{a+b}$. By simple subtraction the intensity of the remaining ideas can be determined.[1] But Herbart has still not arrived at the fact of the threshold of consciousness. The condition under which an idea would entirely disappear below the threshold of consciousness would be $b - \frac{ab}{a+b} = 0$, whence $b = 0$. Only when three ideas, $a$, $b$, $c$ ($a > b > c$), occur can the weakest disappear below the threshold, under the auxiliary assumption that the inhibition sum is now $b + c$.

The fundamental equation for the mechanics of ideas is also derived from a consideration of the inhibition sum.[2] In their original state ideas are entirely uninhibited and constitute an inhibition sum. As the inhibition sum diminishes, the movement of ideas begins. If the inhibition sum is $S$, and $\sigma$ the inhibited quantity after the expiration of a time, $t$, then

$$(S-\sigma)dt = d\sigma.$$

[1] *Psychologie als Wissenschaft*, 1824-5, §§ 41 ff.    [2] *Op. cit.*, § 74.

While in the mechanics of bodies the force determines only the differential of the rate of motion, here it determines the very rate itself. From the integration of the equation follows

$$t = \log \frac{Const}{S-\sigma}.$$

Since when $t=0$ also $\sigma=0$, $const=S$; and for the inhibited quantity we get

$$\sigma = S(1-e^{-t}).$$

In this equation is contained the law according to which the actually inhibited quantity of any inhibition sum, $S$, increases in a time, $t$. By an analogous calculation we can determine the time for the rise of ideas.[1] If $\phi$ stands for receptivity, and if within a time, $t$, a quantity, $z$, of presentation is produced, then the receptivity at the expiration of $t$ is only $\phi-z$. If the force of a disturbance, say, a brightness, is $\beta$, we have the equation

$$\beta(\phi-z)dt = dz, \quad \text{whence}$$
$$z = \phi(1-e^{-\beta t}).$$

To this equation corresponds, in addition to the general principles of metaphysics, the known fact "that, first, every perception requires a short interval of time if the resulting idea is to attain to a finite degree of strength among other ideas; secondly, that a perception prolonged beyond a certain time produces no increase in the resulting strength of the idea." The passage clearly suggests the problem connected with the increase of the sensation stimulus with which subsequent sense psychology was to occupy itself, and, indeed, the ascending curves obtained by empirical measurements occasionally approach the fundamental form deduced by Herbart. Up to a certain point, too, mathematical psychology connected itself again with the Herbartian problem of the statics of ideas in subjecting the prob-

[1] *Op. cit.*, § 94.

lems of the distribution of degree of clearness in consciousness, and of the inhibition or assimilative interaction of ideas, to experiment. Nevertheless, the passages in Herbart's psychology in which he shows signs of abandoning his imaginary mechanics of ideas for actual psychological experience are of rare occurrence. Indeed, it is merely a fraction of this experience, a limited range of certain intellectual processes, with which his psychology deals. Following out his presuppositions to their logical conclusions, Herbart intellectualized mental life to a degree nowhere else reached in the history of psychology.

The Herbartian tradition was continued by a small number of disciples for a number of decades. One of the most important of these, M. W. Drobisch, projected an ambitious programme for psychology, claiming for it an insight into the true nature of reality beyond that of any other science.[1] In the contents of consciousness, in the variety of our ideational, affective, and desiderative life, we observe the inner processes themselves which constitute spiritual life. The first task of psychology is the entire exclusion of metaphysics and the creation of an empirical psychology which should be really worthy of the name. A related problem is the formulation of a mathematical theory of mental life. A third problem consists in the application of the results obtained to epistemological and metaphysical questions. It is in the first of these attempts that the influence of natural science, for which the exact spirit of Herbartian psychology has such a deep affinity, makes itself most definitely felt. The man who contributed most in this direction was Theodor Waitz,[2] who abandoned the Herbartian scheme and regarded psychology as one of the natural

[1] *Empirische Psychologie nach naturwissenschaftlicher Methode*, 1842, 2d ed., 1898, Einl., pp. 9 ff.
[2] *Lehrbuch der Psychologie als Naturwissenschaft*, 1849.

sciences. The Herbartian tradition was maintained more strictly by W. F. Volkmann, who made a conspicuous attempt to prove the services of realism in the realm of psychology.

An intermediate tendency is represented by Hermann Lotze, the most independent of the group of psychologists who usher in the most recent development of psychology. He sought to formulate a physiology of mind but maintained, at the same time, that the results must be interpreted in the light of general psychological conceptions, and this for the reason that he had long ago ascertained secretly, by statistical methods, that the average life of the great positive discoveries of exact physiology had been four years! It is true that Herbart had admitted the existence of physiological conditions of mental states. The significance of the body for states of consciousness is proved by the influence upon them which the body exerts, by the bodily resonance observable in connection with certain psychical states, and by the co-operation of the body in the production of volitional acts. Lotze, however, was the first to take account of the physiological conditions of mental life in any thoroughgoing or extensive way.[1] He did not content himself, for example, with simply placing sensation and feeling side by side, as two elements of mental life, but analyzed the genesis of simple sensation itself into a series of distinguishable stages. In the first place, the external stimulus is transformed into the excitation of the sense-organ; this, in turn, produces the nervous process which is eventually to result in sensation, and, finally, we have the problematic modifications within the brain itself. Here the process emerges from the physical realm. The impression which the excitations within the nervous system pro-

[1] *Cf.* with this the historical retrospect by Külpe, *Grundriss der Psychologie*, 1893, p. 27. [English translation, p. 26. Trs.]

the application of the principles of psychical mechanics. Nevertheless, the general character of the Herbartian speculation was not without aid to these investigators.[1] A thinker trained in the abstractions of the Herbartian system, which dealt only with the general relations obtaining among mutually inhibitive intensive magnitudes, would readily substitute for the latter corresponding factors when these manifested themselves in human society.

The beginnings of ethnic psychology in England were independent of these efforts and were dominated by different conceptions. It was English empirical psychology that was the first to enter the broad field of ethnological phenomena for the purpose of utilizing these phenomena for psychological purposes. The investigations of prehistoric man and the beginnings of civilization by Lubbock and Tylor (1865) opened the way. But it was the psychology of Herbert Spencer, based upon the evolutionary idea, which was bound to transcend the standpoint and to overstep the limits of a merely individual psychology. In spite, however, of the wealth of ethnological data displayed in these and similar works, they tended after all to run to philosophy of history rather than to remain pure ethnic psychology.

These modern developments were anticipated early in the eighteenth century by G. B. Vico (1668–1744),[2] who similarly combined problems of the philosophy of history with reflections in ethnic psychology for his interpretation of the historic process as a process conditioned by psychological laws. It is true that, in so far as he confined himself to a comparison of the life of peoples separated from each other in space and time, his method was merely a method of historical induction; nevertheless, the subjects investigated by

---

[1] See Wundt, *Völkerpsychologie*, I, 2d ed., 1904, Einl., pp. 18 *ff*.
[2] In his work, *Scienza nuova d'intorno alla commune natura delle nazioni* (1730).

esses, which was to serve as the conceptual basis for the explanation of the phenomena of consciousness.

To the Herbartian school is also due the first stimulus to the development of ethnic psychology, which has become one of the most important branches of comparative psychology.

## 3. Comparative Psychology

The term comparative psychology might be said to include those branches of psychology which go beyond the realm of phenomena given in individual self-observation and which depend in the main upon the method of comparison. Ethnic psychology and, in large part, animal psychology come under this classification. The influence of Darwinism which is noticeable in the treatment of a number of special problems is felt mainly in this field. As a special branch of comparative psychology may also be mentioned individual psychology, in so far as it attempts to separate individual from general psychical phenomena by the aid of comparative methods.

### (a) *Ethnic Psychology*

The science of ethnic psychology is usually said to have been founded by Steinthal and Lazarus, who issued their *Zeitschrift für Völkerpsychologie* in 1860. As we look back to those early beginnings from the point of view of the concepts of ethnic psychology originated in recent times by Wundt, the psychical mechanics of Herbart seems the most inappropriate point of departure possible for the consideration of this group of phenomena, particularly since the investigators referred to, in spite of the wide scope of their programme, regarded ethnic psychology merely as a field for the phenomena of mental rivalry. The third and fourth propositions, finally, are attempts to bring into relation the intensity of sensation and the retinal distribution of the stimulus, a question which was later taken up again by Fechner.

In the discussion of the complex functions the moral point of view characteristic of Lotze's thought occasionally comes into the foreground. He applies the law of persistence, which it is so tempting to invoke in support of the retention of memory images in the brain, to the soul itself. The difficulty of understanding how an infinite number of impressions can persist in one substance is no greater in the case of the soul than in the case of the brain. The soul hypothesis, however, satisfies our moral needs more adequately than the other. Lotze accordingly proceeds upon the assumption that memory as well as miscellaneous recognition and the course of ideas are conceivable without the co-operation of the brain.[1] Lotze's psychology here issues in a pure spiritualism, in which the rigor of psychological analysis is combined with a disposition to yield to moral interests and needs.[2]

Among those who have helped to preserve the fundamental idea of Herbart's psychical mechanics is Lipps. Although he shows a closer affiliation with the views of Herbart in his first principal work, *Grundtatsachen des Seelenlebens* (1883), than in his subsequent publications, nevertheless, the aim which underlies all his work is to bring the realm of psychical processes under the reign of necessary law. If one were asked to state the principal difference between the psychology of Herbart and that of Lipps, it might be said to consist in the attempt of Lipps to substitute for the mechanism of conscious psychic processes, such as Herbart contemplated, the mechanism of unconscious psychic proc-

[1] *Op. cit.*, p. 473.      [2] *Cf.* above, p. 30.

duce in the soul might, in the first instance, be an unconscious process, which is then succeeded, as a sixth member of our series, by a simple sensation. As a seventh stage might be mentioned attention, which conscious sensations receive in greater or less degree. With distinctions such as these, derived from the modern physiology of the senses, are combined ideas reminiscent of the Herbartian mechanics of ideas, which lead to a number of general propositions concerning the relation of impressions in the soul, as follows:[1] (1) If two impressions which are qualitatively the same enter consciousness, the result is a simple sensation of double the strength of each taken separately. (2) If two impressions are qualitatively dissimilar, but are at the same time comparable, it depends upon the mental excitation in which they are produced whether they fuse or not. Two colors, for example, if not separated spatially, must fuse. (3) If a number of different nerve-fibres receive an equal amount of the same stimulus, and if the impressions really sum themselves, the intensity of the resulting sensation will be proportional to the sum of the nerve-fibres through which it is excited. (4) If a stimulus of a constant amount is distributed among a number of nerve-fibres, the resulting sensation is much weaker than if the total stimulus is carried by a single nerve-fibre. (5) Disparate stimuli, like colors or tones, do not result in an intermediate sensation, but only in a distribution of attention.

It is remarkable how many psychological problems are affected by the foregoing generalizations. In connection with the first of these propositions, renewed attempts have been made at an elementary construction of sensation. The second suggests presuppositions which were to serve as the starting-points for some purely psychological theories of space. Taken in conjunction with the fifth, it also suggests

[1] *Medicinische Psychologie*, 1852, pp. 230 *ff.*

him—language, myth, custom, and laws—belong without question to ethnic psychology.

### (b) Animal Psychology[1]

The contention of Descartes that animals were soulless automata, a conception popular at the time, was not seriously controverted until the eighteenth century. Condillac ascribed to animals a soul life essentially resembling that of man.[2] There are, according to him, no specific differences between man and the animals as regards mental constitution, the difference consisting merely in the greater range of man's experiences. The narrow range of an animal's experience is due to its low physical development, and particularly to the comparatively low development of its sense-organs. The influence of sensualism, which tends to correlate the range of experience and knowledge with the development of sense-organs, is clearly evident here. Condillac's position was controverted by H. S. Reimarus,[3] one of the early champions of deism in Germany. The instincts of animals are not acquirements due to intelligence and experience but are purely congenital traits. As the bearer of ideals and possessor of intelligence and free will, man, compared with the lower animals, is simply a higher order of being. In his analysis of the animal mind Reimarus accordingly confines himself to the determination of these congenital instincts. He finds ten classes of these, and the adaptations which they severally show furnish him with arguments for the wisdom of the Creator.

The influence of the semitheological doctrines of Reimarus upon natural scientists was practically negligible. His

[1] *Cf.* with the following E. Rádl, *Geschichte der biologischen Theorien*, II, 1909, pp. 427 ff., 214 ff.
[2] *Traité des animaux*, Amsterdam, 1755.
[3] *Allgemeine Betracht. ü. d. Triebe d. Tiere*, 1760.

view of instinct, however, was revived in the nineteenth century in the form of a certain conception growing out of the German philosophy of nature. Starting with the phenomena of the simplest instinctive activities, Fichte had arrived at the notion of the subject as pure activity. For Schelling the animal instincts were the significant activities of the same power which reveals itself most profoundly in art. The metaphysical will of Schopenhauer, too, nowhere reveals itself more immediately than in instinct, and Hartmann bases his conception of the unconscious, which is of such central importance in his system, largely upon the doctrine of instinct. One of the best evidences of the reflex influence of these general philosophical ideas upon psychology are the writings of the physician C. G. Carus,[1] which seek to portray, often by the aid of myth and allegory, the gradual growth of consciousness in the animal world. Man and the lower animals are bound together by many analogies. Observation gives place to admiration of the hidden essence which comes to expression, e. g., in the profound symbolism of the spiral line of the snail; by unbridled analogies the author lifts himself into the realm of metaphysics and of those spiritualistic ideas with which we have already become acquainted.[2]

Natural science, meanwhile, in its more exact forms, took its starting-point from Condillac. Lamarck was prominent among those who developed the notion of evolution which was suggested by Condillac. He enriched the current doctrine by the important addition of the idea that the results of the experiences gained during the life of the individual do not disappear at the death of the individual but are transmitted to the offspring by heredity. The views of the psy-

---

[1] *Psychologie oder Geschichte der Seele in der Reihenfolge der Tierwelt*, 1866.
[2] See above, p. 30.

chical life of animals held by Darwin were somewhat naïve, since he ascribed to animals a soul life essentially similar to man's but existing in a somewhat masked or undeveloped form. Instinct is to be explained as inherited habit, and the differences among instincts are to be accounted for by reference to the same process of natural selection by which we explain differences of bodily structure. Since Wundt's studies in animal psychology,[1] this branch has become more closely affiliated with general psychology. A singular revival of long-forgotten ideas which carry one back to Scholasticism is found in Erich Wasmann.[2] He agrees with Reimarus in separating instinct entirely from intelligence. Intelligent actions differ from instinctive through the presence in the former of the consciousness of end. The absence of the consciousness of end and of the power of abstraction in the lower animals constitute an impassable gulf, according to Wasmann, between man and these lower forms. An effective counter-influence to such views is found in modern experimental animal psychology, which even goes to the opposite extreme, as in Loeb's theories of the chemical reactions of lower animals.[3]

### (c) *Influence of Darwinism*

The influence of Darwin upon psychology was also evident in connection with many special problems. Thus we meet with the attempt to explain color sensations from an evolutionary point of view. After the English statesman W. E. Gladstone and L. Geiger had contended that the Greeks—Homer, for example—had not been able to distin-

[1] *Vorlesungen über die Menschen- und Tierseele*, 1863, 5th ed., 1911. [Engl. tr. (*Human and Animal Psychology*) by Creighton and Titchener, New York, 1895. Trs.]
[2] *Instinct und Intelligenz im Tierreich*, 1899.
[3] See above, p. 42.

guish blue from black or gray from green, H. Magnus[1] sought to show that man was originally entirely color-blind. The order of colors in the spectrum from red to violet is claimed to be the order in which human sensitivity to the various color-tones developed; and Magnus does not shrink from the conclusion that sensitivity to ultra-violet light will at some future time be developed.

Similarly, new points of view were developed in the study of the origin of language. Darwin's own views stood midway between the theory of imitation and that of instinctive sounds, the two theories which formed the most natural approach to a psychological comprehension of the problem of language. He held that language originated partly in the imitation of natural sounds, partly in the instinctive cries of man himself. Starting from a similar point of view, G. Jäger sought to explain the development of human language from the sounds uttered by animals.[2] He describes in detail the stages which occurred, as he supposed, in the development of expression among animals, from accidental to voluntary utterance, from mere motor discharge to communication. The influence of bodily structure, too, is taken into account. Thus quadrupeds, for example, whose chest movements are affected by their mode of locomotion, lack the delicacy in the control of respiratory movements which is requisite for speaking or singing. These biological fancies, however, were soon abandoned again, along with various other speculations, such as the genealogical theories of language of Schleicher, the theory that inarticulate interjection formed the substrate out of which articulate language developed, and the like.

Evolutionary psychology also made a number of attempts, which owe their origin to modern biology, to determine the

---

[1] *Die geschichtliche Entwicklung des Farbensinnes*, 1877.
[2] *Über den Ursprung der menschlichen Sprache*, 1867 and 1869.

elementary psychical attribute of organized matter. We have to do here with the transformation of the problem of determining the psychical element which is co-ordinate with the element of matter, a problem originating in metaphysical psychology, or in the border field of empirical psychology, into the problem of the kind of psychical activity which characterizes various stages of organic evolution. Hering named memory as the elementary psychic characteristic of organized matter.[1] Racial memory is developed in the evolutionary series as a whole, by heredity. The related distinction between individual and phyletic memory subsequently found its way into many psychogenetic considerations, such as those of W. Preyer.[2]

### (d) Individual Psychology

A last branch of comparative psychology occupies itself with individual differences. If we pass over the secular psychology of the Renaissance,[3] the main ideas of individual psychology are found in that versatile era, the period of the Enlightenment. Herder, in 1778, voiced the demand for a "characteristic" psychology. Oddly, he directed his polemic against the *ars characteristica* which had originated in the philosophy of Leibniz and which Ploucquet and Lambert sought to develop into a general science of conceptual signs. Psychology, he urged, should take particular care not to lose itself in such fruitless generalities. Herder recommends as a model for psychologists the physiology of Haller, whose law of muscular sensitivity Herder proclaimed as the fundamental law of sensation. Spirit-filled, like Pygmalion's statue, Haller's physiological treatise is to be raised to the rank of psychology. A year later appeared Feder's inves-

[1] *Über das Gedächtnis als Funktion der organischen Materie*, 1870.
[2] *Die Seele des Kindes*, p. 230.   [3] *Cf.* p. 57, above.

tigations of the will, in which the idea of special psychology was also definitely expressed. These various movements and ideas were voiced in the *Magazin für Erfahrungsseelenlehre*, published by C. P. Moritz, founded in 1782. The whole problem of individual psychology, the psychology of individual differences, has come into special prominence in recent years in its connection with the applications of psychology, particularly to the field of education. An initial problem here, according to L. W. Stern, is created by the fact that psychology, as an analytic science, which isolates mental processes, stands in fundamental contradiction to all those branches for which the mental life, as an individual whole, *i. e.*, as a personality, is of significance.[1] The fact that the divisions of general and individual psychology, on the one hand, and of pure and applied psychology, on the other, cross each other, leads to one of the most actively controverted questions of contemporary psychology.

The various tendencies of comparative psychology which devote themselves to the study of special social groups cannot be followed in detail here. They belong, in any event, mainly to the present. Occasionally we find striking discrepancies between investigations of this sort, which are not always undertaken with purely psychological motives, and exact psychological reflection. Here belong hypotheses like those of Weininger which have achieved an ephemeral reputation, and according to which the specific difference between the sexes is to be explained by reference to the wholly untenable conception of a mental state in which sensation and feeling have not yet become differentiated from each other.[2]

[1] *Psychologie der Aussage*, Heft I, 1903, p. 15.
[2] Weininger, *Geschlecht und Character*, 7th ed., 1905, pp. 127 *f*.

## 4. Influences of Natural Science

The last stage in the development of modern psychology is characterized by the influence upon it of natural science. The effect of this influence was not that the tendencies of explanatory psychology which were motived by purely psychological considerations, an account of which we have already given, were supplanted by the modes of thought characteristic of natural science. Rather did the attentive consideration of the methods of science and of the border problems of psychology and science bring the unique character of the problems of psychology into clearer relief.

The contact of psychology with natural science was thus manifold. That the idea of the regularity of events, which had lent vitality to science since the Renaissance, also served as an ideal in psychology can be proved by the evidence of centuries.[1] It was in the nineteenth century, however, that the growing knowledge of the central nervous system came to the aid of the older efforts to determine the physiological basis for a definitely outlined system of psychological ideas, thus resulting in the so-called modern science of phrenology. But the method of science, too, found its way into psychology. It came from the direction where the problems of science and of psychology find a common meeting ground, that of the physiology of the senses. Here the basis was laid upon which experimental psychology as an independent branch of investigation could be founded.

### (a) *The Newer Phrenology*

Phrenology has a long preliminary history in the various theories regarding the seat of the soul. Only the rôles, so to

[1] *Cf.* Chapter VIII, 1, below.

speak, in these two branches, were in a way interchanged. In the older theories the point of departure was psychology, which accordingly reacted upon brain physiology; and the comparatively meagre knowledge of brain anatomy gave unrestricted play to the most extravagant hypotheses. The psychological motive which led Descartes to locate the soul in the pineal gland, strange as it appears to us nowadays, dominated psychology for centuries. Since we can have only a single impression of an object at any one time, there must be some place where the separate views from the two eyes, for example, or any other such disparate impressions, are united into a single whole before they enter the soul.[1] The organ in which this fusion takes place must, it is evident, be one which is not duplicated in the brain. The motive, however, which prompted Descartes to decide upon the pineal gland was that it was only here that the unification of impressions could be accomplished by means of the animal spirits (*spiritus animales*) which fill the ventricular cavities of the brain. The fundamental idea of Descartes that the coalescence of disparate mental impressions could occur only through their conjunction in some one point of the brain appealed so strongly to the psychologists of the seventeenth and eighteenth centuries that there was hardly an unpaired structure in the brain which was not at some time or other a candidate for the honor of being the seat of the soul. Lancisi and Bonnet held the seat of the soul to be the *corpus callosum*, Digby the *septum pellucidum*, Haller the *pons Varolii;* Boerhave located it in the *medulla oblongata*, Plattner in the *corpora quadrigemina*.

The doctrine of the seat of the soul combined with the faculty psychology which, in comparison with the Cartesian doctrine of the soul as a simple, indivisible substance, already represented considerable analysis, to form the well-known

[1] *Les passions de l'âme*, I, p. 32.

system of phrenology of F. J. Gall,[1] a system which illustrates what varied psychological tendencies meet in the psychology of the latter part of the eighteenth century. Gall transformed the fundamental concepts of faculty psychology into organs of mind. The origin and connection of mental processes were ascribed to nerve vibrations, to which corresponded, on the psychological side, the association of ideas. In addition to various fundamental psychical dispositions or faculties the soul has a number of characteristics, such as intelligence, will, attention, and the like. Each faculty possesses all these attributes. The number of these fundamental traits is said to correspond to the number of instincts, of which Gall enumerated twenty-seven, such as sex, philoprogenitiveness, friendship, cunning, pride, avarice, and the like. Assuming that each of these faculties was matched by a corresponding brain structure, Gall proceeded to elaborate the practical science of phrenology. Since the brain structures in question are located superficially, the skull would show corresponding conformations which can be easily ascertained by tactual exploration, thus affording an objective means for the ascertainment of mental endowment. Although Gall anticipated many modern conceptions, such as those of congenital tendencies to criminality or the tendency of supernormal persons to insanity, his art was commercialized and degenerated into charlatanism.

The untenability of Gall's phrenology was proved in the first part of the nineteenth century by the French experimental psychologists Magendie and Flourens. Flourens ascribed different function-complexes to the *medulla oblongata*, the *corpora quadrigemina*, and to the *cerebellum* and *cerebrum*. The last vestige of the old question of the seat of the soul is found in his influential doctrine of the vital

[1] Gall, *Vorlesungen über die Verrichtungen des Gehirns*. Herausgegeben von H. G. C. von Selpert, 1805.

nodes. The point of the V-formed gray mass at the beak of the so-called *calamus scriptorius*, with which the fourth ventricle passes over into the fissure of the spinal chord, is the seat of life in the sense that its extirpation or injury results in instant death.[1] The psychical functions proper, however, remain localized in the entire area of the cerebral hemispheres. The functions in question are intelligence and will, whose localization he conceived of in such wise that the most minute part of the organs involved could act in place of the whole. Intelligence and will, however, are very complex functions, and it is difficult to see how they can be localized in the smallest structure of an organ so highly differentiated as the brain. The disposition to take refuge in the older-style phrenology in order to escape from these difficulties was encouraged by the partial confirmation of the theory of Gall through the discovery by Broca, in 1861, of the so-called centre of speech. The advance of modern phrenology, as distinguished from the particular system of Gall, consisted, in the first place, in the substitution for the older organs of mind certain special centres or areas connected with certain peripheral functions such as the movements of co-ordinated muscle groups. In the second place, the inner senses of Gall were forced to give place to psychical elements, usually sensations and ideas, which the psychology of Herbart had brought into prominence. It was accordingly assumed that the cortex contained sensory centres for the reception of incoming stimuli and for the initiation of motor innervations. Each of these centres, in turn, contains sensory and idea cells. The latter possess the power of reviving sensations, as the excitement of the sensory cells tends to communicate itself to the idea cells. This was the form of the theory as taught by Meynert and as later applied especially by H. Munk, who gave it considerable currency among brain physiologists.

[1] *Rech. expér. sur les fonct. du syst. nerv.*, 2d ed., 1842, p. 204.

Closer to the results of psychological analysis is a second form of phrenology which separates the areas in which the connections among sensations, and probably also their reproduction and the complex psychical processes, occur from the ideational centres, as special association centres. Thus the psychological services of the association theory find recognition in the field of pure psychology.

The controversy regarding the association centres psychology might well have left to the brain physiologists. Aside from the details mentioned, two results were reached which were of general interest for psychology. In the first place, the question regarding the seat of the soul, which had occupied psychology for centuries, was definitely rendered meaningless by the discovery of the motor areas by Fritsch and Hitzig. In the second place, the results of the study of brain physiology confirmed anew the inconceivable complexity of the apparently most simple mental processes. How many components might be contained in a given mental process of which no trace appears in consciousness was revealed especially by the study of those cases of brain lesion which resulted in the splitting up of mental factors which ordinarily occur together and the disappearance of a given factor from the original complex.[1]

### (b) The Influence of Sense Physiology

In spite of the close relationship which existed between sense physiology and psychology, owing to their common connection with the problem of perception, the results of this relation were for a long time sufficiently meagre. The classical physiologists of the first half of the nineteenth century were themselves obliged to make acquaintance with the psychological aspect of the sensory functions, and for

---

[1] *Cf.* with this Wundt, *Grundzüge der physiologischen Psychologie*, I, 6th ed., pp. 341 *ff*.

this they drew freely upon the philosophy of their time. While psychology generally followed philosophical speculation only too readily, it is a remarkable fact that the transcendental idealism of Kant influenced psychology only indirectly, through sense physiology. Johann Müller, who is one of the founders of the newer sense physiology, at the early age of twenty defended the thesis, *Nemo psychologus nisi physiologus*, a principle to which he remained loyal throughout his life.[1] Rejecting Schelling's philosophy of nature, he returned to the great philosophers of the past, Kant, Spinoza, and, among the younger thinkers, particularly to Herbart. It was especially the Kantian doctrine of space and time as pure intuitions which he incorporated into his theory of perception. In seeking for a physiological substrate of these transcendental functions he found the manifestations of this directly in sensation. The retina, for example, feels itself as spatially extended. Not less characteristic of Müller's psychology is the principle of the specific energy of the senses, which likewise points to certain philosophical presuppositions such as are implied in the recognition of the fact that psychical processes, and sensory processes in particular, are incommensurable with the processes of the external world. The conception of the immediate reality and of the incomparable uniqueness of psychical processes may be said to be a common conviction of the epoch in question. In this, too, perhaps, consists the greater historical significance of Müller when compared with, say, Purkinje, who also ranks as one of the founders of modern physiology.[2] Few of his observations, which extend to nearly all branches of biology, bear his name. In psychology the greater clearness of light rays of short-wave

[1] *Cf.* Stumpf, "H. v. Helmholtz u. d. neuere Psychologie," *Archiv f. Gesch. d. Phil.*, VIII, 1895, pp. 303 *ff*.

[2] Purkinje, *Beobachtungen und Versuche zur Physiologie der Sinne*, 2d ed., 1825.

length in dim light is called the Purkinje phenomenon, and even this phenomenon had been known a long time, although it had not been utilized for the theory of vision. There are numerous precepts in the Koran, for example, which are to be carried out at a certain hour of the day, owing to the fact that red and blue threads become invisible in the twilight.

It was Müller's school which was to give to the world the investigator who closed once and for all the gap between physiology and psychology, Helmholtz, who devoted the main strength of his best working years to investigations in physiological and experimental psychology. The two works upon which his fame mainly rests, his *Handbuch der physiologischen Optik* (1856-66) and his *Zur Lehre von den Tonempfindungen* (1862), were devoted to the psychology of the senses. A mathematical physicist by natural endowment, his principal achievements in the theory of vision and audition are due to his supreme mastery of the mathematical technique necessary for such investigations. Helmholtz's psychological theories, however, have a definite philosophical background, which may be said to be a more profound version of the idealism of Müller, particularly on the epistemological side. Already in his Königsberg inaugural address, *Über die Natur der menschlichen Sinnesempfindungen* (1852), he expounded the view that sense experience is merely a sign of the existence of some objective quality, never a copy which in some way reproduces its real nature. Sensation as merely a symbol of the external world—this doctrine remained fundamental to his main work and served as an explanation of the structure of the organs of vision. During the fifties and sixties of the last century investigation in the field of vision was, indeed, extremely active, as the names of Brücke, Listing, Volkmann, Fechner, Donders, Panum, and others will recall, and this serves to explain, to some extent, how such a work as Helmholtz's *Physiological Optics* could come into existence. Still, the study of it serves only to increase our admiration for the creative energy of its author. The thoroughgoing application of the experimental method, the criteria which underlie the analysis of the complex sense-perceptions, the points of view for the derivation of the psychical products from their elements—these achievements have never been lost to psychology.

With the recognition of the psychical activities involved in perceptions a large group of psychological problems admitting of exact treatment came into view, with the result that sense psychology became in a very genuine sense a model for modern experimental psychology. These psychical activities were thought by Helmholtz himself to be intellectual activities, an elaboration, logical in its beginnings and gradually becoming unconscious, of sensation elements into the constituent parts of perceptions. This empirical point of view, which stood in sharp opposition to the nativism in sense psychology that had grown out of Müller's theories, was developed in close dependence upon a philosophical writer whose *Logic* was one of the most influential works of the middle of the nineteenth century, John Stuart Mill. Mill's empirical logic, which was championed in Germany by no less an investigator than Justus Liebig, met with a friendly reception particularly among natural scientists. It was not the doctrine of association, however, which Helmholtz borrowed from Mill but rather the doctrine, so much controverted, of unconscious inductive and analogical inference, an idea which he utilized for his own theories of perception. That a natural scientist should go to a logician for light on psychological questions bears witness to a truly remarkable dislocation of the boundary-lines of the sciences.

Although Helmholtz was extremely critical of philosophies

of nature, declaring his own allegiance to Mill's inductive method, he himself now and then unwittingly fell into the mode of thinking which he disparaged. The notion of development or evolution he never adopted. His analysis of the human sensory functions, which, in spite of its empirical character, makes no use of the evolutionary principle, occasionally reminds one of the attempts of the philosophies of nature to discover the laws of nature in the activity of human intelligence. The sense physiology of Helmholtz was, of course, intended to be predominantly psychology. But this psychology did not undertake an investigation of the simple psychical processes but assumed certain supposed psychical processes in the complex activities of perception. The eye is for Helmholtz a physical apparatus whose function it is to mediate certain sensation elements, like color, brightness, and so forth. Back of these sensations, however, stands intelligence, which acts upon them like a mental faculty. These conceptions are connected with the attempt, often noticeable in Helmholtz, to dispose of certain psychological problems involved in perception, problems which are not amenable to treatment of the degree of exactitude required by natural science, in the easiest and quickest way possible. In this way Helmholtz sometimes approached perilously near to a popular intellectualism of which psychology subsequently had to free itself.

### (c) *Experimental Psychology*

The problems which we associate with experimental psychology to-day were not clearly defined until very recent times. Most of the beginnings in the transformation of the method of psychology were made by the psychology of the special senses which has just been described. The great physiologist Ernst Heinrich Weber took the idea, which had, indeed, been expressed before, namely, that one must test the instruments of sensation just as the physicist and chemist must test the instruments with which they work, and made it the starting-point for purely psychological investigations. He not only applied this test in his own investigations of the perceptions of space and of pressure, but he also pointed out the psychological conditions of reliability in comparison, as, for example, of the differences in accuracy in the reception of simultaneous and successive stimuli. By varying the interval between the two stimuli and noting the rate of diminishing accuracy with the increase of the interval he even prepared the way for the investigations of memory by the use of exact methods. "Since the opportunity for exact measurements of mental processes comes so rarely," he wrote, "I recommend these investigations to the attention of psychologists."[1] In these noteworthy words we meet with a distinct recognition of the importance of exact experimental investigations. The law which has been for all times associated with the name of Weber was in the first instance merely a result of observation. In his interpretation of this fact he recognizes a peculiarity of the comparison of sensations in the fact that here two magnitudes are not compared with a common standard of measure but directly.[2]

Psychology did not at once heed the admirable suggestions of Weber. Attempts like that of Bonatelli[3] remained isolated until the new ideas were again vitalized by philosophy. In studying the history of psychology one is frequently surprised at the metaphysical framework which supports psychological systems. Nevertheless, it must not be forgotten that many psychological points of view owe their origin

---

[1] *Tastsinn und Gemeingefühl*, 1846, p. 546.
[2] *Op. cit.*, pp. 560 f.; cf. Chapter IX, 1 (b), below.
[3] *Dell' Esperimento in Psicologia*, Brescia, 1858.

to their relation to purely philosophical problems. An illustration of this is Gustav Theodor Fechner, who combined the exact investigation of his time in the psychology of the senses with profound and fantastic ideas derived from Schelling's philosophy of nature. Starting with the problems of the philosophy of nature of Romanticism, which had been obscured by the dominant philosophical tradition and which was kept alive by a few philosophical scientists, Fechner defined psychophysics as the exact science of the relations of body and mind. The idea that body and mind represent the dual manifestations of a fundamentally unitary substance already formed the basis of his *Zendavesta*, published in 1851. His problem was to ascertain the functional relation between the two series of phenomena and, in particular, to establish the law according to which the intensity of mental activity varies with the variation in the intensity of its underlying physical activity. Later he expounded schematically certain fundamental relations between body and mind and between lower and higher forms of spiritual life by aid of the relation between arithmetical series of lower and higher orders.[1] The scheme of geometrical orders led him, by a somewhat uncertain line of thought, to make the relative increase of physical vital energy the measure of the increase of the corresponding psychical energy.[2] With this was connected the idea that the soul would sum these increments, $d\gamma$, just as the kinetic energy of a body is regarded as the sum of its absolute increments, $d\beta$. Thus the fundamental formula, $d\gamma = K \dfrac{d\beta}{\beta}$, and as its integral the formula of measurement was arrived at. Without any thought of the relation of this formula to Weber's law, he submitted a paper on the subject to W. Weber in 1850, who was impressed with the correctness and

[1] *Zendavesta*, II, p. 334.   [2] *Cf. Psychophysik*, 1860, II, p. 554.

keenness of the fundamental idea, although unfortunately it did not agree, as he thought, with the newer discoveries. Fechner at length discovered an empirical foundation in the fundamental psychophysical law for brightnesses, and it was not until after a number of experiments with weights that he discovered the broad basis of empirical facts in the investigations of E. H. Weber.

The science of psychophysics, as Fechner conceived it, is to be distinguished from psychology proper as well as from physics, and aims at the exact determination of the relationship between psychical and physical processes. It begins with the psychophysics of extra-organic stimuli, which seeks to determine the relation between consciousness and the external world and which serves as an introduction to the psychophysics of the bodily organism. For there is a psychophysical activity within the bodily organism which stands intermediate between external stimulus and sensation, and it is the relation of this to the purely psychical activity within that the "inner psychophysics" seeks to determine. To this field are transferred Weber's law and the phenomenon of the threshold, under the assumption that psychophysical activity is proportional to the stimulus. In the further development of these ideas the question of the psychophysical continuity and discontinuity comes distinctly into the foreground. The latter arises when the movements of psychophysical activity occur below a certain limit called the conscious threshold. The result is a number of psychophysical steps or stages. As conscious processes which are distinguishable by us are continuous below our principal threshold, so also our own consciousness is a part of a more general, inclusive consciousness.

With the loosening of the bond with which Fechner had connected ideas from the philosophy of nature with the problem of the measurement of sensations, the fundamental psychophysical problem admitting of exact treatment which remained was that of the relation between the intensities of sensation and stimulus. The restriction of metric psychology to this problem was the more likely to lead to some disappointment since the development of Fechner's methods, which showed a tendency to approach the quantitative determinations of physics, rendered them more and more useless for the purposes of psychology.[1] At the same time there arose a new group of problems calling for investigation according to the new principles of psychical measurement. The course of ideas, the relation as regards clearness of simultaneous contents of consciousness, the processes of recall, which formed, indeed, the original interest of the science of psychical mechanics with its mathematical speculations—all these problems had to be investigated anew by empirical methods as soon as an exact basis for psychological measurement had been discovered. The impulse to these investigations was given by certain remarkable differences in temporal estimation which were noticeable in astronomical observations in the employment of the so-called eye and ear methods. The problem here is to estimate the position which a star passing through the telescopic field occupies with reference to the threads of a micrometer at two successive strokes of a second's clock.[2] In the year 1795 the discrepancy of eight tenths of a second between the findings of the London astronomer Maskelyne and of his assistant Kinnebrook led to the dismissal of the latter. The incident attracted the attention of the noted astronomer Bessel, who recognized the subjective variations in temporal estimation as a fact of general import and studied it somewhat exhaustively under the name of the

[1] *Cf.* Chapter IX, 3, below.
[2] *Cf.* Wirth, *Die experimentelle Analyse der Bewusstseinsphenomene*, 1908, pp. 305 *f.* and 393.

personal equation. He sought a psychological explanation of the phenomena by bringing them into relation with the variability in the temporal succession of the acts of hearing and seeing.[1] Later the phenomena were investigated further with the aid of artificial visual stimuli. Here belong the studies of Hartmann,[2] who also interested himself in the problem of decimal equations, i. e., of the systematic errors occurring in the estimation of the decimals of a linear element which is not further divided.

But even the efforts to exclude these errors through an objective method of registration led to an important psychological discovery. Arago, in 1842, employed the stopwatch to record the moment of the passing of a star; later the electrical contact key was generally introduced as a means of registration. The hope was thus entertained of determining the time of stellar passage with perfect accuracy, a hope which received support from the belief of physiologists of the time that the physiological processes involved in nerve conduction took place with very great rapidity, a rapidity about equal to that of light. Nevertheless, the objective control by means of recording instruments still showed time differences, which were thereupon interpreted as reaction times suited to the special conditions of such transit experiments.[3]

Time differences of this sort were also studied by Helmholtz, although from a different point of view. He started with the physiological problem of determining the rate of conduction in the motor nerves of the frog, which he found to be from 30 to 90 metres a second, a rate quite at variance with that assumed by earlier investigators, including Johann Müller. The problem now was to determine the rate of

[1] *Astronomische Beobacht. d. Sternw. zu Königsberg*, Abt. VIII, 1822, XI and XVIII.

[2] *Grunerts Archiv f. Math. u. Phys.*, XXXI, 1858, p. 24.

[3] Hirsch, *Moleschotts Untersuchungen*, IX, 1863, pp. 183 ff.

nerve conduction in man by means analogous to those employed by astronomers for the study of individual differences. The investigations of Helmholtz on the subject are known to us through his correspondence with his father during the year 1850. A hand movement was to be made as quickly as possible after an electric signal was given. If attention was highly concentrated, the time required was one tenth of a second. Under conditions of fatigue, and if ideation had to intervene before the reaction could occur, the time required was considerably longer, although still regular. Thus the problem of time measurement which was destined to prove so fruitful of results was opened up and was later broadened in its scope by the interpolation of psychical intermediaries by Donders and his pupils.[1]

The different tendencies enumerated, the theories of perception of the sense physiologists, the psychophysical speculations of Fechner, and the investigation of the astronomical registration errors, all alike pointed to the development of a new psychology. Wundt treated them as symptomatic of a new experimental psychology in his *Beiträge zur Theorie der Sinneswahrnehmungen* (1862). He himself penetrated to the very heart of the problem of perception by analyzing perception into its elementary psychical processes, by the aid of the experimental method employed in physiology rather than by the aid of metaphysical speculations. In an introductory section on method he undertakes a general justification of the experimental method in psychology. As an illustration of an experiment which has as its object a purely psychical event, Wundt cites the artificial imitation of astronomical observations, whose conditions he had himself varied by the introduction of a pen-

[1] De Jaager, *De physiologische Tija bij psychischen Processen*, 1865. F. C. Donders, "Die Schnelligkeit psychischer Processe," *Arch. f. Anat. u. Physiol.*, 1868.

dular movement. The interpretation of the temporal discrepancy of one eighth of a second as a psychical constant, which could be either positive or negative, was indeed soon abandoned; nevertheless, the psychological significance of the fact in question was recognized. As a second example is cited Fechner's law, which is to be stated in the form of the purely psychological law: "Where two psychical functions stand in immediate dependence upon one another, the dependent function increases proportionately as the logarithm of the one originally variable," a formulation which later had to be qualified, but which still retains its significance as an attempt at a purely empirical interpretation of Weber's law.

Wundt's own contributions confine themselves to the theory of sense-perceptions, the problem being to trace the genesis of sense-perceptions from sensation. The main points of the theories expounded in this connection, particularly that of the relation of certain sense-impressions and muscular movements, have had to be restated. Other points, such as the assumption of unconscious logical processes, have had to be abandoned in view of a more adequate knowledge of association processes.[1] This early sketch, however, was only a part of a more general tendency in the direction of an experimentally grounded science of mental phenomena, a science which was destined, as Wundt himself had hoped, to become more than an empty name.

With what success the experimental method was extended beyond the field of sense-perception to the more complex ideational processes the monograph of Vierordt, *Über den Zeitsinn* (1868), a document instructive even to-day, bears convincing testimony. Aside from some investigations by students of Vierordt, the only experimental work which preceded this was that of Mach. The spirit of the new method

[1] *Cf.* Chapter XI, p. 5 (*c*), below.

is clearly discernible in the problem set by Vierordt to investigate experimentally the various functions and capacities of the time-sense, as these are revealed in the main sense departments, in ideal construction, and, finally, in the purely conceptual apprehension of temporal magnitudes. The conviction that these were all signs of the beginning of a new era soon gained ground. When Wilhelm Windelband assumed his duties as professor of inductive philosophy in Zürich he was ready to say that psychology had definitely freed itself from the shackles of metaphysics.[1] Psychological investigations were yielding a fundamental insight into the elementary constitution of mental life, and the study of the combinations of these elementary processes really constituted the first beginnings of general psychology. These were, of course, as he recognized, merely beginnings. The question why these constant elements combined according to equally constant and incomprehensible laws is referred to a distant future in which a general metaphysical theory of energy would solve at one stroke the most profound problem of both physical and mental phenomena.

The life-work of Wundt, who, as we have seen, had early voiced the demand for experimental psychology, extends into our own time. He himself classified the tendencies and the corresponding fields of labor of the new psychology under three general heads.[2] Of these the field of sense-perception admits most readily of survey. Here metaphysical and empirical hypotheses[3] have in many cases given way to genetic theories which derive sense-perceptions from the elementary associations between simple sensations. Thus the concept of association, which had during the eighteenth century been wholly confined to memory processes, emerged

[1] *Über den gegenwärtigen Stand der psychologischen Forschung*, 1876.
[2] "Psychologie," in *Die Philosophie im Beginn des XX Jahrhunderts*, 2 ed., 1907.
[3] *Cf.* Chapter XI, 3 and 4, below.

from under the influences of sense psychology with a new significance and scope. In this connection the new principle of original resultants, which asserts that a complex composed of psychical elements may be qualitatively new in the sense that it may show features which were not contained in the original elements and which could not be obtained by a mere addition of these elements, came to be recognized. Once this fact was verified in the realm of the simpler mental processes it was natural to investigate, from the same point of view, the higher and more complex combinations, such as the thought processes and imagination. Furthermore, the methods of sense psychology came to serve as models for psychology as a whole. After the experimental method had been introduced into psychology through the influence of sense psychology, the conviction could easily gain strength that introspection was trustworthy only when subjected to experimental control. The simpler mental processes were, in any case, accessible to methodical and systematic introspection, but quite recently, and often in conscious contrast to the older point of view, the experimental method has been extended far beyond its original field to the most complex cognitive experiences. It is particularly the Würzburg school whose trust in the reliability of controlled introspection led to the disappearance of the earlier and more restricted conception of the scope of the experimental method.

By the aid of such systematic experimental introspection Ach discovered forms of experience in which a complex conscious content was present simultaneously as knowledge.[1] Imageless presentation of such a total knowledge content Ach called *Bewusstheit*, or awareness. Awareness is of two kinds, awareness of meaning and awareness of relation.

[1] N. Ach, *Über die Willenstätigkeit und das Denken*, 1905, esp. pp. 210 ff. and 235 ff.

Since in the awareness of meaning the felt presence of relations on the basis of excited reproductive processes is of first importance for the presented knowledge, awareness of the second order, like the experiences of surprise, confusion, and doubt, can also be called awarenesses of relation in a narrower sense. In the first case, the question is one of relation to a future factual content; in the last, to a past factual content. The awarenesses of the latter class were already known as independent experiences. We have them in Höffding's quality of familiarity (*Bekanntheitsqualität*)[1] or in Volkelt's memorial assurance (*Erinnerungsgewissheit*).[2] The *Bewusstseinslage* or conscious attitude of Marbe has been interpreted by many as an anticipation of the concept of awareness.[3] Ach expressly distinguished these awarenesses from the phenomena of consciousness commonly known as presentations or ideas. Awareness, or *Bewusstheit* in Ach's sense, as simultaneously presented knowledge content, is to be distinguished not only from the highly ambiguous notion of presentation or idea, which is sometimes made to include even the unconscious, but also, and particularly, from imageless ideation. This imageless presentation of knowledge is a psychical experience the existence of which can be demonstrated. Nor is the question one of feelings accompanying ideation: it is possible for an awareness like surprise, for example, to occur without any accompanying feeling tone whatever. The further question whether awareness and feeling are not subdivisions of a common genus is still an open one.

The second field for the labors of the new psychology was

[1] Höffding, "Über Widererkennen, Association und psychische Aktivität," *Vierteljahrsschrift f. wiss. Phil.*, XIII, 1889, pp. 420 ff.

[2] *Zeitschrift für Phil. u. phil. Kritik*, CXVIII, 1901, pp. 1 ff.

[3] Marbe, *Experimentell-psychologische Untersuchungen über das Urteil*, 1901. *Cf.* the historical review of theories in Ach, *Über den Willensakt und das Temperament*, 1910, p. 18.

opened up by the investigations of Fechner, and its problems are those which have grown out of the problem of mental measurement. The fundamental insight that psychical contents were susceptible to exact quantitative determination was at first handicapped by Fechner's belief that the stimulus was the measure of sensation, a belief which involved the insurmountable difficulty of bringing two disparate realms into quantitative relation. How Fechner's point of view became transformed into our present point of view is a matter which must be reserved for later discussion.[1] The recognition of the fact that sensations are measurable only as sensations led to a group of purely psychological problems, and the subordination of psychical processes to the concept of collective object opened up to the method of measurement every field of mental life in which quantitative determinations are possible. In a word, Fechner's psychophysical methods of measurement were transformed into purely psychical methods of measurement.

While sense psychology and psychophysics confined themselves to the investigation of the elementary facts of consciousness, the new psychology developed a third tendency which embraced the investigations of the higher processes of consciousness and of their general connections. After psychophysics had developed an exact and, at the same time, empirical basis of quantitative determinations for a single group of conscious contents, it was only to be expected that the Herbartian idea of mental mechanics would make its reappearance. The conviction, however, unmistakably gained ground that a mechanics of elementary associations of the older style was inadequate to explain the actual connection of conscious processes. Every act of will, no matter how simple, every fluctuation in the degree of clearness of conscious contents, rather pointed anew to the fundamental

[1] *Cf.* Chapter IX, 3 and 4, below.

fact of apperception. The Herbartian psychology had sought to reduce this concept, which was introduced into philosophy by Leibniz, to a product of association. Since apperception was viewed as only a special case of the fusion of ideas, its intimate relation to self-consciousness and will was obscured. The examination of the complex processes, however, gave a new significance to this concept, through which the inner activity, immersed as it is in the flow of consciousness, received a scientific expression. And thus experiment was again proved to be an aid to exact investigation.[1]

Experimental psychology, which owes its birth almost entirely to the German scientific spirit and investigation, soon passed beyond the boundaries of its native country. It has received its most important development outside of Germany in America. Previous to 1880 American books on psychology were written almost exclusively by theologians and educators. While in Germany psychology had long been the battle-ground of competing systems of speculative philosophy, Scottish realism held undisputed sway among the older theological writers of America. The earlier writings of Edwards,[2] Hickok,[3] and Porter[4] in the nineteenth century are typical examples of the species of psychology in vogue. The attempt of Schmucker to introduce into American philosophy the conception of psychology as a theory of ideas received little notice.[5] The influences which gave birth to a new psychology in America were twofold[6] and originated in Germany and England, respectively. One was the experimental psychology of Germany which has been

[1] See Chapter VI, 4, below.      [2] *Freedom of the Will*, 1754.
[3] Hickok, *Empirical Psychology*, 1834; *Rational Psychology*, 1848.
[4] Porter, *The Human Intellect*, 1868.
[5] S. S. Schmucker, *Psychology; or Elements of a New System of Mental Philosophy*, 1844.
[6] *Cf.* J. Mark Baldwin, "Psychology Past and Present," *Psych. Rev.*, I, 1894, pp. 363 *ff.*

discussed in the previous pages. The other was the traditional doctrine of English associationism and Spencer's notion of evolution or development. To a certain degree, this twofold origin is still commemorated in the controversy between the associationists and the apperceptionists.

# PART II

# DEVELOPMENT OF THE FUNDAMENTAL CONCEPTS OF PSYCHOLOGY

## CHAPTER V

### THE IDEA OF PSYCHOLOGY AS A SCIENCE

The history of an empirical science shows not merely a growth of empirical materials but also a transformation, which is not less significant, in the fundamental principles employed in the interpretation of these materials. This transformation is observable even when the alleged self-evidence of the principles in question precludes an historical development. The history of mechanics, for example, shows how so obvious a principle as that of inertia has only comparatively recently supplanted other principles which were seen to be inadequate. But even this principle, together with others which were for a long time accepted as self-evident, has even quite recently been held to be a purely empirical principle which would tend to break down under radically altered conditions, with the introduction of velocities, for example, approximating that of light. The subject-matter, however, of these sciences remains the same; and if one should speak of a change in chemical elements, for example, in virtue of which chemistry would become an historical science in the widest sense, one must remember that the development has been so extremely slow here that it can be practically disregarded in writing the history of chemistry.

The case of the history of philosophy is different. Among the many influences which converge here, one of the most important is that of personal experience. Personal experience, to be sure, plays its part everywhere, but in the philosophical sciences we become so uniquely aware of its influence that the history of philosophy can be defined outrightly as a history of philosophical experiences. And these experiences have, in the course of time, changed their character. Although the central problems of philosophy can be traced throughout thousands of years of reflective thought, the experiences themselves which give rise to a given philosophical problem have become different.

Psychology shows both forms of historical development. It deals with experiences as its special subject-matter, but it does so as an empirical science. Here we have to deal, then, with changes both in fundamental principles and in the subject-matter itself. In the history of psychology, to be sure, the principles of explanation do not appear with the same clearness as, for example, the principles of explanation in mechanics. Nevertheless, it is noticeable that many ideas which are regarded as generally valid by psychologists of to-day were formerly unknown. An example of this would be the notion of the analyzability of complex mental contents into their elements.

Of greater difficulty is the question in what sense experiences undergo changes, thus producing changes in the subject-matter of psychology. Just as it is possible for an individual to put himself back into an earlier period of his life and to recognize it as belonging to himself, without actually re-experiencing the emotional excitements and motives in the form of their previous occurrence, so it is possible for a similar difference to exist between the conscious experiences of people removed from each other by thousands of years. This question need not, however, be dealt with here, since psychology, in so far as it is not individual psychology, confines itself to phenomena of general scope and significance. And it is certain that the elements of mental life and the general forms of their combination have undergone little or no change within the historical period. If the physiological characteristics of man have undergone no change within historical times, it is certain that no changes have occurred in the psychological functions either. The hypothesis of the color-blindness of the ancient Greeks, for example, has not stood the test of critical examination. There is just as little proof of the assumption that the number of sensation qualities in any sense department, or that simple reaction-time, or any other essential attribute of such mental processes which can be rendered precise by the aid of psychophysical constants, has undergone alteration. We do, indeed, find considerable variation in the nomenclature of sensation qualities. Although the discriminable sensation qualities in the higher sense departments were determined with considerable unanimity at an early period in the history of psychology, we find the most diverse opinions concerning those of the lower senses as late as the nineteenth century. Gruithuisen,[1] for example, distinguished fourteen qualities of gustatory sensations, while Valentin[2] recognized only two, sweet and bitter. However, the divergence of opinion here is probably due merely to the difficulties of psychological analysis. The case of the feelings is of a similar nature. If differences of opinion exist here, we may be sure that there has never been a time when such differences did not exist.

Although introspective observation has been much facilitated and refined by the greater differentiation of mental life which has occurred in connection with the progress

[1] *Anthropologie*, 1810, p. 312.
[2] *Grundriss der Physiologie des Menschen*, 2d ed., 1847.

of intellectual culture, the realm of elementary experiences with which introspection deals has remained the same. This change in complex experiences which the history of civilization illustrates is, therefore, not of immediate interest for the history of psychology. We do, indeed, occasionally find a reflex influence of complex experiences upon the conception of the elementary experiences, the significance of an experience thus becoming of decisive importance for the structure of this experience itself.

It is one of the most noteworthy characteristics in the history of psychology that the nature of a psychical event is often determined by the nature of the object upon which the idea or the desire implied in this event is directed. That which can think an eternal truth is itself eternal; that which occupies itself with sense-impressions is, like the latter, transient and perishable. This is the presupposition which led Plato to the division of man's inner life into a higher and a lower part and which was confirmed by a very analogous distinction within the ethical field. If modern psychology describes conscious experiences as a perpetual flux of psychic processes which preserves its continuity amid its changing aspects or phases, it does so only at the end of a long, subjectifying process. While in the natural sciences subjective factors have been reduced, a similar process of reduction has occurred in psychology, only in an opposite direction. We are acquainted with the process of empathy (*Einfühlung*) in which psychic contents are experienced as connected with objective contents. But there is also the opposite process in which a relationship is experienced between psychic states and the objects to which they refer.

In so far as we have an objectification of experiences in the process of empathy, the results of such a process have been largely invalidated by the presuppositions of modern science since the beginnings of scientific reflection. The second form of objectification, the transferrence of the characteristics of objects to experiences, with which we have here to do, extends to a period lying within the history of psychology. Just as we can live over again the state of mind of a primitive man who peopled the winds and the clouds, we can in imagination transport ourselves into the mental condition of one who in the contemplation of supernatural objects feels himself as being another. But the true inwardness of this experience we are able to judge only from its results.

The presupposition mentioned, particularly in the form of the theory of an ontological affinity between that which knows and that which is known, has been from the earliest times one of the ruling ideas of various systems of metaphysical psychology. We find it as a common element in the two great philosophical rivals of ancient Greece, Plato and Democritus. Both alike find within experience a certain kind of knowledge having the character of intuitive certainty, which points beyond the appearances of sense, γνώμη γνησίη. With both thinkers the content of this knowledge is the forms of reality (ἰδέαι). According to Plato, however, the soul can know the eternal ideas because it is coeternal with them and remembers them from association with them in a previous state of existence. In Democritus the ἰδέαι are the geometrical forms of the atoms, and, since the soul itself consists of atoms, it knows objects from the minute images (ἴδωλα) expressing the nature of the atoms which penetrate the soul. These metaphysical interpretations do, indeed, pass far beyond the range of psychology. Their common presupposition, however, is that of the identity between the content of knowledge and its bearer, between object and subject. If this presupposition lapsed in the later and more genuine analysis of consciousness, this was due not only to the changed point of view from which experiences were regarded but also to alterations in the experiences themselves. The elaboration of conceptual ways of thinking tended to accentuate the cognitive aspects of experience, a process analogous to the heightening of ecstatic experience with which the belief in immortality was connected.[1] If we assume that intellectual experiences have lost this character of vivacity in the development of scientific thought, then the subject-matter of psychology, the experiences themselves, would, indeed, have undergone some change within the history of psychology.

Aside, however, from these details, what conditions the development of fundamental psychological concepts is not so much an alteration in the experiences as a development in the point of view from which psychical facts are regarded. Perhaps it is true that psychology has been less successful in penetrating to the facts which are removed from the ordinary realm of experience than the other sciences. This is compensated for, however, by the greater change in the point of view from which mental processes are regarded. In the chapters which follow we shall try to state the more salient features of this development. In addition to the consolidation of the concept of a science of psychology there arises a gradual apprehension of the subject-matter of psychology—namely, consciousness. The different views as to what are the fundamental phenomena of consciousness appear in the attempts at a classification of mental processes. No less have the methods of psychology shared in these changes in point of view. Among the theoretical concepts, finally, one of the most important is the concept of psychical measurement which has in modern times become fundamental for psychology, aiming at exact quantitative determinations.

[1] *Cf.* p. 16.

The development of the concept of psychology takes its start from the older conceptual determinations of psychology, originating within the framework of one or the other of the various philosophical systems. The problem of psychology as a science, which contained the motives out of which the modern concept of psychology developed, is of comparatively recent origin.

## 1. Older Conceptual Formulations of Psychology

Since the concept of psychology as a science has become a problem only in comparatively modern times, the preceding conceptual determinations of psychology corresponding to the general tendencies of psychological thought lose something of their significance. The word psychology does not occur previous to the sixteenth century. Melanchthon employed the term as a title of academic lectures. R. Gockel used it in 1590 as a collective title for the works of various authors. The term became generally known through Christian Wolff, who did so much for the establishment of philosophical terminology. Up to Wolff's time the term psychosophy, apparently introduced by J. J. Becker, seems to have been in use. The term pneumatology is also found in the writings of Leibniz.

If we should attempt to review the older conceptual formulations, we should find in the celebrated *ars magna* of Raymond Lullus, who lived in the latter half of the twelfth century, a special *figura animæ* which purports to represent the whole of psychology. The soul ($S$) was symbolized by a quadrilateral figure. The three principal faculties, *memoria*, *intellectus*, and *voluntas*, are designated by the letters $B$, $C$, and $D$ at three corners of the figure, while the fourth corner was lettered $E$ and represented the unity of the faculties. This relation was represented by the formula,

$B + C + D = E$. Above this figure are superimposed similar squares which turn upon the same centre, at whose corners other faculties are represented by letters, as *memoria obliviens* (*K*), *intellectus ignorans* (*L*), *voluntas diligens vel odiens* (*M*); whence $K + L + M = N$, a new condition. Four such formulas are required to represent the complete nature of the soul. About this whole figure revolves a second concentric one, so that we get in all one hundred and thirty-six *cameræ* (*secunda figura S*). The great esteem in which the art of Lullus was held illustrates the tendency to formalism which has, perhaps, never been developed to the same point as in the philosophy of Scholasticism. If problems could be set and answered by shifting these concentric figures, it is merely a naïve expression of the fact that in the conceptual world every correctly formulated problem has some solution. We know that in mathematics or pure logic, for example, where we have to do with ideal objects, any correctly stated problem can be solved, although the solution might not be explicitly statable. Once having ascertained the significance of the symbols we employ, we operate with these in a purely mechanical fashion. It is in some such manner that we might explain the great vogue of the Lullian system, although it was bound to be shattered by the impact of modern science, so great was the discrepancy between this mechanical method of juggling concepts and the empirical order it purported to represent.

The views which have been held at various periods regarding the question of psychology as a science are clearly reflected in the position assigned to psychology in the more important attempts at the classification of the sciences. In Bacon's classification psychology is defined as philosophy of the soul (*philosophia humana circa animam*).[1] It is divided into a *doctrina de spiraculo* and a *doctrina de anima sensibili*,

[1] *De dig. et augm. scient.*, 1623, IV, 3.

*sive producta.* This branch of philosophy is further divided into a doctrine of the substance and faculties of the soul and a doctrine of the use and the objects of these faculties. The faculties of the sensible soul are those of movement and sensation. In his distinction between the divine and the earthly soul Bacon follows closely the example of Aristotle. Among the faculties of the soul are also named soothsaying and witchcraft (*divinatio* and *fascinatio*), which are regarded as practical applications of psychology. Speaking broadly, then, we find Bacon's conception of psychology including the traditional views of metaphysical and faculty psychology, although it must be conceded that the division of the science of the phenomena of human life was continued pretty largely unchanged in the much later division into physiology and psychology.

The division of psychology on the basis of faculties is also found in D'Alembert, who was the first to undertake a classification of the sciences similar to Bacon's.[1] The fundamental faculties recognized by him are intelligence and will, the object of the former being the true, that of the latter the good. The former gives rise to the problem of logic, the latter to the problem of morals. Since D'Alembert derives the different sciences from the different objects toward which the various sciences are directed, psychology again becomes subordinated to the normative sciences of logic and ethics.

Our source of information concerning the general conception of psychology developed at this time is the article "Psychology," in Diderot's *Encyclopédie*. Psychology is here viewed as a branch of philosophy which defines the nature of the human soul and gives an account of its activities. It divides into empirical or experimental and rational

[1] *Explication détaillée du système des connaissances humaines*, 1752, *Œuvres*, 1821, I, pp. 102 *ff.*

psychology. According to Diderot, empirical psychology is more important than rational psychology and furnishes the starting-point for the latter.

Neither of the definitions mentioned is very definitely motived and must, of course, not be measured by a standard which developed only after the possibility of scientific psychology became itself a problem.

## 2. The Problem of a Science of Psychology

The understanding of the requirements of a scientific psychology was for a long time retarded on account of the fact that psychology was regarded as sufficiently defined as the science of the soul, and it was scientific only in so far as this was possible within the limits set by the metaphysical presuppositions regarding the nature of the soul. Only when psychology became an independent empirical science could the question of its scientific concept arise. This question reduced to the alternative as to whether psychology was in the last resort a species of metaphysics or of physics. In consequence of this alternative, psychology divided into two branches. This partition occurred in the eighteenth century, when empirical psychology was in some quarters regarded as a branch of physics, while the older Leibniz-Wolffian school adhered to the position that it belonged to metaphysics.

The profounder study of the scientific character of psychology on the part of Kant, whose psychological thought was otherwise largely traditional, was of real significance for the development of the science. The distinction between rational and empirical psychology Kant is generally believed to have inherited from Wolff.[1] Wolff, however, deduced the unity and the simplicity of the soul ontologically from the

[1] *Cf.* J. B. Meyer, *Kants Psychologie*, pp. 220 *ff.*

simplicity of substance, while Kant arrived at the idea of the soul as a simple and unitary substance from the unity and simplicity of consciousness. It is an extreme position to maintain with Herbart that Kant's idea of rational psychology was picked out of the air. A more circumspect historical investigation rather shows that the Kantian formulation of rational psychology was derived from the study of Knutzen, Mendelssohn, and Reimarus. Rational psychology, as expounded by Kant, was literally a preoccupation of the period. After the rejection of the paralogisms of rational psychology, nothing remained for Kant but empirical psychology. The investigations of such an empirical psychology constituted for Kant a field completely distinct from his own critical task of discovering the *a priori* elements in metaphysics, logic, and ethics. It is important to notice this, since experience, in the sense of Kant, is the joint product of the material of sensation and of the subjective forms of knowledge, and since investigations of the nature of this experience would seem inevitably to become psychological in character. Nevertheless, epistemological reflection must be distinguished from the observation of the empirical mental facts. The former reveals the *a priori* constituents of experience, the latter the general laws of mental life. Kant draws here an extremely important distinction, which has been wrongly interpreted by certain representatives of modern Neo-Kantianism as the subordination of empirical psychology to the primary problem of epistemology.[1]

Kant denied the possibility of systematic analysis in psychology on the ground that the manifold of inner observation could only be separated mentally but could not be held in separation nor recombined at will.[2] His second objection

[1] *Cf.* 3 (*a*), below.
[2] *Metaphysische Anfangsgründe der Naturwissenschaft*, Vorrede, 1786.

has become better known. It was to the effect that psychology could never become an explanatory science since it did not admit of mathematical treatment. The only possibility would be to apply the law of constancy to the flux of inner changes. But we do not attribute to the soul anything *a priori*, except that it has temporal duration, and with the pure intuition of time we are unable to construct anything, as we can with the intuition of space, since it has only one dimension. Kant follows out the same idea in the criticism of rational psychology, which connects itself with the paralogisms of pure reason. Rational psychology is the attempt to obtain synthetic knowledge *a priori*, such as is obtained from the bare concept of an extended, impenetrable being, in the theory of bodies. But time, as the only form of inner intuition, can give us knowledge only of the change in the determinations of an object, never of the object itself which is determined. The ego would have to be an intuition or a concept of an object in order to yield rational knowledge of the nature of a thinking being, whereas it is in reality merely the form of consciousness.

Kant, accordingly, thought very slightingly of the future of scientific psychology although he regarded its development in the direction of empirical anthropology as very important. Empirical psychology finds its object in the ego, as object of inner experience, or as phenomenon of the inner sense, and thus becomes anthropology or a sort of physiology of the inner sense. The relation of the inner sense to time, however, unavoidably produces uncertainty in empirical psychology which depends upon the deliverances of the inner sense. And since the presuppositions necessary for an experimental psychology are not met, psychology has to content itself with being a systematic natural history of the inner sense.

There are several reasons for Kant's unfavorable opinion

of psychology. One has to remember, in the first place, the state of empirical psychology at the time. Kant's disparagement of contemporary psychologists and of their unconvincing explanations is everywhere apparent.[1] The only writer of whom he expected anything considerable was Tetens, whose principal psychological work, *Philosophische Versuche über die menschliche Natur*, as we learn from a letter of Hamann's to Herder,[2] was constantly before him. The problem of freedom proper, however, Kant writes to M. Herz, Tetens leaves entirely unsolved. The deeper reason, however, lies in the demands which Kant makes of knowledge; he demands apodictic certainty of a science in the strict sense of the word. A consciousness of unconditioned necessity can only be derived from the necessary conditions of our thought, and, since these do not obtain within the realm of empirical psychology, Kant felt obliged to deny to the latter the rank of a science.

Notwithstanding Kant's opinion, however, the history of psychology shows many attempts to apply mathematics to psychology, among which the Herbartian psychology ranks supreme. The very branch of psychology concerning whose future Kant had the most serious misgivings became one of the most popular in the nineteenth century.

Although Herbart's speculations contained many untenable presuppositions, his method of regarding the intensity of ideas in its relation to time is nevertheless based upon an incontestable formal condition of the mathematical treatment of psychical phenomena. The fact that the intensity of psychical processes constitutes a dimension in addition to that of time has been felt even by psychologists who do not share the conclusions of Herbart—men like Wundt, for example—as a weakening of the Kantian objection. Even

---

[1] *Cf.*, for example, *Philosophie als Wissenschaft*, 1794.
[2] May 7, 1779.

more sweeping is the position of Brentano,[1] who insisted upon the indispensability of mathematics in the exact treatment of any science on the ground that we come upon quantities in literally every field of phenomena. If there were no intensities in the realm of psychical phenomena, the theories of psychology would be essentially simpler but not less exact than now.

Comte defended the possibility of the science of psychology from different points of view. Psychology, as we know, was not included in the linear arrangement of the sciences of which Comte was the author. In his *Positive Philosophy* the psychological material is included under the general head of biology. According to Comte, psychology, up to the time of Gall, remained entirely excluded from the great scientific movement originated by Descartes. The positive, that is, the purely scientific, doctrine of the affective and intellectual functions "consists in the experimental and rational study of the phenomena of inner sensibility belonging to the cerebral ganglia which exist apart from all external apparatus."[2] Since it is impossible to observe mental processes during their occurrence, psychology based upon introspection must give way to phrenological physiology in the sense of Gall.

Owing to its obvious misunderstanding of the simplest facts of consciousness, the teaching of Comte did not materially influence the history of psychology, and has consequently remained somewhat isolated. That this displacement of the conception of psychology was not by any means immanent in the positivistic arrangement of the sciences is shown by the classification of Herbert Spencer, which is in many respects similar to Comte's, and in which psychology is included as an independent science following upon biology, and preparatory to sociology. The influence of Spencer's

---

[1] *Psychologie v. empirischen Standpunkt*, I, 1874, p. 86.
[2] English translation by H. Martineau, bk. V, chap. VI.

metaphysical presuppositions is evident in his view of all contents of consciousness as modifications of an ultimately unknowable spiritual substance; and in his division of psychology into objective and subjective psychology, the former exhibiting mental states in their relations to the stages of organic evolution, the latter deriving the simple elements by the analysis of the highest psychical phenomena, namely, the thought processes, we see the influence of his philosophical theory that all mental activity represents a differentiation and integration of states of consciousness.

### 3. The Modern Concept of Psychology

In the controversies regarding the modern conception of psychology the old question whether psychology is metaphysics or physics returns in a new form. Psychology was obliged once more to come to terms with philosophy and with natural science. Only the rôles were now interchanged. The question now was not whether psychology was a philosophical discipline but the opposite, whether certain philosophical disciplines were not rather to be regarded as branches of psychology. As regards the relation of psychology to natural science, with which psychology was seen to have many methods in common, the problem here was to define the boundaries of the subject-matter which rightfully fell to psychology.

The relation of psychology to philosophy was worked out in connection with the movement known as psychologism. The task of relating psychology to natural science led to establishment of criteria according to which the contents of experience were to be divided into physical and mental phenomena.

## (a) *Psychology and Philosophy: Psychologism and Its Opponents*

Since J. E. Erdmann the term psychologism has been applied to the view that psychology is auxiliary to and the basis of the various mental sciences. This position of psychology in the hierarchy of the sciences most modern psychologists would probably accept as an expression of the scientific temper of the time. In the narrower sense, however, psychologism means the view that reality is composed of psychical contents and that the various branches of mental science, particularly philosophy, are accordingly nothing else than psychology. The sole task of philosophy is thus to make a psychological analysis of the content of experience. Of the different varieties of psychologism it is the epistemological variety in the form expounded by John Stuart Mill that has been most widely discussed.

Arguments for or against a psychological tendency in epistemological questions had, of course, been current before Mill's time. Kant had, in substance, taken a stand against psychologism when he distinguished the psychological explanation of judgment from its validation.[1] Beneke, on the other hand, was not less emphatic than later epistemological psychologism in proclaiming psychology as the basis of the whole of philosophy. In modern times the discussion has centred around the influential empirical logic of John Stuart Mill.

In his controversy with Sir William Hamilton, Mill held scientific logic to be a part or branch of psychology.[2] Its normative character consists merely in the fact that it is a practical art rather than a pure science. In the dispute over psychological logic, which thus became the centre of

[1] *Über Philosophie überhaupt*, p. 167.
[2] *An Examination of Sir William Hamilton's Philosophy*, 5th ed., p. 461.

the controversy, the distinction between the ideal character of purely logical laws and the empirical character of psychological laws was brought out with illuminating distinctness, as, for instance, in Sigwart's excellent *Logik* (1873-8),[1] which, however, again made concessions to psychologism in the doctrine of the twofold character of the fundamental laws of logic as at once natural laws and normative laws of thought. Nevertheless, there seems to be a growing recognition of the fact that the general conditions of the objects of thought which logic investigates are of a different nature from the thought processes which belong to psychology, a distinction which underlies a fundamental differentiation of the respective tasks of logic and psychology.[2] Psychology would be interested, as Windelband says, to determine how an idea arises; logic, on the other hand, would inquire whether the idea is valid, that is, whether or not it is true.[3] We should thus arrive at a definition of psychology such as that of Edmund Husserl, who in his attempts to determine the basis of pure logic emphasized the character of psychology as an empirical science by assigning it the task of investigating descriptively the subjective experiences or contents of consciousness according to their fundamental kinds or forms of complication, and of determining genetically the manner of their origin and decay, the causal forms and laws of their formation and transformation.[4] In his own analysis, indeed, a strongly logistic tendency made itself felt, calling forth the sharp criticism that his psychology merely afforded an opportunity for the application of pure logic.[5]

[1] [English translation, 1895. Trs.]
[2] *Cf.*, *e. g.*, B. A. Riehl, "Logik," in *Kultur der Gegenwart*, I, 6, 1908, p. 76. On the modern psychology of thought, see the dissertation of E. Dürr, "Literaturbericht," pp. 1 *ff.*, *Arch. f. d. ges. Psychologie*, VI, 1906.
[3] *Präludien*, 1884, p. 23.
[4] *Logische Untersuchungen*, II, 1901, p. 336.
[5] *Cf.* Wundt, *Kleine Schriften*, I, 1910, pp. 569 *ff.*

This complete separation of these subjective experiences or contents of consciousness from the objects at which they are directed is the result of a long process of development. Originally this separation between mental acts and their objects was not made at all, in so far as this was possible in view of the rest of experience. For a long time, accordingly, we find a reflex influence of the objects of mental activities upon the alleged structure of those activities themselves.[1] The thought processes or the processes of volition were not regarded as constituent parts of the concrete stream of mental events, but rather as events which were to be measured by reference to a standard or norm like truth or goodness. We have an illustration of this in the definition of D'Alembert cited above.[2] On the other hand, the reverse process took place also; the object of mental activity was resolved by psychologism into the activity itself. The logical law was now declared to be a natural law of psychology, and the conceptual relation expressed in a thought was interpreted as merely an intellectual experience. For the purely logical relation expressed by the law of contradiction, namely that contradictory predicates cannot belong to the same subject at the same time, psychologism substituted the real incompatibility of two mutually contradictory acts of judgment as empirical mental processes in the same mind. It was only in contrast with these various forms of usurpation that the view of mental states as independent realities emerged.

Of course, efforts were hereby not excluded to maintain a connection between psychology and epistemological problems, a connection which would seem to be inevitable, owing to the fact that all processes of knowledge are presented in individual experience. Paul Natorp declared the subject-matter of psychology to be the subjective aspect of experi-

[1] *Cf.*, p. 144.  [2] *Cf.* p. 149.

ence, prior to all processes of objectification. Now, since the fundamental laws of objectification and the laws which immediately complete the process of objectifying the phenomena are different from each other in the same sense in which the *a priori* constituents of consciousness are different from the empirical, it is possible to distinguish a purely *a priori* part of psychology, which can be referred to philosophy as a correlate to the purely objective criticism of knowledge.[1] A still closer affiliation of psychology with philosophy is found in H. Cohen. The task of psychology within the general field of philosophy is to deal with the problem of the unity of social consciousness. It is true, psychology describes consciousness according to its elements; but these elements are necessarily hypothetical, since it is impossible for one who operates with consciousness to lay bare that with which consciousness really begins.[2] This hypothetical character of the elements of consciousness, to be sure, seems to conflict with the characterization of mental elements expressed elsewhere;[3] still, it must be remembered that the fundamental conception of psychology as a philosophical science which is in question here is distinctly different from the conception of an empirical science, which also represents the result of the effort to articulate psychology with natural science.

### (b) *Psychology and Natural Science: Differentiation of Physical and Psychical Phenomena*

To the definition of psychology bequeathed by metaphysics as the science of the soul has been opposed the definition of it as the science of mental phenomena.[4] The latter defi-

---

[1] *Einleitung in die Psychologie nach kritischer Methode*, 1888, pp. 43, 124.
[2] *Logik der reinen Erkenntniss*, 1902, p. 16.
[3] *Cf.* Chapter VII, 3, below.
[4] *Cf.* F. Brentano, *Psychologie v. emp. Standpunkt*, I, pp. 10 *ff.*

nition was prompted by the same motive as prompted critical reflection to discontinue the old definition of physical science as the science of bodies, and to substitute therefor the definition of it as the science of physical phenomena. The insight which was obtained early in the history of philosophy that the objects of what is called external perception are only phenomena Locke once illustrated by a celebrated psychological experiment. Having warmed one hand and cooled the other, he plunged both into the same vessel filled with water, with the result that one hand perceived cold while the other perceived warmth. But since warmth and cold could not exist simultaneously in the same water, he regarded the phenomenal nature of these perceptions as proved.

In the application of this concept of appearance to the realm of inner perception, which came much later, an effort was made to avoid the implication that mental contents were the states of a substance. This is illustrated in the definition of psychology accepted by John Stuart Mill,[1] who asserted the task of psychology to be the investigation of the course of mental states, which was controlled, according to him, by the well-known laws of association.[2] In connection with complex phenomena the question arises as to whether they can be explained as the joint products of mental processes or whether they are to be regarded as novel formations. The phenomenalistic point of view, however, disclaims any intention of limiting the task of psychology.

The definition of psychology as the science of mental phenomena has been represented on the Continent by Franz Brentano.[3] Brentano is particularly interested in the criteria according to which mental phenomena can be unambiguously distinguished from physical. The characterization of mental phenomena as distinguished from physical

[1] *Logic*, VI, chap. 4, § 3.   [2] *Cf.* p. 101, above.   [3] *Op. cit.*, 101 *ff.*

has often been merely negative. Originally the distinguishing feature was spatial. Physical phenomena had extent, while mental phenomena, thinking, willing, and the like, had neither extent nor any other spatial characteristic. This served as the differentiating mark in the metaphysical systems of Descartes and Spinoza, and it was adopted by Kant, who regarded space as the form of outer sense. Still more recently inner experience has been defined negatively by Bain on the basis of the absence of spatial attributes.[1] The objection has been urged against this criterion that there are also physical phenomena which do not have the attribute of extent. Tones and odors have always been denied an original spatial quality. Berkeley even denied spatial characteristics to color, Plattner to taste impressions, and many psychologists from Hartley to Herbart and Spencer have not admitted that space is an original attribute of any phenomenon of the outer sense. Convinced of the inadequacy of these negative definitions, Brentano endeavored to find some positive characteristics of mental phenomena which would distinguish them unequivocally from physical. The most important one of these he found to be the "intentional" character of psychical phenomena: they are phenomena which intentionally contain an object. A second characteristic given by Brentano is that they are discoverable only by introspection, thus reverting in a peculiar way to the old doctrine of inner sense.[2]

In addition to this phenomenology of consciousness represented by Brentano and his school there is observable a second main tendency which determines the relation between psychology and natural science by the point of view from which an item of experience is to be regarded. The example of natural science suggested to psychology a treatment of its objects in analogy with the treatment of natural science.

[1] *Mental Science*, 1868, Intr., chap. I.   [2] *Cf*. p. 84, above.

Thus Rickert maintained that psychology must transform the manifold of psychical experience into a conceptual order, just as natural science substitutes a conceptual order for the manifold of sense experience.[1] This demand was most completely met by Münsterberg. For Münsterberg the object of psychology, like the object of natural science, is a product of abstraction. It came into existence logically through the fact that reality was objectified, the value objects of the actual ego thus detached from the subject, and actuality transformed into experienceable processes. Within this objectified world natural science and psychology were differentiated in such a manner that the latter had to do only with objects which exist solely for the activity of one subject.[2]

On the other hand, the necessity for such a conceptual translation has been denied on the ground of the direct, immediate reality of the experience to be thus transmuted. This position has been taken by Wundt, who has defined psychology tersely as the science of immediate experience, thus supplementing natural science, which is the science of mediate experience. Faithfully as this view of psychical facts as a sphere of reality of equal validity with the reality of mediate experience champions the rights of psychology in its relation to natural science, nevertheless the epistemological presuppositions underlying this distinction, in consequence of which conscious experience and objects differ only according to the point of view adopted, have often been controverted, particularly by the representatives of act psychology.

In recent times decided doubt has been cast upon all these distinctions. The modern opponents of metaphysics have tried to drive the old metaphysics out of its last lurking-place.

[1] *Grenzen der naturwissenschaftlichen Begriffsbildung*, I, pp. 183 *ff*.
[2] *Grundzüge der Psychologie*, 1900, p. 202.

This tendency produced the empiriocriticism of Mach and Avenarius,[1] which recognized everything which we immediately feel as a complete experience. While the customary distinctions between physical and psychical lead to manifold ambiguities, the new definition of the psychical asserts the object of psychology to be that aspect of a complete experience of an individual which is dependent upon the individual for its existence. Instead of the older opposition of nature and spirit bequeathed by naturalistic modes of thought, we now have as the constituents of our psychical life psychical experiences, determinate sensations of color, tones, and so forth, which stand on precisely the same footing as the contents of inner experience.[2] In the terminology created by Avenarius, which substituted for the individual the nervous part system $C$, this definition tends to assume a materialistic hue, from which, however, it later freed itself by the suppression of the insidious system $C$.

The enticing doctrines of empiriocriticism have occasionally been responsible for an unhistorical polemic against psychology like that of R. Willy, for example, who has expressed the opinion that psychology is at the present time undergoing a crisis, and has sought to show that the systems of Wundt, Rehmke, and Brentano really rest upon a metaphysical spiritualism.[3] The point of his criticism is that the attempts to assign psychology a special subject-matter, like Rehmke's psychical concrete or Brentano's psychical phenomena, do not, in spite of their pretence at pure empiricism, escape spiritualistic metaphysics. But psychology, which has so often been the target of epistemological attacks of this sort, will survive this criticism also, deeds being more convincing than words.

[1] *Vierteljahrsschrift f. wiss. Phil.*, XVIII, 1894, 137, 400; XIX, 1895, pp. 1, 129.
[2] *Cf.*, e. g., H. Cornelius, *Einleitung in die Philosophie*, 1903, pp. 177 ff.
[3] *Vierteljahrsschrift f. wiss. Phil.*, XXI, 1897, pp. 79, 227, 332.

One question as to the future. If psychology, according to the modern conception developed here, is to bear the same fundamental relation to the mental sciences as physics bears to the natural sciences, there must exist in connection with psychology a certain border realm similar to the philosophy of nature affiliated with natural science. It might be contended that the history of metaphysics, in which philosophical points of view have dominated, shows plainly enough how widely the latter are relinquished by the modes of thought of a truly empirical psychology. Still, there is a second way in which the phenomena of consciousness can be considered, a way which has its counterpart in the investigation of the presuppositions of the exact sciences. As one investigates here the basis of hypothetical constructions and the significance of axiomatic assumptions, so it is possible to raise the question in psychology as to the nature of the fundamental hypotheses employed, and whether there are also in this field propositions of axiomatic significance. The history of epistemology and of ethics illustrates the abundant attempts to discover primitive relations among contents of consciousness which exhibit axiomatic character. These have always been measured by a logical or ethical norm. Thus it was taught, for example, that there existed a necessary connection between the true knowledge of a moral good and the act of will directed to the production of this good. For concrete volitional experiences, however, no such axiomatic principle obtained. A few such propositions which have a principial significance for empirical psychology have indeed been exploited,[1] and we shall come upon them again in the discussion of the special fundamental concepts of psychology. Nevertheless, the problem itself belongs to the future. It is possible that reflection upon the hypothetical principles underlying psychology will open to us vistas

[1] *Cf.* p. 142, above.

as far-reaching as the theory of relativity, for example, in modern physics.[1]

[1] [For the latest conceptions of psychology as discussed at present, particularly among American psychologists, *cf.* esp. Angell, "Behavior as a Category of Consciousness," *Psych. Rev.*, 1913, pp. 255-270, and Watson, "Psychology as the Behaviorist Views It," *Psych Rev.*, 1913, pp. 158-177. Trs.]

# CHAPTER VI

**THE SUBJECT-MATTER OF PSYCHOLOGY: CONSCIOUSNESS**

Considering how far back reflection on psychological questions extends, the real subject-matter of psychology was late in receiving conceptual formulation. As qualities or functions of a metaphysically defined soul, psychical contents were mere manifestations, much in the same way that natural processes were the manifestations of physical bodies which acted as their bearers. It was only when psychical contents were viewed in their immediate reality as parts of a unified field of experience that psychology acquired a definite subject-matter. The development of the concepts of consciousness merely means, therefore, the gradual apprehension of psychical contents in their immediate reality as conscious experiences. The question whether the concept of consciousness is wide enough to include the entire range of psychical events has given rise to controversies concerning the limits of consciousness, which have centred principally about the question of the significance of the unconscious in psychology. Another and different problem was that of the range of consciousness, which led to the consideration of the graduation of conscious contents according to degrees of clearness. The latter connected itself mainly with the accentuation of special conscious contents in the experience of attention.

### 1. The History of the Concept of Consciousness

#### (a) *Early Developments of the Concept*

The problem of consciousness can hardly be said to have existed for the philosophy of antiquity. It is true that

Plato points to the necessity of reflection (φρόνησις) and of self-knowledge, but the notion of self-knowledge is much too narrow to serve the purpose of defining the boundaries of the subject-matter of psychology. The consciousness to which Plato refers is the consciousness of what our experience objectively signifies. Here, too, we see how the object at which psychical activities are directed becomes normative for those activities themselves.[1]

The limitation of ancient psychology referred to reveals itself with particular clearness in Aristotle's attempt to determine the boundaries of the psychical. Psychology, according to Aristotle, has to do with the phenomena of life in plant, animal, and man. But we find no criterion by which we are to distinguish psychical phenomena from vital processes in general. Even in the consideration of specific psychical contents there is no attempt to point out any common characteristic which belongs to them as contents of consciousness. Neither the arrangement in a hierarchy of lower and higher functions, in which the conscious functions are naturally classed together, nor the distinction between the perception of a sense-impression and the perception of this perception itself, between the thought of an object and the thought of the thought,[2] yields any formula which comprehends the whole of consciousness as such. Suggestions of the concept of consciousness are found in Aristotle only in connection with the metaphysical treatment of the fact of self-consciousness, as in that memorable passage in the *Metaphysics* which describes the nature of God.[3] God alone, who is pure activity (*actus purus*), thinks himself, his thought being his sole object.

The characteristic thought of, in the first instance, merely as self-consciousness was destined to expand into the general concept of consciousness. This step, as has been shown,

[1] *Cf.* pp. 144 *f.*, above.   [2] *Cf.* p. 72, above.   [3] XII, 8, 9.

was not taken until Neo-Platonism.[1] The Neo-Platonic interpretations of the concept of consciousness were partly based upon the thesis that that which cannot know itself cannot know anything else. According to Plotinus, the soul comes to self-consciousness through its vision of the Nous. The result of this act is an identity of the νοῦς, νόησις and νοητόν. This is a description of the experience of self-consciousness which is at once mystical and sensuous. More important, however, is the fact that Plotinus ascribed to the Nous, which he defined as a manifold containing within itself the principle of unity,[2] the attribute of self-consciousness (συναίσθησις αὐτῆς), and thus gave general currency to an expression which had occurred only occasionally in writers like Alexander of Aphrodisias and Galen. From now on the definite separation between consciousness and the unconscious possession of an idea becomes customary among the Neo-Platonists. To the activities of sensation, presentation, etc., is superadded an accompanying consciousness (παρακολούθησις) which is further described as an activity of reflection (ἀνακαμπτούσης τῆς διανοίας).

While, therefore, the distinctive character of consciousness as such remains unrecognized, the problem of consciousness emerges more distinctly than before. The emphasis upon the inner man in the teachings of Christianity was also bound to assist the process of psychological self-reflection. In Augustine the knowledge by the soul of itself is one of its most assured possessions. Even if we should doubt the existence of the outer world, this very doubt would assure us of our own psychical existence. The fact that Augustine found an epistemological basis in the immediate deliverance of self-consciousness, an insight of great moment to the future of philosophy, shows how vitally he grasped the fundamental psychological principle involved.

[1] Siebeck, *op. cit.*, I, 2, pp. 337 *ff*.   [2] *Enn.*, V, 9, 6.

For a thousand years, however, this thought remained undeveloped. It became merged with the doctrine of the inner sense, as in Thomas Aquinas, for example, who, notwithstanding his theory of inner perception,[1] gave the colorless description of self-consciousness as an act of knowledge in which spiritual substances return upon themselves.

### (b) Development of the Modern Concept of Consciousness

The discovery of consciousness as a fundamental psychical fact was not made before Descartes. It is true that Descartes was influenced in many of his psychological views by that bold empiricist Vives.[2] Nevertheless, his distinction between extended and thinking substance was tantamount to the designation of the field of psychical phenomena or contents of consciousness as a permanent subject-matter of psychology. It has been asserted that psychology, in so far as it was not metaphysical, had not made any important advance over Aristotle up to the time of Descartes. It is certain, in any case, that the discovery of Descartes introduced a characteristic difference between modern psychology and the psychology of Aristotle. Descartes clearly enunciated the truth that the appearance of a psychical content was identical with the consciousness of the same.[3] This has remained the point of departure for empirical psychology; it was already self-evident for Locke that to have ideas and to be conscious of them was one and the same thing.[4]

In keeping with its origin in epistemological considerations, the Cartesian concept of consciousness has partly

[1] See p. 74, above.
[2] This has been emphasized particularly by Höffding, *Geschichte d. n. Phil.*, I, p. 259.
[3] *Princ. Phil.*, I, 9.
[4] *Essay on the Human Understanding*, bk. II, chap. I, § 9.

been refined in modern psychology in an epistemological direction, and it has partly been freed from the strictly intellectualistic character given to it by Descartes, according to whom all conscious contents consist in cognitive processes. It was not until these modifications occurred that the concept was wide enough to include equally all psychical phenomena.

The first of these developments led to considerable differences in point of view in the treatment of self-consciousness. The empirical point of view which sought to resolve the fact of self-consciousness or the ego into empirically given contents of consciousness was never more brilliantly represented than by David Hume. The upshot of his criticism was the total rejection of the idea of soul substance, on the ground that such a substance always presupposed the spatial connection of the contents of consciousness with something extended or inextended. Just as little are we able to discover in personal identity or the ego the principle of unity within consciousness, as philosophers have claimed. "Our notions of personal identity proceed entirely from the smooth and uninterrupted progress of the thought along a train of connected ideas."[1]

The opposite tendency reached its climax in post-Kantian philosophy. Kant's much admired doctrine of the unity of transcendental apperception found in self-consciousness that relation between the contents of consciousness and a self which Fichte erected into a philosophical principle. Ever since the Neo-Platonists compared this inexpressible relation between the ego and the contents of consciousness with the relation between the centre of the circle and the circle itself, many thinkers have sought to give an answer to this riddle which continues to stand at the threshold of psychology. They were all surpassed by Fichte, however, when

[1] Hume, *Treatise of Human Nature*, bk. I, part IV, § VI.

he undertook to evoke the whole universe from the bare fact of this relation to the ego. The glorification of the fact of self-consciousness which his constructions implied aroused the protests of more cautious psychologists. Fichte's doctrine of self-consciousness may be summed up in the following formula: The ego is that which thinks itself. Herbart proved the unsoundness of this formula by showing that it involves an infinite regress. The "itself" can, in turn, be nothing else than the self, so that the Fichtean proposition is equivalent to the proposition: the ego is that which thinks itself, etc., *ad infinitum*.

Of greater significance for psychology was the extension of the concept of consciousness to include all psychical phenomena already suggested in Leibniz's important doctrine of the grades of consciousness, in virtue of which all conscious states pass into each other by continuous transitions. To express this unique character of consciousness Leibniz employed a terminology partly invented by himself. He used the old word *perceptio*, in the first place, to indicate the unconscious, passive state of the monad, in which it represents only the external world. Opposed to this is the conscious state, designated by the newly coined word *apperceptio*, which is that activity of the monad through which it becomes aware of its own perceptions. The word consciousness, meanwhile, passed into philosophical usage as a translation of *conscientia*. This has, in spite of many shifts of meaning, retained the ethical significance of conscience, illustrating how the concept of consciousness is foreshadowed in the terminology of ethico-religious reflection. It is true that the Stoics already used the philosophical terms συνείδησις (consciousness) and συναίσθησις συστάσεως (self-consciousness), with which Seneca first associated the term *conscientia*. In *conscientia*, however, the ethico-religious significance of conscience remained predominant, for which the much-disputed term *synteresis* was used in the Middle Ages. The etymology of this word, as we learn from Albert von Bollstädt, was already in dispute in Scholastic philosophy. Attention has recently been called to the fact that τήρησις was used by certain physicians of the latter half of the Middle Ages as the *terminus technicus* for observation. According to the use of συναίσθησις or συνείδησις by Stoicism, and still more by Neo-Platonism, συντήρησις would thus, in the first instance, have meant self-observation. If the derivation suggested here is correct, the history of this concept offers an instructive example of the fact that a term of purely psychological import which had been restricted to an ethico-religious signification had its original meaning restored only by the roundabout way of translation.

## 2. The Concept of the Unconscious

### (a) *Representatives and Opponents of the Notion of the Unconscious*

The concept of consciousness in Leibniz was so comprehensive as to include the notion of the unconscious as well. The idea of *petites perceptions* gave rise to the idea of a monad filled at each moment with an infinite number of perceptions. Since any number of intermediate stages may exist between a given grade of consciousness and the state of unconsciousness, the *petites perceptions* need to be only relatively unconscious. Leibniz gives a number of reasons why the *petites perceptions* do not possess the degree of consciousness of ordinary conscious contents. They are either too weak to rise to consciousness or they occur in such large numbers as to make the consciousness of the separate ones impossible. Finally, they may be crowded out by other particularly strong contents of consciousness.

It is possible that Leibniz is here influenced by the older view of Malebranche,[1] who had deduced the original unconsciousness of so many ideas from the impossibility of their simultaneous apperception. These are reflections which anticipate later views in a remarkable way and which illuminate strikingly the significance of this concept of degrees of consciousness for the subsequent efforts of psychical mechanics.

But with the sharp separation of *perceptio* and *apperceptio* and the recognition of *perceptiones insensibiles* Leibniz approaches the conception of the unconscious, while he abandons completely the idea of a hierarchical arrangement of conscious contents on the basis of degrees of clearness, assuming the existence of innate and, in the strict sense, unconscious mental contents. In the polemic with Locke, who takes his stand on the ground of psychological experience, the rationalism of Leibniz gains the upper hand. In the criticism of Locke's theory of knowledge Leibniz maintains the existence of innate and unconscious contents said to contain the principles of theoretical and practical reason. The notion of these unconscious contents approaches to some extent that of psychical disposition, and Leibniz, indeed, sought to render their existence vivid by comparing them with memory contents.[2]

Leibniz's doctrine of unconscious psychical contents readily passed over into a number of very diverse psychological tendencies, he himself having thrown out suggestions for various applications of the idea. It was introduced into association psychology by the elder Mill, who spoke of sensations which, on account of habitual inattention, do not rise to the level of consciousness at all. Hamilton pointed to unconscious intermediate links which we are

[1] *Rech.*, III, 27, and VI, 1, 5.
[2] *Philosophische Werke*, ed. Gerhard, V, p. 75.

obliged to assume in order to make the connection of our ideas intelligible, and Lewes went still further with the claim that the great majority of conscious processes ran their course unconsciously. In Maudsley, finally, unconscious psychical activity became a fact so incontrovertible as even to demand the physiological treatment of psychology.

The concept of the unconscious is developed in a different direction by Herbart. According to Herbart, those ideas are unconscious which lie below the threshold. True, they do not represent actual presentation, which can take place only above the threshold, but only a tendency to presentation. At the same time they act upon one another according to the same laws which govern actual presentations. As an auxiliary conception which was meant to explain conceptual processes, the idea of unconscious inference came to play a part in the later spatial theories of Helmholtz and Zöllner. The many-sided utility of the concept of the unconscious shows itself, finally, in the fact that it was invoked to extricate the ego doctrine of Fichte from the difficulties in which it had become involved in connection with the problem of self-consciousness. Schelling in this way arrived at a purely speculative deduction of the unconscious.[1] The production of the world can never be comprehended by beginning with an ego already conscious of itself. But the ego which has become conscious of itself can look back upon a moment of its own activity in which it was not as yet conscious of itself, and thus the beginning of the ego's activity retreats into the realm of the unconscious. With all his appeal to the facts of psychological experience, large concessions were later made to the notion of the unconscious by Hartmann in his *Philosophy of the Unconscious*.

[1] *Werke*, Abt. I, vol. III, pp. 348 *f.*

# THE SUBJECT-MATTER OF PSYCHOLOGY

Over against this large number of champions of the doctrine of the unconscious we find a second group of thinkers, no less influential than the former, who oppose the doctrine. It was rejected by the leading English psychologists, J. S. Mill, Bain, and Spencer, and by H. Lotze in Germany. Ulrici also denied the existence of unconscious psychical activity, although his own concept of consciousness, of course, differs from the usual one.[1] Fechner's fundamental psychological law, indeed, led him to a point beyond which a conscious correlate of psychophysical activities disappears. Nevertheless, he evaded the assumption of unconscious sensations and ideas by holding that only the psychophysical activities persisted.[2] Wundt, who in his earlier psychological writings[3] still admitted unconscious inference, which seemed to be so important for the theory of perception, later took stand against the assumption of unconscious psychical activity. In order to satisfy the demands of explanatory psychology Lipps, indeed, fell back upon unconscious psychical processes. The appearance of these processes, however, are, even in Lipps, always accompanied by consciousness.

## (b) Arguments for and against the Unconscious

The various lines of thought in the controversy over the unconscious can be best followed if presented in the form of the arguments for and against the unconscious which were put forward by the participants in the discussion of the question.[4] As is the case in so many fundamental concepts of psychology, the demand made was partly one of

[1] *Cf.* p. 80.  [2] *Elemente der Psychophysik*, II, 1860, p. 438.
[3] *Beiträge zur Theorie der Sinneswahrnehmung*, 1862. See also his *Lectures on Human and Animal Psychology*, 1863.
[4] *Cf.* F. Brentano, *Psych. v. emp. Standpunkte*, 1874, pp. 137 *ff.*, which the present discussion partly follows.

explanation, partly one of description. The arguments accordingly fell into two classes, in the first of which the unconscious is invoked in the service of causal explanation, and in the second of which difficulties are pointed out in the pure phenomenology of consciousness which cannot, it is held, be solved without having recourse to the hypothesis of unconscious psychical phenomena. The difficulties raised by the demand for causal explanations were obviously greater than those presented by the task of pure description. An unconscious psychical process was accordingly invoked either as the cause of an empirical conscious process, or else the attempt was made to prove the existence of unconscious psychical processes on the basis of an inverted causal relationship.

The former and more natural use of the unconscious is the one most frequently found. Thus Sir William Hamilton argued for the existence of unconscious ideation from the occasional absence of a series of intermediate terms in the revival of a previous train of association.[1] However, no one who agreed with Hamilton in his assumption has been able to show that this explanation is the only possible one. The same applies to F. A. Lange, who explained the phenomenon of the blind-spot by supposing that the eye unconsciously infers the color which it should actually see. The theories of space of Helmholtz and Zöllner operated with the notion of unconscious inference, without utilizing the auxiliary aids employed by the psychology of the time in order to do justice to the facts without invoking unconscious intermediate links. Maudsley and Lewes sought to show by the phenomena of reproduction that experiences which rose to consciousness in dreams or in recollection may originally have existed as unconscious psychical phenomena. All these arguments finally combine in Hart-

[1] *Lectures on Metaphysics and Logic*, I, Lecture XVIII.

mann, who, indeed, goes beyond immediate experience in so far as he regards conscious and unconscious phenomena as heterogeneous, the hypothesis of the unconscious thus losing much of its significance for empirical psychology. Unconscious psychical phenomena do not conform to the laws of experience but dissolve into an eternally unconscious and unique reality possessing wholly transcendental attributes.[1]

The second line of speculation which views unconscious psychical acts as the effects of conscious psychical acts is encountered less frequently. A consideration of this sort goes back to Leibniz. An ocean wave produces the roar of the breakers, but if it is only a drop of water which falls we hear nothing whatever. But we must have an auditory sensation even in the latter case, for the noise of the wave consists of the simultaneous noises of the single drops which compose it. An analogous idea is utilized by Ulrici for visual sensations. Although very small objects are not perceptible, they nevertheless yield some visual impression. For larger objects are perceptible only because the visual perception is the result, as it were, of a number of sense-impressions which separately are so weak as to escape attention.[2] This conclusion has been contradicted by the pretty generally recognized principle of modern psychology that the sum of effects is not merely quantitatively different from the separate members or components, but qualitatively as well. The fact that the after-image shows details which were not observed in the original image was also cited by Ulrici in support of the assumption of unconscious sensations.[3] Helmholtz, too, has given a circumstantial account of similar phenomena.[4] Still, it has never been proved that

---

[1] *Philosophie des Unbewussten*, 2d ed., pp. 473 *ff.*
[2] *Gott und Mensch*, p. 294.
[3] *Op. cit.*, pp. 285 and 304.   [4] *Phys. Optik*, p. 337.

the sensation in question was actually unconscious, and the newer analysis of the processes of attention has suggested less hypothetical explanations of the phenomenon concerned than the one here employed.

More convincing than the lines of reflection just enumerated was the assumption that the strength of the consciousness accompanying a given psychical activity stands in a functional relation to the strength of the latter. With sufficient diminution of the degree of strength of the psychical phenomenon, consciousness could disappear entirely. It was on the basis of such considerations that Beneke admitted the existence of unconscious psychical activities.[1] The doctrine did not make much headway, however, as the notion of psychical measurement, which the idea of the strength of psychical activity suggested, tended in Fechner to ignore unconscious sensations and to put in their place the vague notion of psychical disposition. Brentano, moreover, broke the force of the argument for the unconscious by considerations of a purely psychological character.[2] The intensity of presentation is always equal to the intensity with which the presented content appears. The intensity, therefore, of the presentation of a presentation must be equal to the intensity with which this presentation itself appears. In virtue of the veridical character of inner perception, the apparent intensity of conscious presentations and their actual intensity coincide. We thus arrive at the conclusion that in the case of any conscious presentation the strength of the presentations referring to it is equal to its own strength. This line of reflection is really less significant as a refutation of Beneke than as a characteristic of Brentano's psychology. A conclusion which at the outset is not by any means self-evident will follow necessarily from presuppositions every one of which must be admitted

[1] *Lehrb. d. Psych.*, 2d ed., § 57.   [2] *Op. cit.*, p. 157.

if one accepts as one's point of departure the conception of Brentano's psychology as the doctrine of psychical phenomena given in inner perception.

The other principal line of evidence for unconscious psychical activities depending upon the presuppositions required in a purely descriptive account of conscious phenomena made capital of the enormous complication which the assumption that any psychical activity was a conscious activity was said to necessitate. If an unconscious psychical phenomenon is an impossibility we should have to assume, in addition to the presentation of a tone, the presentation of this presentation. The second presentation, in turn, if it is to be conscious, requires another presentation of itself, and so on, the simple act of audition thus forcing upon us the assumption of an infinite number of such psychical activities. Reflections of this sort arose particularly in connection with the doctrine of the inner sense. This difficulty connected with the doctrine of the inner sense had already been pointed out by Aristotle in the *De Anima*. The first writer to deduce from this difficulty the existence of unconscious psychical activities was Thomas Aquinas.[1] In modern times Herbart referred to the fact that among the various masses of ideas, each of which apperceived the preceding one, one must hold the ultimate or highest place, and that it cannot itself be apperceived.[2] For Herbart, of course, the existence of unconscious ideas was already assured on other grounds. Although the difficulty of indefinite complication of mental states has often been discussed, it has seldom supplied a real argument for the existence of unconscious psychical phenomena. Attempts have sometimes been made to solve this problem without resorting to the assumption of unconscious psychical phe-

[1] See p. 74.
[2] *Psychologie als Wissenschaft*, Teil II, Absch. II, Kap. 5, § 199.

nomena by asserting that the psychical activity and the objects toward which it is directed are one and the same phenomenon. Bain, for example, asserted the same identity of activity and object in the various kinds of sense-impressions as he believed to exist in the so-called affective sensations. A closely related position is that of J. S. Mill. We see foreshadowed here the concept of consciousness as immediate experience in which the two terms of act and content, usually kept distinct, are identified, as, for example, in the psychology of Wundt.

Starting from his own point of view, Brentano undertook the solution of the problem in a different manner. He made his beginning with the question as to the relation between the presentation of an object and the presentation of this presentation, and he found the idea of a peculiar coalescence of the object and its accompanying presentation a common one among psychologists. Aristotle had already made the observation that a conscious phenomenon must include within itself the consciousness of itself.[1] More clearly than in the case of sense-perception, he described the peculiarity of inner experience in his *Metaphysics* to the effect that knowledge, sensation, opinion, and reflection were always directed toward something else, but secondarily also toward themselves. Practically all authorities who deny unconscious activities agree with this description in the main. So J. S. Mill, for instance, according to whom sensations apprehend themselves, and Lotze, according to whom a consciousness of psychical phenomena accompanies the phenomena. Ulrici, too, regarded all our sensations as at the same time sensations of ourselves; and even in Beneke the accompanying consciousness was treated as a special attribute of the psychical phenomenon, given with the latter.[2] In Brentano's psychology, after the statement that every psychical phenomenon is the consciousness of

[1] *De Anima*, III, p. 2.   [2] *Lehrb. d. Psych.*, 2d ed., § 57.

an object, the opposite question, whether every psychical phenomenon is the object of consciousness, is raised in the paradoxical form whether an unconscious consciousness exists. If the term unconscious is here understood in the passive sense of an object of which one is not conscious, an unconscious consciousness is as free from contradiction, as, for example, an unseen act of seeing.[1] Analysis, however, tended to abandon the notion of an unconscious consciousness in the above sense, since it showed that the presentation of a tone, for example, and the presentation of this presentation are one and the same thing.[2] The foundation seemed thus to be removed from under the notion of the unconscious from the standpoint of the pure phenomenology of consciousness also.

### 3. The Range of Consciousness

Aside from these attempts to draw the boundary-lines of consciousness, certain other considerations regarding the range of consciousness have been of no less importance. While the determination of the boundaries of consciousness tended naturally to become a speculative question, the problem of this content of consciousness tended from the first to take on an empirical and special character and preceded to some extent the development of the concept of consciousness itself.

The fact that only a limited number of psychical contents could be present in consciousness simultaneously forced itself upon the attention of observers at a very early stage of scientific reflection. Diogenes of Apollonia is reported to have referred to a competition among the various sense departments for a part in a limited amount of mind stuff.[3]

[1] *Op. cit.*, p. 133.     [2] *Op. cit.*, p. 167.
[3] For a history of the attempts to determine the range of consciousness, see W. Wirth, *Die experimentelle Analyse der Bewusstseinsphänomene*, 1908, pp. 56 *ff*.

For a long time scientific curiosity regarding the problem in question seems to have been satisfied by the assertion of Aristotle that several objects could be apprehended simultaneously, to which he added certain other observations concerning the relation of similar and opposite ideas.[1] It was not until the time of Scholasticism that we find in John Buridan a more careful investigation of the possibility of a plurality of simultaneously existing psychical states.[2] Buridan asked the question, a question new to his time, as to the degree of clearness with which simultaneous presentations could be perceived. Now every perception, no matter how simple, is composed of a multiplicity of parts. As a rule, it is not the parts which are perceived, but the whole. When the object is very large, on the other hand, the parts are perceived more distinctly than the whole. If a number of sensations are presented simultaneously the distribution of clearness among them is not uniform. These observations of Buridan, fragmentary as they are, stand out in clear relief against the attempt often made in the Middle Ages to limit thought (*intelligere*) to one presentation at a time, an idea revived in the Herbartian school of psychical mechanics and ironically called the needle-eye theory of consciousness.

In modern psychology the problem of the range of consciousness arose in connection with certain epistemological distinctions in Locke, to whom the narrowness of consciousness was a familiar concept, and who discussed the psychological distinctions between clear and obscure, distinct and confused ideas.[3] A chiliahedron and a figure of nine hundred and ninety-nine sides can be distinguished if we confine ourselves to that part of the two ideas indicated by the final digits, as, for example, when we consider that

---

[1] See p. 89.   [2] *De sens.*, 21.
[3] *Essay on the Human Understanding*, II, chap. XXIX, esp. § 14.

the number of sides is divisible by two in the one case and not in the other. A difficulty arises, however, when we try to distinguish the two figures by their actual appearance in perception, since we can form no distinct images of the two figures in the mind, as we can, for instance, of a figure of four and one of five sides. Aside from the insight that there was some sort of limit to the number of clear, simple ideas contained within a complex idea, the statement that this limit was not exceeded by four or five such component parts has acquired a special significance from later experimental verifications.

With much sympathy and intelligence Bonnet subsequently undertook to deal with the question, which arose in many different connections, as to whether a number of presentations could appear in consciousness simultaneously. He took a decided stand against the Wolffian school, which tended to take the older Scholastic view of the restricted range of consciousness. The arguments of the Wolffians were partly metaphysical, as when they reasoned that it would contradict the notion of the simplicity of the soul if it could be modified variously at one and the same time; they were partly based upon the consideration of the temporal succession of ideas in consciousness, which made it impossible for more than one idea to arise in a given moment of this temporal series. Bonnet, on the contrary, asserted that all the higher psychical processes, the intellectual as well as the conative, presuppose the existence of a plurality of simultaneous ideas in consciousness. Bonnet's observations are significant also for the distinction drawn by him between the range of consciousness and the range of attention. In the visual field, for instance, a large part of the contents of focalized consciousness shows an approximately even distribution of clearness.[1] For the determination of

[1] *Essai de Psychologie*, 1755, chap. XXXVIII.

the range of attention Bonnet depended upon the same method which had earlier led Locke to assert the impossibility of imagining a chiliahedron. He stated it as a constant of visual imagination that only five or six simple contents, like the sides of a geometrical figure, could be grasped simultaneously with a maximum of attention.

The first attempts at an experimental, quantitative determination of the range of consciousness were made by Sir William Hamilton.[1] Hamilton sought to ascertain how many instantaneously presented visual stimuli could be grasped at once, evidently proceeding on the assumption that the range of consciousness could be determined by simply counting the objects, like balls, for instance, which had been momentarily exposed. It was not until much later that it became clear that what Hamilton was investigating was not the range of consciousness but the range of attention. Hamilton's constant, meanwhile, which never exceeded six impressions, has not only not been modified by later investigations, but it approximates also the earlier results obtained by purely introspective methods, in spite of the fact that the conditions of Hamilton's investigations were very different from those of Bonnet's, since in Hamilton's experiments a degree of consciousness sufficient for reproduction had to be attained, while Bonnet sought to ascertain the greatest possible range of simultaneously presented ideational contents.

## 4. The Graduation of Consciousness: Attention

One of the most general characteristics of consciousness is described by the fact that within the field of conscious contents as a whole a narrower circle of so-called contents of consciousness rises into comparative prominence. The

[1] *Lectures on Metaphysics and Logic*, I, p. 254.

graduation of consciousness according to degrees of clearness was already a familiar aspect of the concept of consciousness in Leibniz, and the genesis of the notion of degrees of clearness in the Leibnizian psychology has already received some attention in previous pages.[1] The relation existing between the fluctuation of attention and the clearness of conscious contents was also presupposed in the earlier efforts to construct a theory of psychical mechanics. It was Herbart who, starting with the conception of a competition among ideas and refining upon the Leibnizian terminology, designated the ideas showing the greatest amount of clearness by the general name of apperception.

A new point of departure for the consideration of the problem of attention grew out of the connection of the problem of attention with that of abstraction, a connection which maintained itself for many centuries in the form of the so-called empirical theories of abstraction. In contrast with the antiquity of the problem of abstraction, which goes back to the early beginnings of the doctrine of general ideas, attempts to give a psychological account of abstraction belong to comparatively recent times.[2] Oddly enough, we meet with them in a work conceived in the spirit of Cartesian rationalism, the *Logique de Port-Royal*.[3] The distinction is here made between the abstract and the general. The abstraction made in connection with a single object is a preparatory step toward generalization proper. On account of the circumscribed scope of consciousness it is able to grasp a complex object only by viewing separately the various sides which the object presents. This isolation of the separate sides of the object through abstraction is thus characteristically brought into connection with the

[1] See p. 171, above.
[2] *Cf.* K. Mittenzwey, in Wundt, *Psychologische Studien*, II, 1907, p. 358.
[3] *L'art de penser*, 1662. Edit. nouv. par Fouillé, 1879.

narrowness of consciousness. Great as was Locke's subsequent contribution to the description of the processes of abstraction, he never succeeded in giving a psychological explanation of the activities in question. It is true that he specially mentioned the fact (to use his own illustration) that the mind observes the same color in chalk or snow to-day that it yesterday received from milk. But the reason for this he never gave.[1] A purely empirical solution of the problem as to the manner in which this abstraction takes place was given by Hume. When we distinguish the form of a body from its color we view the body from the different points of view which result from the different series of resemblances into which the characteristics observed arrange themselves.[2] With this the problem of abstraction was solved to the extent that the older question of generalization gave way to that of abstraction in the case of the single presentation. The nature of this process of abstraction, however, reduced itself again in Hume to the play of the mechanism of association.

A new phase of the problem, developed in contemporary French psychology, brought the process of abstraction into relation with that of attention. The idea that attention isolates a given sense quality from the rest, thus resulting in abstraction, goes back to Condillac. In its essential features this view was still represented, at the beginning of the nineteenth century, by Laromiguière.[3]

More important were the attempts of Bonnet to make an analysis of the process of attention, although he still depended largely upon the ideas of the nerve-fibre psychology.[4] The distinction between sensation and reflection as two different sources of ideas Bonnet derived from the psy-

[1] *An Essay on the Human Understanding*, II, chap. XI, p. 9.
[2] *Treatise of Human Nature*, I, § VII.
[3] *Leçons de philosophie*, II, 3d ed., 1823, p. 321.
[4] *Cf.* p. 94, above.

chology of his time. The ideas of reflection arise in consequence of the action of attention upon the nerve-fibres with which the ideas in question are associated. That true perception arises only in this way Bonnet illustrates by the example of a preoccupied philosopher who is taking a walk through the woods. Most of the impressions from his surroundings glide over the surface of his consciousness, only those attracting the attention which are important for his welfare.[1] Bonnet's theory of abstraction, with its emphasis upon attention, has in its main features served as a model for many other treatments of the subject. In Germany, Lossius interpreted it in a peculiar manner in terms of physiological processes.[2] Since the soul is unable to think without the action of nerve-fibres, even general concepts must have physiological correlates. In three partially identical presentations, $Am$, $An$, and $Ap$, $A$ is represented by a common nerve-fibre. If this is excited alone, the result is a general idea common to all three presentations.

Through such reinterpretations the empirical theory of abstraction became pretty far removed from the psychological problem of attention. The insight into the connection between the isolation of mental contents accomplished through attention and the distribution of degrees of clearness was reserved for English psychology. We meet it in the turn which Hamilton gave to the problem of abstraction. Whether considerations of this kind had any significance for the logical side of the problem of abstraction is not important here. What is of importance for the doctrine of attention is the process of abstraction in the sense of the isolation of the contents observed, and Hamilton located the central point of the problem by bringing it into relation to the circumscribed scope of consciousness. Since atten-

---

[1] *Cf.* J. Speck, *Arch. f. Gesch. d. Phil.*, XI, 1898, p. 181.
[2] *Physische Ursachen des Wahren*, pp. 156 *ff.*

tion can grasp only a small number of impressions simultaneously, and these only imperfectly, the turning of the attention toward a given impression means the withdrawal of it from the rest.[1] Meanwhile, attention is described as a will act conforming to a definite psychological law, the law, namely, that the greater the number of impressions simultaneously presented to consciousness the less the intensity with which each of the separate impressions is felt. Attention was thus recognized as consciousness of a higher degree or strength. It is true that we still have an identification of the range of attention with that of consciousness.[2] Nevertheless, the two characteristics which Hamilton found in the experience of attention, namely, the increased clearness which attention involves and the close relation of attention to will, have been incorporated into the modern concept of attention as its most important characteristics. Freed from its long entanglement with the problem of abstraction, the concept of attention or apperception has become one of the fundamental concepts of psychology, illustrating not only an elementary aspect of consciousness but the simplest form of conation as well.

To what extent experimental methods have entered this field is illustrated by the work of W. Wirth, whose experimental investigations were based on the thought that an exact determination of degrees of consciousness could be obtained from the apperceptively conditioned changes in psychical magnitudes, such, for example, as a difference-threshold.

The most important result of the evolution of the concept of consciousness as a whole is the extension of the narrower connotation of consciousness as inner awareness to include the whole phenomenological constitution of the

[1] *Lectures on Metaphysics and Logic*, 5th ed., 1870, p. 258.
[2] *Cf.* p. 184.'

ego, or the totality of psychical experiences. In this way the concept of experience was extended beyond its original meaning as the inwardly perceived so as to include what the ego actually constructs. The difficulty, however, that the ego of pure apperception in the Kantian sense, as the locus of relations for all conscious contents, cannot itself be a conscious content standing on a level with other contents has given rise to serious misgivings.[1] This difficulty has only recently led Natorp to argue that consciousness means object for an ego and that this object relation cannot again become an object. In order to solve this difficulty, a number of psychologists have suggested a new definition of consciousness according to which consciousness is a general term for psychical activities.[2] Now, these activities can be directed upon the phenomenological ego just as well as upon other objects. This shift in the meaning of the concept of consciousness which the purely descriptive efforts of these psychologists effected brings us to the subject of the classification of the contents of consciousness.

[1] *Cf.* p. 179, above.
[2] E. Husserl, *Logische Untersuchungen*, II, p. 342.

# CHAPTER VII

## CLASSIFICATION OF THE CONTENTS OF CONSCIOUSNESS

Attempts to classify psychical phenomena according to their chief differences arose at a much earlier period than the formation of a concept which would express their common characteristic, namely the concept of consciousness. The differences in the content of consciousness forced themselves on the attention first of all, long before their common participation in one unified conscious existence was noticed. The older classifications were, therefore, not made on the same basis as the later ones. For these latter were based upon characteristics which only appear when the separate psychical contents are regarded as being contents of consciousness belonging to one whole. Nevertheless, the striving toward an appropriate classification of the contents of consciousness has always been in psychology the sign for the rise of empirical thought.

The individual classifications of varying extent with which psychology busied itself are subordinate to the problem of a general classification of the contents of consciousness, which deals with the highest classes or genera of the contents of consciousness. Now, if a classification is built upon ideas of similarity, it generally becomes ambiguous, since each content of consciousness may be grouped differently according to different ideas of similarity. What determines the grouping is the choice of a definite principle of classification. We can, therefore, best orient ourselves by means of a survey of the most important principles of classification upon which in the history of our subject the attempts at classification have been based. Many of these principles are still exerting their influence at the present day. This is especially the case with that principle out of which the concept of a psychical element has arisen—a concept that has been so important in modern classifications.

## 1. Survey of the Most Important Principles of Classification

Before the application of empirical principles of classification we find many primitive attempts to do justice to the diversity of psychical facts. The metaphysical psychology, to which the problem of classification was really foreign, was inclined most often to dispose of it by presupposing different substrata for the phenomena. In the theory of the divisions of the soul, the necessity for classification finds a naïve expression, inasmuch as the principle of unity in regard to the experiences of each such division of the soul is maintained.[1]

The empirical classifications can be arranged under three heads. Most often the principle of non-derivability has been used, according to which the highest classes were formed of contents of consciousness which could not be derived from each other. Under this head comes also the differentiation of the contents according to their origin, in so far as their non-derivability is an immediate consequence of the difference of their origin. Not so openly acknowledged and, therefore, more often unconsciously effective, is the principle of intentional relationship, by means of which the fundamental divisions are made according to the way in which the contents of consciousness are related to

[1] *Cf.* p. 46.

their intentional object. Superior to these two principles is, lastly, the principle of analysis, which takes as its point of departure the division of all contents of consciousness into complex and simple.

### (a) The Rise of Psychological Classification

The division of conscious experiences was suggested in the first instance by expressions used in speech. For a long time this motive for classification escaped psychological analysis, as is seen in the ramifications of the old faculty psychology. In the earliest divisions of metaphysical psychology we note that here also non-scientific points of view dominate, mostly in the form of analogies with principles of division that man had employed upon the things of his environment. The threefold division is an ancient possession of mankind. Even the Indian theory of the soul mentions three kinds of psychical content: (1) *Guna*, or spirit, also called *satva* (sense of truth) or *âtman* (breath); (2) *radschas* or *manas* (energy), also called *ahankara* (feeling of self); (3) *tamas* (darkness), as the symbol of passion or desire. This threefold division is a connecting-link in a long chain of analogy, which begins with the three gods, Indra, Varuna, and Agni, is continued in the three elements of nature—light, air, and earth—and which ultimately terminates in the threefold division of society into Brahmans, or priests; *Kschatrijas*, or warriors; and *Vaiçjas*, or workers. Similarly the twofold division into higher and lower functions of the soul corresponds to the pairs of opposite words found almost in every language, as in Hebrew *ruach* and *nephesch*, in Greek νοῦς and ψυχή, in Latin *animus* and *anima*, and in Slavonic languages *duch* and *duše*.[1] In the older divisions of Greek psychology ethical considera-

[1] O. Willmann, *Empirische Psychologie*, 1904, pp. 11 ff.

tions join with these language influences and help determine the division. Plato's division was based upon the two chief differences in the direction of moral strife and expressed clearly the conflict between the demands of reason and those of the sensual desires in man.

The classifications of Aristotle are the first that begin to show some understanding of the peculiar nature of psychic content. Of his principles of division, that one has most psychological importance according to which he divides psychical activities in relation to their object. In Scholastic terms, it is the method of intentional in-existence that causes the difference between thinking and desiring. These two activities are not directed toward different objects but toward the same object in a different manner. The same thing may be at once object of thought and of desire.[1] The decisive characteristic is no longer the difference in the substratum, or bearer, but rather the relation to the intentional object. With this we see the foundation of a principle of differentiation that has been dominant for many centuries.

The ideational and the volitional worlds were in this way empirically separated. The effect of this point of view of intentional relationship is seen in the fact that that group of experiences which do not so readily show such a relationship, *i. e.*, the feelings, were neglected in this classification, and only very much later were they recognized as a special psychical division. We owe the first thoroughgoing psychological description of the affective experiences to Augustine. Influenced probably by his own enhanced affective life, he grouped the feelings in an independent division alongside of ideas and will.[2] In the Middle Ages, however,

---

[1] *De Anima*, III, 10; *Metaphysics*, XII, 7.
[2] *Cf.* Siebeck, *Beiträge zur Entstehungsgeschichte der neueren Psychologie*, Giessen, 1871.

these beginnings were lost sight of because of the dominance of the Aristotelian twofold division. In Thomas Aquinas's famous theory of the emotions we find simply the traditional opinion that feeling is only a modification of desiring. A separation of the feelings from the volitional processes begins first of all with Duns Scotus, who classed pleasure and pain as "passions," and differentiated them from acts of will.

The speculations of the German mystical philosophers arrived in quite a different fashion at an understanding of the affective processes. It is true that these mystics had a great many problems in common with Scholastic philosophy, but they experienced these problems differently. Master Eckhart started with the discussion whether the will or the intellect was the superior power, and he settled this in his own peculiar fashion by lapsing into an emotional state beyond will and intellect in which both of the latter coalesced into one unity. Since Scholastic philosophy had no expression for such experiences, he coined the word *Gemüt*.[1] This was the signal for the further naming and emphasizing of the affective experiences. It was a long time, however, before scientific psychology was at all influenced by these important presentiments of the pious mystics.

## (b) *The Principle of Non-Derivability*

The new concept of consciousness made possible the conception of psychical phenomena as belonging to an independent field of experience, and from this conception there arose a number of different points of view for purposes of classification. Only after consciousness had been found to be a common characteristic of psychical contents could

[1] ["Feeling and Will; the Sum Total of Affective-Conative Processes," Titchener, *Am. J. of Psych.*, VII, p. 81. Trs.]

the content of consciousness be classified according to purely phenomenological attributes. This new standpoint is clearly seen in Locke's classification of the contents of consciousness.

Locke first of all divided his "ideas," which coincide with our modern conception of the contents of consciousness, into complex and simple, and classified the latter according to their origin, that is to say, according to the manner in which they enter into consciousness. This principle of classification naturally came to him because he had presupposed that the mind was at first absolutely blank, a *tabula rasa*. In this manner he arrived at the following four classes:[1] (1) Ideas that come into the mind by one sense only (simple sensations); (2) ideas that come into the mind by more senses than one (*e. g.*, extension, form); (3) ideas that are to be had only from reflection or introspection (thinking and willing); (4) ideas that are suggested to the mind by all the ways of reflection and sensation (*e. g.*, pleasure, existence, energy, time).

The greatest misgivings arise, of course, in regard to the last class. The differentiation between ideas of reflection and those that enter the mind by means of sensation points forward to the later differentiation between the subjective and objective sides of consciousness. Again, Locke's method of first considering the simple ideas became common in much of the psychology from his day onward. His simple ideas are already elements in the sense that they can neither be produced nor destroyed by the mind. They are things given to us in experience, and when this is not the case they cannot be produced by any power of even the most sublime genius.[2] We must also remember that the different origin of these classes of ideas brings with it their reciprocal non-

---

[1] *Essay on the Human Understanding*, II, chap. III, § 1.
[2] *Op. cit.*, chap. II, § 2.

derivability, which is caused by the simple character of these ideas. We find, therefore, in Locke the origins of the most important points of view which have been used in later psychological classifications.

Nevertheless, in spite of all this, the old Aristotelian twofold division into thinking and willing continued to exist for a long time. It was, in fact, the chief ground of division in the psychology of Wolff, who also used, in addition to this, the popular division into higher and lower activities of the soul. In English psychology Hume continued the twofold division, and it was retained right down to the time of Reid and Brown. The latter subordinated it, however, to the division of all content into outer and inner affections: the first class comprised all sense-perceptions, and the second contained intellectual mental states and affective states (moral phenomena).

It was not until the psychology of the German Enlightenment that a new terminology came into being. In Tetens and Mendelssohn[1] feeling is recognized as a third class alongside of intellectual and volitional processes. Tetens separates sensation and feeling clearly, inasmuch as he explains the former as a copy of the object and the latter as a change in the perceiving subject.[2]

A more thoroughgoing foundation for the division into knowing, feeling, and willing is found in Kant, especially in his treatise entitled *Über Philosophie überhaupt,* which gives the best summary of his general psychological views. These classes, he maintains, are fundamental for the reason that they are neither derived from each other nor can any one be traced back to the other. Such a method of reasoning was peculiarly adapted to the old faculty psychology, because the phenomena, the sum total of which

---

[1] *Gesammelte Schriften,* II, p. 295.
[2] *Philosophische Versuche,* I, pp. 214 *f.*

went to form such a class, were considered *a priori* as effects of a single faculty and, as such, had to resemble each other to a very great extent. The faculties themselves, however, had to be independent and absolutely heterogeneous if differences in mental life found in our inner experience were to be explained by their activity.

In so far as the discussion of this division was carried on in the Kantian school from the standpoint of the faculty psychology it loses interest for us. Krug, for example, maintained that only two faculties were necessary, namely, ideation and endeavor, because the activity of the human mind was exerted in two directions—outward and inward. It was Hamilton, however, who gave a more serious vindication of the Kantian classification. He strove to justify the position that feeling should be considered as an independent class, since there exist states of consciousness that cannot be classified as belonging either to thought or to active endeavor.[1] In spite of this co-ordination of the three classes there remained, nevertheless, an order of precedence, in which knowing took the first place. For, if we consider which one of the three classes is least dependent on the others, it is at once clear that knowing is the only one that could lay claim to be an independent entity. In the second place comes feeling, which can at least be thought of as taking place without volitional processes. The remaining class always presupposes the co-operation of the two others.[2]

After Herbart's attempt to abolish all multiplicity of mental faculties it was Lotze who was most pronounced in his defense of the Kantian threefold division. He did not wish or attempt to support that strict division which regarded knowing, feeling, and willing as three lines of development

[1] *Lectures on Metaphysics*, II, p. 423.
[2] *Op. cit.*, I, p. 187; II, p. 431.

absolutely independent of each other. In comparing mental phenomena, however, he was driven to make the hypothesis that, in the dependence of experiences of these different classes on each other, the first process acts as a kind of inducing motive to the succeeding process, but does not cause it, while at the same time there is some power or force at work which gives its assistance, but which escapes our observation. If the soul were nothing else than a thinking or imagining being, there would be no sufficient reason why anything else except this special activity should be called into being. There would be no reason for feelings of pleasure and pain. Any inner change, however dangerous it might be for the soul's own existence, would simply be observed or perceived by it, just as it simply observes any other conflict of forces.[1] This description of Lotze is worthy of note because it is an attempt to give a purely psychological foundation to the fundamental thought underlying the Kantian threefold division.

There is another form of the threefold classification that uses for its general principle of classification the popular psychological distinction between actual sense-impressions and their reproduction or mental images. This is not met with so often in the history of psychology, although just such a threefold division, which regards as ultimate elements sensations, images, and feelings, is to be observed in modern psychology.[2] If we pass over the primitive explanation which was satisfied with the old theory of the inner sense, inasmuch as it referred the differences between sensations and their reproductions to the outer and inner senses,[3] we see at once that this question was not of special importance for faculty psychology, because it was presupposed that the soul had an immediate consciousness of its different activities. Locke was content merely

[1] *Mikrokosmos*, I, pp. 193 ff.   [2] See below, 2.   [3] *Cf.* pp. 71 f.

to affirm that the soul was passive in sensation and active in reproduction. This same opposition occurs again in Leibniz,[1] who regarded sensation as passive, because of its vagueness, and the image or thought process as active.

Purely psychological characteristics for such a differentiation were first sought by the English Sensationalists. It is obvious that motives prompted by their theory of knowledge led them to fix upon a clear distinction between sensation and the reproduction of sensation. Berkeley had already noted a long list of criteria that distinguished sensations from images: intensity, vivacity, duration, and orderly coherence.[2] And Hume also attempted in different ways to make it clear why it is that we experience mental images as different from sensations. He found, for example, that the most vivid reproduction is clearly inferior to the most vague sensation. This is an opinion that Spencer repeated a hundred years later.[3] French Sensationalism did not make the distinctions quite so fine, for, following the example of Condillac,[4] the difference between vivacity and intensity was neglected, and the two were considered identical. Alongside of this purely psychological determination of the difference, there have always arisen attempts at a physiological explanation. Hartley translated Hume's description into the language of his vibration hypothesis, and he gave it the interpretation that the breadth of the oscillation of a sensation always exceeded the breadth of the oscillation of the reproduction. When such a naïve, materialistic explanation was no longer tenable, the opposition between the sensory and motor nervous systems was made use of, as, for example, in the writings of George, who took into account the physiological knowledge of the nineteenth century.

[1] *Monadologie*, 49.
[2] *Treatise*, 30.
[3] *Principles of Psychology*, I, § 49.
[4] *Traité des sensations*, I, 2, 9.

of consciousness to the object is always the same or similar, whereas between the classes this relation is essentially different. For the separation of ideation and judgment, which is the most surprising thing in this new threefold division, Brentano gave an indirect proof. If no such fundamental difference in their intentional relations existed, then the difference must lie either in the content, to which they both refer, or in the degree of perfection, in which the same content may exist in our minds as ideation or as judgment. Since, however, neither of these is the case, the difference can only be one of intentional relation.

This threefold division is connected in a peculiar manner with Brentano's theory of the inner consciousness. Each psychical act, however simple, can be looked upon as idea of itself, as knowledge of itself, and as feeling of itself. In this we see clearly Brentano's striving to make the three kinds of intentional relationship the necessary forms by means of which anything comes to consciousness and thereby give his three chief classes a logical connection in conscious life. To thoroughly appreciate this classification, one must remember his concept of the "psychical phenomenon"[1] in which the use of this principle of intentional relation is obviously foreshadowed. Besides this, the use of this principle gave his logical tendencies plenty of scope, inasmuch as the most important function of logical thinking, *i. e.*, judgment, became one of the fundamental classes of the mental processes.

### (d) *The Principle of Analysis*

When we call to mind how comparatively late in the history of psychology any reflection as to the conditions of psychological analysis arose, we cannot be at all surprised

[1] *Cf.* p. 84.

to affirm that the soul was passive in sensation and active in reproduction. This same opposition occurs again in Leibniz,[1] who regarded sensation as passive, because of its vagueness, and the image or thought process as active.

Purely psychological characteristics for such a differentiation were first sought by the English Sensationalists. It is obvious that motives prompted by their theory of knowledge led them to fix upon a clear distinction between sensation and the reproduction of sensation. Berkeley had already noted a long list of criteria that distinguished sensations from images: intensity, vivacity, duration, and orderly coherence.[2] And Hume also attempted in different ways to make it clear why it is that we experience mental images as different from sensations. He found, for example, that the most vivid reproduction is clearly inferior to the most vague sensation. This is an opinion that Spencer repeated a hundred years later.[3] French Sensationalism did not make the distinctions quite so fine, for, following the example of Condillac,[4] the difference between vivacity and intensity was neglected, and the two were considered identical. Alongside of this purely psychological determination of the difference, there have always arisen attempts at a physiological explanation. Hartley translated Hume's description into the language of his vibration hypothesis, and he gave it the interpretation that the breadth of the oscillation of a sensation always exceeded the breadth of the oscillation of the reproduction. When such a naïve, materialistic explanation was no longer tenable, the opposition between the sensory and motor nervous systems was made use of, as, for example, in the writings of George, who took into account the physiological knowledge of the nineteenth century.

[1] *Monadologie*, 49.
[2] *Treatise*, 30.
[3] *Principles of Psychology*, I, § 49.
[4] *Traité des sensations*, I, 2, 9.

The problem as to the relation between sensation and reproduction is solved at last in the simplest manner by means of the presuppositions of Herbart's psychology. Here they turn out to be simply different periods in the history of the same idea. Sensation is the idea from its development to its first disappearance, and reproduction is the idea from its reappearance in consciousness to its next disappearance.[1]

Under these circumstances there was no decisive motive that might lead to a division of sensation and image into two absolutely independent classes. We see, therefore, that the most universally acknowledged consequence of the principle of non-derivability is the threefold division into feeling, willing, and thinking.

### (c) *The Principle of Intentional Relationship*

The principle of non-derivability was subjected to the keenest criticism by Brentano,[2] even though we can trace back to him many of the principles mentioned above. If two psychical phenomena are to be looked upon as belonging to absolutely different classes, simply because we cannot *a priori* draw a conclusion from our capacity for the one to our capacity for the other, we must not only, along with Kant, Hamilton, and Lotze, separate thinking from feeling and desiring but also seeing from tasting. Why, we must even go further and separate red vision from blue vision as from a phenomenon that belongs to another ultimate class. In fact, if we look closely, we see in those thinkers the unconscious influence of the characteristic of intentional in-existence used by Aristotle in his classification.

Kant makes the distinction between knowing and desir-

---

[1] For this description see Volkmann, *Lehrbuch der Psychologie*, I, § 80.
[2] *Psychologie vom empirischen Standpunkte*, I, pp. 246 *ff.*

ing consist of a difference in their relation to the object; and the peculiarity of feeling is supposed to be due to the fact that in this case merely a relation to the subject exists. Reciprocal non-derivability follows as a necessary consequence of this difference in intentional relation; but not in all cases of non-derivability need the intentional relation be of another kind. This latter principle of classification is, therefore, superior to the other. We find the same opinion in Hamilton. In the phenomenon of knowing, consciousness distinguishes between a known object and a knowing subject; in the case of the feelings, however, consciousness is itself fused with the psychical state. And, lastly, in the case of desiring or willing there is, just as with knowing, a relation to an object, but knowing and desiring are differentiated just by the difference in their relation to the object. This last point of view seems to have been decisive for Hamilton. The man who most thoroughly followed out the consequences of this principle of the non-derivability of faculties was Lotze, and he was roused to do this by the polemic against Herbart. He did not draw back from the logical consequences, for he maintained, for example, that the faculties of seeing and hearing were different, original, and independent faculties.[1] And yet, since he classed the images of tones and colors in the same class, it would seem as though another point of view had been at work in his division into three classes.

In place of the principle of non-derivability, Brentano, therefore, took the principle of intentional relations in order to determine the chief classes of mental phenomena. He found in accordance with the different ways of intentional in-existence three main classes—ideation, judgment, and emotion. He vindicated this division by appealing to inner experience, and held that within the same class the relation

[1] *Mikrokosmos*, I, p. 198.

of consciousness to the object is always the same or similar, whereas between the classes this relation is essentially different. For the separation of ideation and judgment, which is the most surprising thing in this new threefold division, Brentano gave an indirect proof. If no such fundamental difference in their intentional relations existed, then the difference must lie either in the content, to which they both refer, or in the degree of perfection, in which the same content may exist in our minds as ideation or as judgment. Since, however, neither of these is the case, the difference can only be one of intentional relation.

This threefold division is connected in a peculiar manner with Brentano's theory of the inner consciousness. Each psychical act, however simple, can be looked upon as idea of itself, as knowledge of itself, and as feeling of itself. In this we see clearly Brentano's striving to make the three kinds of intentional relationship the necessary forms by means of which anything comes to consciousness and thereby give his three chief classes a logical connection in conscious life. To thoroughly appreciate this classification, one must remember his concept of the "psychical phenomenon"[1] in which the use of this principle of intentional relation is obviously foreshadowed. Besides this, the use of this principle gave his logical tendencies plenty of scope, inasmuch as the most important function of logical thinking, *i. e.*, judgment, became one of the fundamental classes of the mental processes.

### (d) *The Principle of Analysis*

When we call to mind how comparatively late in the history of psychology any reflection as to the conditions of psychological analysis arose, we cannot be at all surprised

[1] *Cf.* p. 84.

that the distinction between simple and complex contents of consciousness is of recent origin. Along with this there are the peculiar terminological difficulties with which psychology has had to contend from the very beginning. Expressions denoting complex processes, such as idea, emotion, etc., become fixed in a language long before those denoting the simple processes. It was Wolff, in Germany, who helped to make general the word "*Vorstellung*" as an equivalent of the English word "idea." The German word "*Gemüt*" comes from the original stem "*mut*," and was used for a long time and even by Kant as synonymous with "*Seele*" or "*Bewusstsein*." The mystic philosophers gave it a different and peculiar meaning which we have noticed before.[1] Of a much later date is the differentiation between the simple contents of consciousness, which in our modern terminology we are accustomed to separate as sensation and feeling. From the seventeenth century onward the two words were used almost synonymously. In the philosophy of the Romantic period and afterward we begin to note an ambiguity of meaning, for, on the one hand, feelings, as the most immediately experienced subjective states, stand in a kind of opposition to the peripherally conditioned sensations; while, on the other hand, especially among the physiologists, the feelings are restricted to certain kinds of sensation, *e. g.*, the sensations of the skin, the organic sensations, etc.

The principle of division into simple and complex contents of consciousness, bequeathed by John Locke, has remained one of the common characteristics of English psychology. And yet even in England the threefold division was in a way retained by Lewes, who supported it with a doubtful analogy between the psychological spectrum and the optical spectrum. The three principal colors

[1] *Cf.* p. 194.

led on the psychological side to a threefold division into sensation, thought, and movement (*sensation, pensée, mouvement*), and the first of these depended upon sensorial, the second upon cerebral, and the third upon muscle energy. Bain also accepted the threefold division into thinking, feeling, and doing.[1] But, alongside of this, he set up the more important division of psychical phenomena into primitive and such as developed out of the primitive. It was Spencer, however, who was the first to carry out this evolutionary principle thoroughly. The mental activities of the developed consciousness fall into two groups—cognitive (memory, reason) and affective (feeling, will). The simple contents of consciousness, which in Spencer's terminology are designated "feelings," can be separated into emotions, which belong to the centre of consciousness, and into sensations, which belong to the periphery of consciousness. This division is supported by a second division, which, taking an analytic point of view, separates the feelings from such parts of consciousness as can be called, in general, relations between feelings. A "feeling" represents any part of consciousness, which is an individual entity marked off from the neighboring parts of consciousness by qualitative differences and which to introspection appears homogeneous. A "relation," on the other hand, is not taken up with any perceptible part of consciousness. It disappears at once along with the elements if one abstracts from these. A second essential difference between these two kinds of conscious experiences consists in the fact that a feeling of relationship cannot be analyzed into parts, whereas an ordinary feeling permits at least of an imaginary analysis into similar parts.

These ideas were influential in forming the concept of the psychical element, a concept which has been decisive

[1] *The Senses and the Intellect*, p. 2.

in modern forms of classification, although even here the older principles in many cases still exert their influence.

## 2. Modern Forms of Classification

The differentiation of complex and simple contents of consciousness has been decisive in different ways for the classifications of modern psychology. Many attempts start with the idea of finding principles of opposition which will be equally binding for complex and for simple contents. Here belongs the psychology of Lipps, who set up a number of such principal oppositions. The first of these oppositions is that between experiences of the ego and conscious experiences which are not experiences of the ego; alongside stand the no less fundamental oppositions between act and receptive experience, and between act and activity. These oppositions, and especially the first of them, show a certain relationship to the distinction between subjective and objective contents of consciousness, although this latter division is much more consciously dependent upon presuppositions derived from the theory of knowledge.

Husserl went back to the researches of Brentano in regard to intentionality. By separating the experiences of consciousness into acts, *i. e.*, intentional experiences, and not-acts, he arrived at a type of classification to which the fundamental oppositions set up by Lipps would have led. The position to which Husserl relegates the feelings is, however, peculiar. The separation of all conscious experiences into intentional and non-intentional would be merely an external point of view if experiences of the same descriptive genus showed at times intentional relation to an object and at other times no such relation. At the first glance such a state of affairs seems actually to exist in relation to the class ordinarily called feelings. Undoubtedly, there are intentional feelings, *e. g.*, joy in a certain thing. As examples of non-intentional feelings, it is usual to mention the sensational feelings, *e. g.*, the pain of a burn on the skin, the pleasurable taste of a certain food. The difficulty can be solved by maintaining that these "feelings" do not belong to the same descriptive class as those of pleasure and displeasure. And, accordingly, Husserl divides the totality of feelings into affective sensations and affective acts. This solution of the riddle of the feelings by means of the division of experiences into sensations and acts, *i. e.*, into two different classes, is seen also in other proposals for a method of classification. We see it, for example, in Stumpf,[1] who reckons the sensational feelings as affective sensations and classifies them along with the sensations.

Jodl[2] tried in a circumspect manner to bring the old threefold classification of feeling, willing, and thinking into line with modern ideas. Conscious activity is neither cognition alone nor volition alone nor feeling alone; it is rather the combination of the spontaneity and receptivity of an organic being. We should, therefore, no longer seek for separate kinds of activities, for it is rather the case of a single psychical activity appearing in various aspects. Just here lies the chief difference of a classification in the modern sense, in contrast to the older standpoint of the faculty psychology. Jodl finds in every psychological activity three such moments—the impression from without working inward; the response from within working outward; and an inner connection between these two links of the chain. Thus result sense-impressions, feelings, and volitional tendencies as the three chief kinds of conscious reaction of organic beings to the impressions of the surrounding world.

If we turn aside from this attempt to find the fundamental classes that are necessarily connected with conscious reaction,

[1] "Über Gefühlsempfindungen," in *Zeitschr. für Psychologie*, Band XLIV, 1907, p. 1.
[2] *Lehrbuch der Psychologie*, 1896, p. 130.

there yet remains the possibility of grouping the elementary contents from the point of view of our direct experience of them. According to this principle, Ebbinghaus[1] arrived also at a threefold division of psychical contents; but he took as the fundamentally different classes of experience sensations, images, and feelings. This point of view of the immediately perceived differences in the kinds of experience would seem at the first glance to lead necessarily to a perfectly uniform and unambiguous classification. Strangely enough, however, it has given rise to very different ultimate classes. The fundamental distinction between sensations and their reproductions or images has been questioned, and questioned by a classification that also appeals to immediate experience and decides upon a twofold classification of the contents of consciousness. In Wundt's psychology sensations and feelings form the two classes of elementary contents, a division which agrees with the fact that immediate experience contains two factors—an objective content of experience and the experiencing subject.

In contradistinction to all other attempts at classification, the theory that there are two principal kinds of elements in consciousness, the subjective and the objective, rests upon the universal fact of consciousness that the imaging subject can distinguish or differentiate itself from its images. If this principle of division is acknowledged there arise further questions as to the relation in which these different kinds of elements may stand. Would it be conceivable that psychological analysis should lead to the discovery of a greater number of elements? If we are dealing solely with empirically given elements, then it must be possible to conceive of a greater number of elements, just as it is possible to conceive of a greater number of color sensations than those contained in the color circle. Such

[1] *Grundzüge der Psychologie*, I, 1902, pp. 167 *f.*

color sensations cannot be represented in a concrete (*anschaulich*) manner, but they are thinkable exactly in the same sense as any abstract (*unanschaulich*) multiplicity is, *e. g.*, space in more than three dimensions. The twofold division of conscious experiences into subjective and objective seems to be a perfectly unique kind of division. It has often been shown that sensations and feelings cannot as independent component parts fuse together into one whole called conscious experience. And the opposite opinions that those classes are nothing else than characteristics or different sides of the same conscious experience, leads into great difficulties in facing the problem of making clear this union of the subjective and objective sides of consciousness. As an analogy the union of the intensity and quality of a tone might be made use of. But these two characteristics have a bearer, or substratum, namely, the tone. Whether consciousness could be in this sense considered the substratum of feeling and sensation remains yet to be settled. Possibly the combination which the elements of consciousness form together is just as inconceivable (*unanschaulich*) as the combination of a real and imaginary number into one complex number, $a + bi$.

The discussion of this position throws a new light upon those attempts which aimed at finding one single class of psychical elements. This they achieved in considering sensations as the most readily isolated component parts of conscious life. The historical background of this line of thought is formed by the intellectualism of Herbart, who recognized only simple ideas and identified these absolutely with sensations. In recent years Münsterberg[1] has modified this theory in a surprising manner. He starts out from the standpoint of method, from the possibility of the communication of psychical contents. The two com-

[1] *Grundzüge der Psychologie*, I, 1900, p. 309.

munications that it is raining outside and that I am happy are from the point of view of method absolutely distinct. The first case of outer sense-impression can be explained by direct description of the content of consciousness; but in regard to the latter I can never really tell if that which the other calls a feeling of joy may not be what I call anger. Psychology has therefore to resort to indirect description, and it does this by considering the total content of consciousness as a combination of elements which in the images of sense-impressions show noetical relations to the physical world. Such elements are, however, nothing else than sensations. If two sensations are similar to each other we are driven to the conclusion that each of them is divided into parts, some of which are common to them both. Now, since each sensation shows some similarity with some other and is never unique, it therefore follows that no sensation represents a psychological atom and that each is composed of elementary component parts. These thoughts lead to an atomic theory of consciousness which goes far beyond the claim of sensation to be recognized as a psychical element which is not further divisible. They lead us to seek the true elements of psychical life beyond sensation. Of course, Münsterberg cannot maintain that psychical processes are in absolute reality nothing but sensations; he admits they are unities, but in our analysis of them we may arrange them in some new form. Thus an image is made up of elements in the sense that there is a special logical value in the notion of an image as being a combination of elements.

All these modern forms of classification have started with the principle of analysis, and they have ended logically in the problem of the psychical element, and, as we have seen, this element has changed its rôle very often in the classifications we have described.

## 3. The Concept of the Psychical Element

The demands which led to the modern concept of the psychical element are in direct opposition both to the traditional faculty psychology and to the more recent contention that a simple content of consciousness, as, for example, the simple idea of Herbart, can exist in and for itself. Much rather are we to conceive of the parts of our continuous psychical experience as incessantly entering into all kinds of relations with one another. The elements, however, are what lie beneath these. They cannot be further analyzed, although they may appear in any combination.

In this manner Wundt established the concept of the psychical element. In opposition to this, however, the description of consciousness as "a stream of thought" was used. According to Dilthey[1] this continuous flow of the contents of consciousness forms an impediment to the use of any kind of "element" concept. A slight change in the concept is brought about when the elements are looked upon as mere artifices for the purposes of abstraction, and in this form the concept has been made the foundation of many popular presentations of psychology, as, for example, in the psychology of Rehmke.[2] In the controversy over this concept an analogy between the physical and psychical atoms was often made use of, but this analogy fails precisely in the most important point.[3] The psychological elementary concepts ought not to be compared with the analysis of matter into atoms, but rather with the analysis of a movement into its components or into the momentary velocities of a moving point. These are the only things

---

[1] "Ideen über eine beschreibende und zergliedernde Psychologie," in *Sitzungsbericht d. Berl. Akad.*, No. 53, 1894.
[2] J. Rehmke, *Allgemeine Psychologie*, 1904.
[3] *Cf.* Wundt, *Grundz. d. physiolog. Psychol.*, I (6 Aufl.), 1908, p. 417.

that would at all correspond in the department of physics. The continual change of conscious experiences hinders the determination of psychical elements just as little as a velocity changing from point to point hinders the determination of the momentary velocity at any single one of these points.

The question as to the kind and number of such elements becomes, then, a purely empirical one. Taking this position, psychology cuts itself completely loose from all the enticements of a metaphysic of consciousness, which sees in the classes of the content of consciousness the expression of ideal regularity according to law. This question of the psychical elements is not merely a question of a new grouping of long-known contents of consciousness. In recent years we have seen how systematic introspection has led to the discovery of a class of experiences up till now totally disregarded, the so-called states of awareness,[1] which, according to the opinion of Ach, must be considered as an independent class along with the previously recognized classes. This explains, in a way, the difference of opinion which at present exists as to the number and nature of the psychical elements. Even though attempts at classification can be traced back to the oldest period of psychological thought, yet the problem of the psychical element implicit in them is the product of the last few years.

[1] *Cf.* pp. 136 *f.*

# CHAPTER VIII

## PSYCHOLOGICAL METHODS

In the development of psychological methods, as in the development of the methods of any science, we can divide the methods into two kinds: those that procure a knowledge of the facts, *i. e.*, the practical or working methods, and those that serve to work up special facts, *i. e.*, the theoretical methods. Scarcely any other science has had those of the first kind ever questioned, but psychology has had to fight for their recognition. In the controversies as to the relation between introspection and observation, theoretical view-points have mostly predominated. And the same is true of the attempts that arose from this; namely, to base psychology upon physiology. It was only the development of psychical methods of measurement that led to real working methods, which had as their aim exact and, as far as possible, quantitative results.

### 1. Observation and Introspection

That psychological facts are given only to our inner experience can never be seriously questioned. And there are many psychologists of the present day who are of the opinion that introspection alone is perfectly sufficient to obtain a knowledge of them. Scientific introspection is, of course, considered to be a special art, which is more full of content and more systematic than common introspection. The apparatus it makes use of is no other than that which always stands and has always stood within the reach of every man. It becomes more and more refined in proportion as the conscious life itself becomes richer and more varied, but a real history of these methods can scarcely be said to exist.

It is possible that the irregular course of the history of psychology, interrupted by so many leaps and bounds, may have something to do with this peculiarity of introspection. The continuity of psychological thought has often been broken. How often a pre-Raphaelite return to long-forgotten forms of thought has followed a period of the keenest hopes and anticipations! Is not the fact that each single individual, by means of his introspections, has access to all psychical phenomena a temptation and an urgent motive to begin all over again from the very first? Certainly the theory of the inner sense, which arises in a certain historical relation with introspection, busied itself with the peculiarities of introspection. But this did not result in a development of the achievements of introspection, but only, on the one hand, in a kind of hinting in a fantastic way at such possibilities, and, on the other hand, in drawing a distinction between the methods of introspection and those of the so-called outer observation.

Even though we may acknowledge that introspection is the presupposition of every psychology, nevertheless introspection was by no means the beginning of scientific psychology. It is through nature that man has not only got to know himself but has also learned to observe himself.[1] It is no mere chance that the first psychological knowledge among the Greeks comes from mathematicians and physicists. Of course it is true that many universally valid facts of human psychical life appear also in mythological ideas and in the concrete expressions of such in art. But it

[1] *Cf.* H. Ebbinghaus, *Kultur der Gegenwart*, I, 6, 1908, pp. 175 *ff.*

was first of all the methods which had been used in the scientific research of outer phenomena that led to a theoretical psychology, the first outlines of which Plato, the founder of logic and ethics, formulated, at least for thought and volition.

This same connection can also be seen in the important influence that the example of the methods of natural science has had upon the formation of modern psychology. Even before practical psychological methods were formed in analogy to the latter, the idea of strict and universal regularity in mental phenomena was recognized. The great metaphysicians of the seventeenth century, Spinoza and Leibniz, were convinced that mental phenomena agreed with the phenomena of outer nature in regard to the strict regularity of their course. The association psychology must be given credit for having turned this belief to account by formulating certain psychological concepts which were of great help for empirical psychology. Hobbes explained the strict regularity of our thought processes by means of the continuance of material movements in the brain and thereby created in the mental sphere an analogy to the physical principle of inertia. A century later Newton introduced into physics the idea of attracting forces, and then we find in the psychology of Hume also a kind of attraction of ideas. Inertia and attraction were able to explain the mechanical principles of the outer world. Founded on analogies with these, the concept of association in the mental sphere seemed to be designed to do the same for mental phenomena. Last of all we have Herbart, who went furthest with these mechanical analogies. Filled with the conviction that the regularity of mental life was similar to that of the heavens, he provided his ideas with all the characteristics of elastic bodies, which, enclosed within a narrow space, exerted pressure upon each other.

In spite of all this, such analogies left a great deal of room free for the building up of psychology itself. But, in more recent developments of the science, this was in danger of being limited by a direct transference of the methods of natural science to psychology, and this transference led so far as to give rise to the demand that psychology must be methodically based upon physiology.

## 2. Physiology the Basis of Psychology

The influences of the natural sciences upon the methods of psychology are certainly not the only ones under which the latter have come, for the differences in method have certainly not been less than the differences in the general trend of psychology. And yet these influences have been of the greatest importance for our science at the present day.

The opportunity for a direct attack by the natural sciences was given when the question as to the relation between observation and introspection had been decided in the sense that the latter could never become a scientific method. Out of this arose the demand to seek the methodical basis of the science of the soul in another department of science, and the most natural department was, of course, brain physiology. Comte's protest against introspection[1] lost much in force because of his questionable suggestion that psychology should be based upon phrenology as Gall had defined the latter. In contradistinction to this, Maudsley demanded that psychology be theoretically based upon physiology. In a criticism of J. S. Mill's work on Hamilton he proposed with great determination to substitute a purely physiological method in place of the method of introspection to which Mill had assented.[2] In his chief work, *The*

[1] *Cf.* p. 154.
[2] This criticism appeared in *The Journal of Mental Science*, 1866.

*Physiology and Pathology of the Soul*, he contended that it was impossible to attain any results by the old method; such an undertaking, he says, is just as hopeless as trying to illuminate the universe with one tallow candle. Maudsley supported his contentions partly by means of the current arguments of materialism. Material conditions are at the bottom of all psychical life, and, naturally, physiology is best able to give an account of these. The organic metabolism of the brain is always influencing consciousness; nothing is, therefore, more certain than that psychical phenomena are dependent upon physiological conditions. More important, however, are the peculiar but purely psychological reasons that Maudsley brings forward. Since conscious life is not a continuous activity, consciousness cannot give sufficient information about the static states of the soul. Only physiology can teach us about the inactive state of the soul, which is not accompanied by consciousness. But even of the activities of the soul themselves, the most important take place without consciousness. This last argument involves itself at best in a contradiction, since the hypothesis of unconscious psychical processes presupposes a certain amount of purely psychological knowledge.

A similar attempt was made in Germany on the part of Horwicz, which tried to avoid such contradictions. After more or less lengthy discussions as to method,[1] he admitted in his *Psychologische Analysen auf physiologischer Grundlage* (1872 to 1878) the necessity for a kind of introspection, but only for the sake of a preliminary orientation of the total mass of psychic activities. But it is the physiology of the bodily organism which is the real foundation, for the organization of the soul corresponds to the organization of the body. It is by the physiological method that the scientist arrives at a division of psychical phenomena; and so in the same

[1] *Zeitschr. f. Philos. u. philos. Krit.*, Bd. LX, 1872, p. 170.

way should he determine the number and the characteristics of the mental elements and the laws of their combination. This important support that the physiological method was promising psychology has an analogy in the relationship between some other sciences, all of which can be traced back to the influence of Comte's classification of the sciences, where each one served as handmaid to a superior science, and where all were arranged in an ascending series from the least important to the most important. In this scale, psychology is related to physiology as physics to mathematics or as geography to astronomy. Against all this it has been objected that even if physical and psychical phenomena were still more closely connected, the absolute heterogeneity of the two kinds of phenomena would make every conclusion carried over from the one department to the other merely an analogy. And, in fact, the psychology of Horwicz is built upon the insecure foundation of analogies. The chief part is played by the concept of assimilation in the physiological and in the psychological sense; a further analogy exists between the opposition of sensory and motor nervous activities on the one hand and the general division of our total psychical life into theoretical and practical activities on the other. Upon this Horwicz builds a division of psychical phenomena which in the main agrees with that "really perfectly correct skeleton of mental life which was set up by Wolff." That such conclusions drawn from analogies could become a proof of or, worse still, a substitute for a psychologically determined division merely goes to show to how great a degree Horwicz had lost sight of the aims of psychology in his great admiration for the successes in the field of physiology.

In quite a different sense did the physiological method become an aid to psychology in the physiological psychology of Wundt. That this is in the first instance psychology and that it attempts to investigate the processes of consciousness in the combinations they form among themselves—all this follows from Wundt's definition of psychology which was quoted above.[1] Physiological psychology attempts to deduce the psychical from the physical phenomena of life just as little as, for example, microscopical anatomy might attempt to give an explanation of the capacities of the microscope from the facts of anatomy. Physiology is drawn upon partly for supplementary purposes, as, for example, in questions as to the physical basis of mental life, but this latter is not bounded by these facts but leads right on to the other problems of psychology that border upon philosophy. But partly and chiefly do we mean by physiological psychology the incorporation of the experimental methods developed by physiology. Of these experimental methods in the broadest sense the most important part has been played by the methods of psychical measurement, which from the very beginning centred around the problem of a psychical scale.

### 3. The Development of the Methods of Psychical Measurement

Nowhere do we see more clearly than in the development of the methods of psychical measurement what an influence upon the development of a method its subordination to some theoretical point of view may exert even though the latter may in later years have to be sacrificed. It is certain that there is not one of the methods of psychical measurement that did not exist in its broad outlines before the time of Fechner. Yet it was only through him that these methods became a recognized part of experimental psychology. Even the concept of the psychical measure is much older than

[1] See p. 162.

the psychophysics of Fechner.[1] And yet it was Fechner who was the first to bring the experimental methods into relationship with the problem of a psychical measure and in this way lead to a theoretical discussion of these methods. Not the discovery of a new method of procedure but merely a change in the point of view led to the rise of the methods of psychical measurement.

The common starting-point of all these methods lies in those methods which are used to determine the size of physical quantities. Everywhere where the inaccuracy of sense-impressions led to unavoidable mistakes in observation, there arose the necessity of approximating to the objective values as nearly as possible by means of increasing the number of observations. The systematic application of these methods of eliminating error to the problem of the determination of psychical measurement was left for Fechner to take up in his psychophysics. The classification and the names that Fechner gave to these methods of measurement have been repeatedly modified according to the peculiarities of the methods that have appeared most characteristic. For example, Ebbinghaus divides the methods into those of stimulus determination and those of judgment determination; G. E. Müller into the methods of constant changes and of limits; and Wundt, who kept longest to Fechner's division, recently divided them into gradation and enumeration methods.

In the development of the methods there has been a gradual differentiation between those two chief groups, which became clear according to the problems allotted to them by Fechner. Now, according to Fechner, all methods exist for the purpose of bringing into relation definite parts of the scale of sensation with definite parts of the stimulus scale, so as to be able to measure sensation by some unit.

[1] See below, Chapter IX.

In calling these methods of measurement "psychophysical," Fechner hints at the fundamental duty of psychophysics. The just-noticeable difference was taken to represent the unit of sensation. The methods could either find these units directly or arrive at them by calculation. The methods of the first kind, which because of their more natural procedure are in general the older, can be called the gradation methods (*Abstufungsmethoden*). In contradistinction to these the methods of the second class were grouped together under the name of the "error" methods, a name which is not at all happy in describing the difference between the two classes. For every method has to reckon with unavoidable errors of observation and becomes in its exact manipulation an error method. And, in fact, the old experiments which attempted to find directly the just-noticeable difference have been mostly worked over again in new ways under the influence of the discussions arising out of the theory of error.

### (a) *The Older Forms of the Methods*

Ernst Heinrich Weber came upon his most important discoveries in the sphere of psychical measurement with the help of the simplest and most natural of methods. He tried to find directly the least stimulus difference that could just be noticed. Since it was by experiments of this kind that Weber proved the law that bears his name, the method of least differences held for a long time the first place. As so often happens with investigators, who see for the first time in broad outline a new field of science, Weber anticipated or pointed the way to almost all the methods of psychical measurement that were later developed. When in determining the sensitivity of the sense of touch he placed weights simultaneously on the finger and the forearm, whereupon the weight on the forearm appeared lighter, he was working according to what became later known as the method of equivalents.[1] He also let the same weights, which were in the ratio 39 : 40, be lifted many times, and maintained, on the ground of the frequency of the right judgments, that the majority of people would be able to distinguish by means of muscle-sensations two such weights without a previous long period of practice; in this he anticipated the method of right and wrong cases.[2]

The method used with such success by Weber was called by Fechner the method of just-noticeable differences and ranked first among the methods for measuring difference sensitivity.[3] In its use, for example, in investigating the fineness with which differences of weight can be distinguished, the method consists in determining the extent of the difference in the weight that is necessary in order to be just-noticeably perceived. Fechner saw the chief advantage of this method in the fact that the just-noticeable difference could be immediately perceived as the same for the sensation. The extent of the just-noticeable difference certainly leaves some free play to the subjective judgment, even though one may, so to say, come to some agreement with oneself as to the feeling of a small and just-sufficiently sensed difference and be able to reproduce this with sufficient accuracy in different tests. Now, although Fechner calls this method the most important tool of psychophysics, yet it is clear that he felt that its results are really of a preliminary nature, and that a real decision can be reached only by those methods that are founded upon the principles of the theory of error.

Alongside of the method of just-noticeable differences has often been placed the method of mean gradations. The

[1] *Tastsinn und Gemeingefühl*, p. 548.   [2] *Cf.* p. 128.
[3] *Elemente der Psychophysik*, I, 1860, pp. 71 *ff*.

chief idea of this method is to determine equally large differences of sensation by immediate judgment. In this way this method forms a natural continuation of the problem as formulated by Fechner for the methods of measurement. Instead of taking the roundabout way of just-noticeable differences, it appeared much more profitable to investigate the relations between the systems of stimulus and sensation by means of judging more than noticeable differences. Plateau[1] had been the first to use for psychical measurements in this sense the possibility of determining a sensation midway between a stronger and a weaker one with a fair degree of certainty. He asked eight persons who had had practice in painting to determine a gray midway between a pure white and a deep black, and he found the result to be almost identical with all of them. We cannot here go further into the numerous modifications of these methods, as, for example, the method of double stimuli introduced by Merkel[2] whereby a stimulus is to be found that gives twice as strong a sensation as a given stimulus. The theoretical importance of such a mean sensation is determined by one's general opinions of psychical measurement.

### (b) *The Influence of the Theory of Error*

After the method of just-noticeable differences Fechner ranks the method of right and wrong cases and the method of average error. The two latter attempt to determine the relation between the immediate results of observation and the values sought by psychical measurement on the basis of the theory of error. In the determination of absolute sensitivity the method of mean gradations goes over into the method of equivalents, where the observer has to

[1] *Bulletins de l'académie royale de Belgique*, t. XXXIII, 1872, p. 376.
[2] *Phil. Stud.*, Bd. IV, 1888, p. 545.

choose a stimulus that appears the same as a given one, other things being equal (*e. g.*, on a different part of the skin). In using the method of average error the observer has to arrange two stimuli so that they shall be equal; the average error made in doing this is brought into relation with the difference-threshold. The method of right and wrong cases calls for numerous judgments upon one and the same stimulus lying near to the difference-threshold. Rather hypothetical discussions in the theory of error are required in order to come to any definite conclusions as to the nature of the difference-threshold from the relation $\left[\dfrac{r}{n}\right]$ between the number of right cases ($r$) and the total number of cases ($n$), which results from employing this method.

In these methods also Fechner was not without predecessors. Especially in photometrical determinations had the importance of the average error been previously shown. Steinheil[1] had considered the average error, which was made in arranging two similarly bright fields in the prism photometer, as a measure for the possibility of differentiation of two brightnesses. And the method of right and wrong cases had been used in experiments as to the possibility of determining the differences of tone intensity, which had been carried out by Renz and Wolf under Vierordt's direction.[2]

The theoretical discussion, however, first arose because Fechner treated these methods according to the principles of the theory of error. In order to be able to draw definite conclusions from the size of the average error as regards the certainty of the observation, a knowledge of the distribution of the errors or of the law of error is necessary. The first attempts to arrive at the true value of a quantity from

---

[1] *Elemente der Helligkeitsmessungen am Sternenhimmel*, 1837. *Cf.* below, Chapter IX, 1 (*b*).

[2] *Vierordt's Archiv*, 1856, Heft 2, p. 185.

quantities that contain errors of observation are met with in the eighteenth century.[1] Roger Cotes (1722), in an investigation of the errors of values obtained in observation, compared the errors to weights of reciprocal value, which are to be added on to the separate points; the centre of gravity of such a system coincides then with the true value. The importance of the arithmetical mean of a series of observations of the same objective quantity was first recognized by Thomas Simpson in 1757. He showed also how the reliability of such a mean value increased with the increase of the observations. Lambert, in 1760, reached more accurate conclusions in his photometrical investigations. If negative and positive errors appear equally often, and if, further, the supposition is valid that large errors occur less often than small ones, then the arithmetical mean is the truest value. In Lambert's *Theorie der Zuverlässigkeit der Beobachtungen und Versuche* there are fairly arbitrary presuppositions as to the calculation of the mean.

A test of the method of finding the mean by the more accurate help of the theory of probability is first found in Lagrange.[2] Daniel Bernoulli, in a publication of the Saint Petersburg Academy on the compensation of errors of observation (1778), tried to supply the want of a special form for the law of the distribution of error. For the probability ($y$) of an error ($\Delta$) Bernoulli established the equation:

$$y = \sqrt{r^2 - \Delta^2}.$$

If we imagine the separate values $\Delta$ arranged along an abscissa, then the probability curve is a semicircle with the radius $r$ and the centre $\Delta = 0$. If $a, b, c \ldots$ are the observed values and $x$ the most probable value, then the er-

---

[1] *Cf.* the sketch of the history of the theory of error in G. F. Lipps, *Die psychischen Massmethoden*, 1906, pp. 33 *ff*.

[2] *Miscellania Taurinensia*, Bd. V, 1770–1773.

rors of observation ($\Delta$) are represented by the differences $a-x$, $b-x$, $c-x$.... The value $x$ itself is determined by the condition that the product

$$\sqrt{r^2-(x-a)^2} \cdot \sqrt{r^2-(x-b)^2} \cdot \sqrt{r^2-(x-c)^2}$$

be a maximum. With this Bernoulli had given a formal solution of the problem, but his law of error took for granted the same finite field of error for all series of observations. It was impossible by means of it to do justice to the differences in the certainty of observations, which are seen in various distributions of the errors as when they crowd around the middle value or are scattered over a larger area.

A strictly valid theory of error was first obtained by Gauss.[1] Assuming that by repeated immediate observations of a quantity the arithmetical mean of all the observations is the most probable value, he deduced for the probability ($y$) of an error ($\Delta$) the famous formula

$$y = \frac{h}{\sqrt{\pi}} e^{-h^2 \Delta^2},$$

where the parameter $h$ gives a measure for the accuracy of the observations. If, again, the observed values are denoted by $a, b, c, \ldots$ and the most probable value by $x$, then in this case the product

$$\frac{h}{\sqrt{\pi}} e^{-h^2(a-x)^2} \cdot \frac{h}{\sqrt{\pi}} e^{-h^2(b-x)^2} \cdot \frac{h}{\sqrt{\pi}} e^{-h^2(c-x)^2} \ldots$$

must be a maximum. And this is the case if the sum of

$$(a-x)^2 + (b-x)^2 + (c-x)^2 \ldots$$

be a minimum. And with this Gauss arrived again at the method of least squares, which he had used since 1795, and

[1] *Theoria motus corporum cœlestium*, 1809.

in regard to which he could prove that it retained the best combination of observations with any law of error.[1] An analogous method of treating observations without the substitution of a law of error had already been developed by Laplace in his *Théorie analytique des Probabilités* (1812). But it was Gauss who showed definitely that the mean error of a series of observations ought not to be defined as the mean of the simple errors but as the mean of the squares of the errors. And thus the problem of finding a measure for the reliability of a series of observations, which was first attacked by Lambert, was solved finally by Laplace and Gauss, not only in a special sense by the help of Gauss's Law of Error, but also in a general sense by the use of the mean of the squared errors.

Fechner took advantage of the help afforded by the theory of error and he worked upon the supposition that the pure errors, which remain after being separated from the constant errors, follow the ordinary laws of error. In that case the pure mean error could be set in reciprocal relation to the absolute value of the difference sensitivity. In the method of right and wrong cases he arrived at the relation between the relative number of right cases $\left(\frac{r}{n}\right)$ and the distribution curve of the errors by the consideration that a right judgment would always occur if the error process would allow the difference ($D$) between the two stimuli to appear in its true sense. Judgments of equality Fechner divided equally between the right and wrong cases, so that he had only to deal with two categories of judgment. If, then, the error process follows the laws of Gauss, then

$$\frac{r}{n} = \frac{1}{2} + \frac{h}{\sqrt{\pi}} \int_0^{hD} e^{-h^2 D^2} \, dD.$$

[1] *Theoria combinationis observationum erroribus minimis obnoxiæ*, 1821.

It follows further that out of $\frac{r}{n}$ we can calculate $h$, and this is a measure for the difference sensitivity. Since Fechner valued the usefulness of his methods in the main with respect to testing Weber's Law, the knowledge of this value $h$ was sufficient. If it remained constant as long as the stimulus difference $D$ kept the same relation to the normal stimulus, then the constancy of the relative difference sensitivity was guaranteed and with that the validity of Weber's Law. Besides this there resulted a purely mathematical relationship between the method of right and wrong cases and the mean error from the hypothesis that the measure of precision ($h$) is identical with the measure of precision resulting from the mean error $\frac{1}{\Delta_m \sqrt{\pi}}$.

The most important changes in these methods resulted from the different ways in which the judgments of equality could be regarded. G. E. Müller, in his *Grundlegung der Psychophysik* (1879), introduced a new point of view in regard to method, inasmuch as he made a distinction between the fact of there being a difference-threshold and the occurrence of chance errors of observation. The judgments of equality ($z$) are not equivalent to plus or minus judgments of difference. They seem rather to point to the fact of the threshold ($i$) being present, whereas the other judgments come within the scope of the error process. In this way he arrived at the following equations:

$$\frac{r}{n} = \frac{1}{2} + \frac{h}{\sqrt{\pi}} \int_0^{h(D-i)} e^{-h^2 D^2} dD;$$

$$\frac{z}{n} = \frac{h}{\sqrt{\pi}} \left( \int_0^{h(D+i)} e^{-h^2 D^2} dD - \int_0^{h(D-i)} e^{-h^2 D^2} dD \right).$$

The relation between the values $h$ and $i$ would thus become an empirical question to which an answer could be given by means of experiments.

The most recent developments of the methods of measurement have been in part influenced by the attempt to find an analytic presentation of the frequency of judgments which shall be free from the special presuppositions of Gauss's Law of Error. Indeed, Fechner had tried to give due attention to the asymmetry of a series of observations. In an asymmetrical distribution the arithmetical mean no longer coincides with the most probable value. The deviations must, therefore, be calculated from the "density value" or median. We have, then, an error curve on both sides of the median, and its course is the same as the error curve that is common to both sides in a symmetrical distribution. With such a two-sided or divided Gauss's Law Fechner tried to represent asymmetrical types of distribution in his posthumous *Kollektivmasslehre* (1897).[1]

On the other hand, along with the distrust of the usefulness of such mathematical aids, the inclination grew up to determine psychical values without making use of complicated formulæ by means of a so-called immediate method. In the "method of many cases" there are not only the above-mentioned categories of judgment but also the cases of decided difference, of more-than-just-noticeable difference. It had been found necessary to give a different treatment to these different classes of judgments, and this led to the attempt to substitute for the analytic representation of the frequencies of judgment a frequency curve formed from the empirical distribution of the judgments and then to make the area enclosed by such a curve, called by G. E. Müller the ideal area, the basis for further calculation. This emancipation from one-sided mathematical presuppo-

[1] *Cf.* G. F. Lipps, *op. cit.*, pp. 89 *ff*.

sitions naturally led to an expansion of the field in which the methods of psychical measurement were used. And this was not only true for experiments according to the impression method, for which the methods of measurement were at first particularly adapted, but also for many experiments according to the expression method.

### (c) Connection with the Expression Methods

These, the most recent methods of experimental psychology, were originally physiological or registration methods, the use of which for psychological purposes had arisen out of chance observations. We have already remarked briefly on the reaction method;[1] but the other expression methods also arose out of physiological investigations. After the observations of C. Bell[2] on the bodily expressions of the separate affections, the work of Darwin[3] is the best known. He found such an intimate connection between the emotions and their forms of expression that the latter could scarcely exist if the body remained passive. But the real psychological importance of the organic changes for the rise of the emotions was first pointed out by William James. The same idea was worked out in greater detail by C. Lange,[4] who brought seven of the most important affections, *e. g.*, disappointment, anxiety, fright, etc., into relation with definite changes in voluntary innervation, which are seen in dilation or expansion of the blood-vessels.

The chief advance in method and technique is closely allied to the work of Mosso and Féré. Mosso gave psychology the plethysmograph, which he originally used for the purpose of measuring changes in the flow of blood to

---
[1] *Cf.* p. 132.
[2] *The Anatomy and Physiology of Expression*, 1806.
[3] *The Expression of the Emotions.*
[4] *Über Gemütsbewegungen.* German translation by Kurella, 1887.

the brain. This was done in an indirect manner, namely, by measuring the corresponding fluctuations in the volume of blood in one of the larger limbs.[1] This secondary purpose of the plethysmograph then became changed into its chief purpose, and the plethysmographic curve became one of the most important aids for registering the symptoms of the feelings and the affections. Féré[2] investigated chiefly muscle capacity and the distribution of blood in the organism during simple sensory impressions. He found that each pleasant sensation was accompanied by an increase and each unpleasant one by a decrease of energy in the muscle, and similarly that each feeling of pleasure was accompanied by an increase and each feeling of displeasure by a decrease in the volume of blood in the limbs. The experimental results of Féré only partly coincided with the observations drawn by Lange from practical life. This, along with the very small number of results in this field up to that time, led Lehmann[3] to make a more thorough investigation of the feelings, which at once changed the whole point of view for the expression method. The theoretical discussion of the results obtained by Lehmann led to numerous investigations of the symptomatology of the feelings and the emotions, and with these results every new theory of feeling had to reckon.[4]

The narrower group of expression methods known as the reaction methods are more susceptible to treatment by the use of the mathematical methods of psychical measurement. Here there took place, on a smaller scale, the same process of development as all methods of measurement go through in their metamorphosis from physical to psychical

[1] Mosso, *Über den Kreislauf des Blutes im menschlichen Gehirn*, 1881.
[2] *Sensation et Mouvement*, p. 64.
[3] *Die Hauptgesetze des menschlichen Gefühlslebens*. German translation by Bendixen, 1892.
[4] *Cf.* Chapter XII, 1.

methods. At first interest centred only in absolute reaction times under varying circumstances. To-day the distribution of the separate reactions and their relative values have become of no less importance for the interpretation of psychical behavior.

# CHAPTER IX

**PSYCHICAL MEASUREMENT**

The principle of psychical measurement belongs, in the main, to the most recent psychology. The real foundation of psychical measurement by Fechner is preceded by a fairly long preliminary history. Out of the controversy over Fechner's psychophysics two new theories of psychical measurement arose, the differences between which can be most clearly perceived in their explanation of the facts connected with Weber's Law. These are the theories of G. E. Müller and W. Wundt.

## 1. Early History of Psychical Measurement

Although we can speak of the concept of psychical measurement only since the time of Fechner, yet the formulation of such a principle was prepared for by many things before his time. Remarks as to the possibility of psychical measurement arose particularly in connection with the question as to whether mathematics could be used in the field of psychology. A theoretical discussion of the underlying idea precedes the strict conceptual formulation of it by Fechner, and this mostly centred round the question as to whether ideas of measurement were applicable in connection with psychical phenomena. Besides a few really empirical attempts at measurement, this early history of psychical measurement shows also the grouping together of these observations into a law, *i. e.*, Weber's Law, which from that time on became the principal fact in the field of psychical measurement.

## (a) The Earliest Suggestions of Psychical Measurement

The opinion that psychical phenomena cannot be mathematically represented is of very early origin.[1] We find it already in Malebranche[2] in his statement that we can have clear ideas of number and extent, but that in comparing mental states we can perceive clearly only differences in quality which can never be represented by a quantitative expression. Malebranche drew a sharp line of distinction between the physical stimulus and the corresponding mental state. The relations between our tone sensations certainly point to regular relations with the objective number of oscillations, but the differentiation of different tones takes place not by means of clear ideas but by means of the feelings.

Leibniz further prepared the way for the use of the mathematical point of view, inasmuch as he carried over to sensation qualities the principle of continuity, which he had formulated with such clearness for mechanical phenomena.[3] The sensation quality of yellow or of white comes under the concept of a continuous, extended quantity. Of course, Leibniz thought that he was here dealing only with an analogy of his concept of quantity, which in metaphysics and, therefore, in psychology could not be directly used.

In the eighteenth century our problem centres around the question as to whether psychical phenomena, in their character of intensive quantities, could be classed under concepts of measurement which presuppose a summation of elements. After Wolff had set up the demand for a science of psychometry, Ploucquet[4] questioned very decidedly the possibility of

[1] *Cf.* Itelson, *Arch. f. Gesch. der Phil.*, Bd. III, 1890, pp. 282 *ff*.
[2] *Recherche de la vérité*, 1675, XI.
[3] *Math. Schr.*, edited by Gerhardt, Bd. VI, pp. 99 *f*.
[4] *Commentatio de Arte Characteristica, Einleitung zu Methodus calculandi in logicis*, 1763.

using the number concept in regard to intensive quantities. He opposed the universal characteristic set up by Leibniz as well as the psychometry of Wolff. The intensity of any sensation can in no way be made up of parts. If I add to a certain light a less intensive one, the first light does not thereby become brighter, as it ought to if the two lights were simply added. Kant for some time entertained the thought of such a composition of sensations out of a number of equal parts. He promised in a letter to Schütz (1785) to add an appendix on the theory of the soul to his *Metaphysical Foundations of Natural Science*. The basic principle of the anticipations of sense-impressions ought to help us to a "Mathesis intensorum." It is well known that the mathematical principles of pure reason teach us "how phenomena, according to their appearance or according to the reality of their perception, can be produced according to the rules of a mathematical synthesis, and that, therefore, in the one case as in the other, number values can be used. I can, for example, put together and decide *a priori* that the intensity of the sensations of sunlight is equal to, say, two hundred thousand times the brightness of the moon." Kant, meanwhile, did not draw any conclusion of interest to psychology from this, for precisely the supposed impossibility of using mathematical concepts of size became his chief argument against the possibility of psychology being regarded as a science.[1] It is possible that the influence of Ploucquet led to this change in his opinions.

Just about this time Eberhard[2] came surprisingly near to Fechner's principal thought. He finds, in connection with the limitation of mental power, "that the comparison of the values of images according to the degree of clearness

---

[1] *Cf.* pp. 151 *f.*
[2] *Allgemeine Theorie des Denkens und Empfindens*, 1776 and 1786, p. 66.

leads to a mathematics of the soul. In the comparison of sensations with each other the unit of measurement would have to be an unnoticed image which, of course, would be useless for this purpose just because it is unnoticed."

In the nineteenth century the old arguments for and against psychical measurement are repeated. Galuppi[1] opposed the possibility of adding sensation intensities with the argument that quantitative determination always belongs to the object of sensation but never to the sensation itself. Others regarded the possibility of psychical measurements as quite natural and agreed to it as a matter of course. In the long-forgotten *Psychologie* of Eschenmayer we note the remark that "a perfect theory of the senses must bring everything qualitative that works upon our senses into measurable relations subject to the calculus, and each quality must possess a certain value in dynamics." [2]

### (b) *Weber's Law and Its Preliminary History*

The anticipations of Weber's Law do not take us back into the field of the old psychology. Here, if anywhere, we see the origin of one of the most important laws of psychology based upon the experiences gathered during observations made for the purposes of natural science.

Errors of observation and the inaccuracy of our sense-perceptions led to an investigation of the subjective factors of sense-perception. Older than the attempts to arrive at a quantitative determination of the capacity of human sense-organs is the knowledge that there certainly exists a limit to their capacity. Even if we neglect for the moment the very general recognition of the relativity of sensation, we can trace a special form of this thought, which to-day gets

[1] *Saggio filosofico sulla critica della conoscenza*, 1819.
[2] *Op. cit.*, 1822, p. 48.

the name of the determination of the difference-threshold, right back to the Scholastic Buridan. He pointed out various changes of our perceptions due to purely subjective conditions, as, for example, the fact that gray near black seems whiter than gray near white. In this connection he notes that not every minute addition to the outer stimulus corresponds to a change in the sensation, and this is really a recognition of the fact of the difference-threshold.[1]

The first quantitative experiments in modern times were performed in the field of visual sensations. Lambert set himself the task, in his *Photometry*,[2] to determine the capacity of the eye for the differentiation of brightness. Since light cannot be measured by a photometer, like warmth by a thermometer, we have to depend solely upon our eye for the determination of the intensity of light, and the judgments of the eye are unreliable for various reasons. The contractions and dilations of the pupil, the changes in sensitivity of the optic nerve according to the surrounding illumination, are all causes that may give rise to illusions. And, besides these things, it is a common characteristic of all sensations for the stronger to suppress the weaker. A candle in the sunlight seems to possess no brightness, and yet the light of this same candle may so suppress the light that rises from decaying wood as to make the latter appear as if it did not exist.[3]

His further investigations are based upon his "axiom of photometry," according to which a phenomenon is the same as long as it affects the same eye in the same way. If the eye looks at two juxtapositive objects at the same time, it is able to give a judgment as regards likeness or difference;

[1] *De anima*, II, 14, *f.* 12 *c*: *sic etiam de luce tu non percipies statim parvum augmentum lucis.*

[2] *Photometria sive de mensura et gradibus luminis, colorum et umbræ*, 1760.

[3] *Op. cit.*, p. 10.

but a definite statement of the degree by which two brightnesses differ is not possible. This remark is of special importance for us because of the later controversy, which arose out of the conception of the more than just-noticeable difference. If, however, the eye judges two brightnesses as equal, we are forced to assume that the brightnesses closely approximate equality. And yet there is always a minimal difference present which escapes observation. In order to determine this difference, Lambert illuminated a perfectly white and smooth wall by means of a candle. Shielding the eye from the direct light and standing some distance away, he measured off the region within which, according to the judgment of the eye, the brightness of the wall appeared to be constant. The size of this region of no longer noticeable difference decreased with the absolute brightness; even the relation to the first brightness was not a constant quantity, for it increased from .04 to .07 with the decrease in brightness. This problem, which led Lambert right up to the facts of Weber's Law, was not pursued further by him; he was satisfied in showing that this unnoticeable or just-noticeable difference in brightness was very small.

Bouguer, a contemporary of Lambert, possessing perhaps less talent for scientific observation but more favored by luck in his experimental work, carried on similar experiments on the differentiation of given brightnesses.[1] His method has become known under the name of Bouguer's shadow experiment. One source of light ($L_1$) is gradually moved backward from a rod ($s$) until the shadow of this becomes unnoticeable on a field illuminated by a second source of light ($L_2$), of the same intensity as $L_1$, from a constant distance. In this way Bouguer found that a given light intensity must be increased by $\frac{1}{64}$ if the increase is to be

[1] *Traité d'optique sur la gradation de la lumière par Lacaille*, 1760, p. 51.

noticeable. And this proportion proved itself to be independent of the light intensity. Just as a loud noise prevents us from hearing a weaker one, so in the presence of a bright light we are not able to see another of much less intensity if both of them affect the same part of the retina. Arago[1] later repeated these experiments of Bouguer and extended them by making use of colored lights. He declared positively that the just-noticeable relative difference remained constant for different brightnesses.[2]

In an extensive investigation on electrical photometry, Masson[3] described a new and simple method for the determination of the just-noticeable difference. He set in rotation white disks, upon which a short piece of a narrow black sector of variable breadth was introduced. By means of fusion there appeared on the disk a gray band, which by varying the breadth of this black sector could be reduced until just noticeable. These disks of Masson have found their place in psychophysics and have proved themselves very useful. The independence of the size of the sector (thus reduced to a gray band just-noticeably different from the background) from the intensity of the absolute brightness shows immediately that the just-noticeable relative brightness differences are constant, and this is precisely the problem of Weber's Law.

The usual immediate judgments of the brightness differences of stars in astronomy were a further cause prompting to photometrical investigations. Since the time of Hipparchus the stellar magnitudes had been divided into classes according to the impression of their brightness. Each class was separated from the next by a supposed equal degree of brightness. Since the investigations of J. Her-

---

[1] *Ann. de Chim. et de Phys.*, 1845, t. XIV, p. 150.
[2] *Populäre Astronomie*, edited by Hankel, I, p. 168.
[3] *Ann. de Chim. et de Phys.*, 1845, t. XIV, p. 150.

schel, which have now been authoritative for a long time, the true brightnesses of these stellar classes form a decreasing quadratic series of the form 1, $\frac{1}{4}$, $\frac{1}{8}$, $\frac{1}{16}$. . . . Fechner later expected to find, by the right choice of the mean brightness of a star of the first magnitude, that the data observed could be represented with greater truth by a diminishing geometrical progression.[1] The meaning of a constant brightness proportion for the different classes of stars could, however, only arise out of the fundamental laws of Fechner's psychophysics. More immediately leading to the facts of Weber's Law were the investigations of the accuracy with which such photometrical determinations of the objective brightness of stars could be made. Steinheil[2] tested on the prism photometer the dependence of the size of the error, which is made in equating two light intensities, upon the size of the intensities to be compared. His observations showed that it is possible to arrange a similar brightness on two fields with great exactness. The uncertainty of each separate judgment of this kind does not exceed $\frac{1}{38}$ of the total brightness, however great or little this may be.[3] Here, then, we find formulated for light intensity that fact which Weber recognized as a universally valid one.

In accordance with the wide range which Weber's Law covers, we note that its preliminary history branches out into very different directions. All the experiments we have so far considered were based upon the peculiarities of the sensations. In the theory of the feelings, however, we find also an independent starting-point for similar considerations which have a mathematical tradition, although the feelings would certainly prove themselves one of the most

[1] *Elem. d. Psych.*, pp. 160 ff.
[2] "Elemente der Helligkeitsmessungen am Sternenhimmel," in *Abh. d. math.-physik. Kl. d. Königl. bay. Akad.*, 1837.
[3] *Op. cit.*, p. 14.

unsuitable departments for the empirical confirmation of any such mathematical laws. In the dependence of the so-called "fortune morale" upon the "fortune physique" we have even an anticipation of the formula in which Fechner expressed the facts of Weber's Law. Bernoulli[1] formulated the principle that the value of external possessions is to be measured by the increase which accrues to the possessor. Any increase in value is merely an increase that is proportional to the external goods already possessed. He expressed this principle by a differential formula and by the logarithmic relation that results. Later on, Laplace[2] argued from the difference between the absolute and relative value. If the latter is reciprocal to the total possessions ($x$) to which it is added, then the increase of the "fortune morale" can be expressed by $\frac{k \cdot dx}{x}$, where $k$ is a constant.[3] If $y$ denotes the "fortune morale" corresponding to the "fortune physique" ($x$), then it follows that $y = k \cdot log\, x + log\, h$; the arbitrary constant $h$ can be found from the two dependent values $x$ and $y$. And, lastly, Poisson[4] arrived at the same thought. He called the relative increase in value "espérance morale" in contrast to "espérance mathématique." Above all, the practical application of this principle seemed of importance to him, although to us it appears very peculiar with its supposed proof of the rules of practical life by means of the integral calculus.

Weber himself formulated the law which bears his name in 1834, basing it upon experiments that he had carried on in different departments of sensation. If we notice a difference in comparing two values, we do not perceive the difference of the values but the relation of the

[1] *Specimen theoriæ novæ de mensura sortis*, 1738.
[2] *Théorie analytique des Probabilités*, p. 187.
[3] *Op. cit.*, p. 432.
[4] *Recherches sur la probabilité*, p. 72.

difference to the two values we are comparing.[1] In the now classical monograph *Der Tastsinn und das Gemeingefühl* (1846), he summed up the results of his investigations on the smallest just-noticeable differences of lines and weights, and laid it down that the recognition of the just-noticeable difference is dependent entirely upon the relation of the difference to the total value.

As supposed evidence he also brought forward the results of Delezenne, who thought he had proved that a tone always becomes just-noticeably out of tune at the same relative difference in the number of oscillations. The investigations of Delezenne at the end of the eighteenth century had followed the dispute between Marpurg and Kirnberger, the supporters of the arhythmic and rhythmic theory of temperature. Among a great number of fruitless theoretical discussions the idea arose that possibly because of the imperfection of the organ of hearing the ultimate deviations from the pure interval, which can never be avoided on an instrument, remain unnoticed.[2] It is strange that, in spite of this appeal to psychological experience, experimental investigation was not taken up in Germany. Delezenne was the first to start his famous experiments in order to contradict the statement of Galin that one could never get any exact knowledge of the length of the strings that produce the tones of the scale.[3] In contradistinction to these only the most recent investigations have proved that the absolute difference-threshold is constant.

In comparison with the earlier formulation of the law of

[1] *Ann. Anot.*, p. 172: *In observando discrimine rerum inter se comparatarum non differentiam rerum sed rationem differentiae ad magnitudinem rerum inter se comparatarum percipimus.*

[2] *Cf.* the article "Temperatur," by Sulzer, *Allgemeine Theorie der schönen Künste*, 1778, Bd. II, p. 283.

[3] "Mémoires sur les valeurs numériques des notes de la Gamme," in *Recueil des travaux de la soc. des scienc., de l'agric. et des arts de Lille*, 1826 et 1827, pp. 1 *ff*.

1834, the later one undoubtedly shows a certain restriction of the law. It does not include so many of the facts of experience as the former did, and yet in its generalization of the observed facts it remains a splendid example of Weber's cautious but, nevertheless, always ingenious method of investigation. Above all, this regularity in the phenomena did not yet appear to him as a principle for the measurement of sensation. He rather looked upon the immediate recognition of the relations between whole values as a most interesting psychological phenomenon.[1] He did not in any way anticipate the conclusions which later on Fechner drew from this law. It was for Weber only applicable to the value of the just-noticeable difference.

### 2. The Founding of Psychical Measurement by Fechner

The decisive step leading from all these separate cases to the conception of a new principle was taken by Fechner. In him the older attempts to find a mathematical principle of measurement and the newer experimental methods and ideas meet.[2] First of all, Fechner developed a principle of measurement for sensitivity in connection with facts of experience. We are able, for example, to make an attempt at measuring the size of those stimuli which produce equally large sensations or equally large differences of sensation. But in these concepts of absolute sensitivity and of difference sensitivity assumed here we have not yet arrived at a principle for the measurement of sensation. If the size of the sensation could be considered proportional to the size of the stimulus, then it would be easy to pass on to some kind of measurement of the sensations. Such an assumption is, however, not proved by any facts. To find such we must first of all discover the function existing between

[1] *Op. cit.*, p. 561.    [2] *Cf.* p. 129.

the two elements, stimulus and sensation, and to do this we have to depend upon the judgment of equality within the field of sensation—the only judgment possible in our experience. In theory, then, this measure of sensation must be obtained by dividing up the sensation into equal increments, out of which the sensation is built up, beginning with zero. The number of these increments is determined by the number of the corresponding additions of stimulus, which are able to produce equal additions of sensation. To arrive at this function we make use of Weber's universally valid law that equal relative additions of stimuli correspond to equal additions of sensation.

The following is the most important of the mass of formulæ which Fechner worked out: If $\beta$ is the stimulus to which a very small addition, $d\beta$, is made, then the relative increase of the stimulus is $\dfrac{d\beta}{\beta}$. Let the sensation dependent upon the stimulus $\beta$ be called $\gamma$, and a very small change in the sensation be $d\gamma$. Weber's Law can then be expressed by the equation $d\gamma = \dfrac{K.d\beta}{\beta}$, where $K$ is a constant. This equation was called by Fechner the fundamental formula. If we integrate we get $\gamma = K \, log \, \beta + C$, where $C$ is the constant of integration. If $C$ is determined by the condition that the sensation $\gamma$ disappear at the threshold value of the stimulus $\beta = b$, then we have $0 = K \, log \, b + C$ and, therefore, $C = -K \, log \, b$ and $\gamma = K \, (log \, \beta - log \, b)$. This equation is the measurement formula. Its formulation would be illusory if the fact of the threshold did not exist. For example, if the sensation disappeared only when the value of the stimulus was nothing, then we would get for $C$ an infinite value and no finite expression could be given for any sensation value.

We need yet another formula as a measure for the sensed

differences. Let $u$ be the difference that is sensed between the sensations $\gamma$ and $\gamma'$, and $\phi$ the corresponding stimulus relation $\frac{\beta}{\beta'}$, and, further, let the relative threshold $v$ have the same relation to $\phi$ as the simple threshold $b$ to the stimulus $\beta$, then it follows that $u = k \ (log \ \phi - log \ v)$. This equation, the so-called formula for difference measurement, could be looked upon as the one approximating most closely to Weber's ideas. And yet what is for Fechner most important in Weber's experiments is not the fact that a just-noticeable difference in sensation follows a relatively proportionate stimulus, but rather the supposedly equivalent fact, namely, that in such a case an equal difference in sensation is observed. Only the analogy between the difference-threshold and the stimulus-threshold allows this formula for the measurement of difference to be deduced from the first or measurement formula.

For Fechner an important supplement to Weber's Law was his so-called parallel law, which stated that if the sensitivity for two stimuli changed in equal proportion the sensation of their difference remained the same. This law forms one of the bridges between outer and inner psychophysics, since it carries over Weber's Law to the psychophysical activity produced by the stimulus. This inner psychophysics of Fechner has remained a realm of shadows. But the underlying thought of his outer psychophysics, his bold coupling of the psychical to the physical world by means of an elegant mathematical formula, even if it was to be contradicted later, started a movement of psychological thought the after effects of which are still with us at the present day.

## 3. Discussions Arising out of Fechner's Psychophysics

### (a) Objections and Attacks

The two decades following the publication of Fechner's *Psychophysik* (1860) are filled with polemics directed against his proud system of thought.[1] We find at first attempts made so to transform Fechner's formulæ that they may more accurately represent the facts of observation. A need of this kind was felt by Helmholtz[2] in the field of visual sensations in regard to the upper and lower deviations from Weber's Law, which are much greater than Fechner had supposed from his own experiments. To do justice to them, Helmholtz formulated the following differential equation:

$$\delta\gamma = \frac{c \cdot \delta\beta}{(a+\beta)\,(A+\beta)}.$$

In this equation $c$, $a$, and $A$ are constants; $a$ is the weak inner excitation independent of the outer stimulus; $A$ is a very high value. If $a$ disappears in regard to $\beta$, and $\beta$ in regard to $A$, the equation is transformed into Fechner's fundamental formula. Integration leads to:

$$\gamma = \frac{c}{A-a} \cdot \log nat \frac{a+\beta}{A+\beta} + Const.$$

This formula of measurement is based upon Fechner's considerations of the scope of the stimulus; but besides this it indicates the maximum of the relative difference sensitivity. If Helmholtz ever did agree with the psychophysical interpretation that Fechner gave to Weber's Law,

[1] For a summary of these controversies, see Fechner, *Revision der Hauptpunkte der Psychophysik*, 1877, and *In Sachen der Psychophysik*, 1882.

[2] *Physiol. Optik*, 1867, p. 313.

it was obviously, as in this case, the alleged simplicity of the explanation which had attracted him.[1]

Aubert[2] raised much severer objections against the validity of Weber's Law. Without going beyond the range of thought involved in Fechner's psychophysics, he stated the results of his experiments on the supposition that the values $\frac{\delta\beta}{\beta}$ stand in inverse relation to the logarithms of $\beta$, if the logarithm of $\beta$ for a certain definite small value of $\beta$ and also the corresponding $\frac{\delta\beta}{\beta}$ is put equal to 1.

Numerous objections, which were directed against the assumed experimental verification of Weber's Law, were brought forward by Mach.[3] But more important was his contention that the formulæ of outer psychophysics could not by any means be carried over to inner psychophysics. The sensation depends directly upon the stimulus but, on the other hand, indirectly upon the psychophysical activity. This psychophysical activity or nervous excitation and the sensation run continually parallel with each other and cannot be anything else than proportional to each other.

This proportional relationship between sensation and psychophysical activity introduced into the discussion by Mach was made by Bernstein[4] the foundation for a purely physiological interpretation of Weber's Law. Bernstein recognized Fechner's formulæ of measurement but put the sensation proportional to the number of ganglion cells in the brain, through which the nervous excitation passes. Let the whole space which it fills be called $S$ and its density

---

[1] *Cf.* pp. 126 *f.*
[2] *Physiologie der Netzhaut*, 1865, pp. 49 *ff.*
[3] "Über die physiologische Wirkung räumlich verteilter Lichtreize," in *Wiener Sitzungsber.*, 1868, Bd. 68, p. 11.
[4] "Zur Theorie des Fechnerschen Gesetzes der Empfindung," in *Reichert-Duboissches Archiv*, 1868, pp. 388 *ff*. *Untersuchungen über den Erregungsvorgang im Nerven- und Muskelsysteme*, 1871, pp. 166 *ff.*

$a$. Then according to our fundamental hypothesis the sensation $\gamma$ will be measured by $\gamma = a \cdot S$. Further, $S$ must be expressed as a function of the stimulus $\beta$ and of the threshold value $b$, with which the nervous excitation $y$ disappears on the border of the circle through which it radiates. The loss that $y$ suffers after it has passed through the spatial element $\delta s$ must, because of the weakening of $y$ due to its spreading out, be put proportional to the growth of $as$ to $a\delta s$, to the intensity of $y$ at the border of the space measured by $s$, and, thirdly, to a constant $k$, which takes into consideration the specific resistance of the central elements. Therefore, we have $\delta y = -k \cdot a \cdot y \cdot \delta s$
and
$$log\ nat\ y = -kas + Const.$$
If $y = \beta$, then $s = 0$; and if $y = b$, then $s = S$. Therefore
$$k \cdot a \cdot S = log\ nat\ \frac{\beta}{b}.$$
Using our first equation, we now get
$$\gamma = \frac{1}{k} \cdot log\ nat\ \frac{\beta}{b},$$
which expresses the empirical facts of Weber's Law. The most doubtful of Bernstein's presuppositions is that the nervous excitation becomes weakened through each cell in proportion to its intensity as it reaches each cell, because the nervous impulse is nowhere limited by any such law. Of course the fact of the stimulus-threshold is advanced and made to mean a degree of nervous excitation that is too small to be carried along to the brain; but this external analogy does not help much. In spite of this, Bernstein's hypothesis was the model for a whole series of attempts at a physiological interpretation.

Of more importance than such hypothetical physiological constructions were the discussions as to the purely psychological consequences of Fechner's law. One line of thought, which was very often to be repeated later, was based upon the method of middle gradations used by Plateau.[1] Plateau maintained that the sameness of the impressions of a copperplate engraving in very different illuminations could be best explained by the fact that the relations of the sensations and not their differences remained constant. Plateau put the formula of measurement in this form:

$$\gamma = k \cdot \beta^p,$$

where $p$ and $k$ are constants and $p$ always smaller than 1. The fundamental formula must therefore take this form:

$$\frac{\delta\gamma}{\gamma} = p \cdot \frac{\delta\beta}{\beta}.$$

In general, Brentano shows his agreement with such a formula when he explains the fact of Weber's Law by saying that every increase of sensation is noticeable as equal if it retains the same relation to the intensity of the sensation to which it is added.[2] Apart from this, Brentano questioned altogether the possibility of using any principles of measurement in regard to psychical phenomena. This position is a necessary consequence of the point of view of which he made use in distinguishing between psychical and physical phenomena.[3] This hypothesis of a constant relation between two just-noticeably different sensations gained a fairly wide recognition. Überhorst[4] expressed it by saying that similar sensations, which can just be differentiated, always differ from each other by a small fraction of their own intensity. This was the form that many psychologists considered the simplest expression of Weber's Law.

Delbœuf's[5] position has been somewhat changeable. He originally assumed that each sense-organ, even without being

[1] *Cf.* p. 222.   [2] *Psychol. v. emp. Standp.*, 1874, p. 90.
[3] *Cf.* pp. 84, 160 *f.*
[4] *Die Entstehung der Gesichtswahrnehmung*, 1876.
[5] *Etude psychophysique*, Bruxelles, 1873.

affected by a stimulus, was in a state of excitation (c). To avoid the threshold and negative sensation values he put

$$\delta\gamma = K \cdot \frac{\delta\beta}{c+\beta},$$

from which we get

$$\gamma = K \log \frac{c+\beta}{c}.$$

This hypothesis seemed to be verified by experiments which he carried on in reference to brightness according to the method suggested by Plateau, and Fechner welcomed this as a specially convincing verification of his law.

Delbœuf[1] himself, however, later arrived at other conclusions. He formed the idea that the oscillatory activity of the sensory nerves, the value of which he denoted by $p$, tries to get into equilibrium with the activity ($p'$) of the outer stimulus. A sensation exists as long as the equilibrium is not attained, and according as $p$ or $p'$ has the upper hand there results a negative (*e. g.*, cold, dark) or a positive (*e. g.*, warmth, light) sensation. As long as the nerve has not yet reached a state of equilibrium along with the stimulus it remains in a state of strain or tension. The sensation is proportional to the work $T$, by means of which the change of the inner oscillatory state and of the position of the parts takes place; and this work $T$ is to be determined in the same manner as, for example, in the isothermal change of pressure and volume of a gas. According to which we have

$$\gamma = c \cdot \log \frac{p'}{p},$$

where $c$ is a constant. Delbœuf considered Fechner's conception of a negative sensation as particularly contradic-

[1] *Théorie de la sensibilité*, Bruxelles, 1876; "La loi psychophysique, Hering contre Fechner," *Revue philosophique*, 1877, pp. 225 ff.

tory. Such a negative sensation is absolutely impossible, since a sensation must necessarily be something. Delbœuf's own formulæ were all very carefully constructed, so that no negative sensation values might be deduced from them.

The difficulties arising out of the concept of negative sensations form the chief argument of Langer[1] against Fechner's law. Negative sensation values must certainly be, according to Langer, such that, when added to equally large positive values, they will give the value $0$. Suppose we have two finite stimuli, one of which produces the sensation $\gamma$, and the other the sensation $-\gamma$ below the threshold; then, if both act at the same time, the sensation $0$ must result. Since this is known not to happen in experience, Langer thought that sensations below the threshold should be called "small sensations," which, because of their slight intensity, are not able to rise to consciousness. The stimulus-threshold would then become a sensation-threshold, and thus the difficulty would be solved in a manner similar to Wundt's solution.[2]

The most numerous attacks on Fechner's law were due to Hering.[3] Weber's Law, he contends, is not a correct deduction from the experiments; for these latter merely prove that the difference in sensation remains always just noticeable with constancy of the relative difference in stimulus. It is quite arbitrary to assume that with different degrees of stimulus the just-noticeable difference in sensation is the same. A second difficulty lies in the considerable empirical deviations from Weber's Law; as long as these deviations cannot be explained as arising from the peculiarities of the sense-organs, nor yet the necessity of the law theoretically proved, then Weber's Law must be con-

[1] *Grundlagen der Psychophysik, eine kritische Untersuchung*, 1876.
[2] See below, pp. 262 *ff*.
[3] " Über Fechners psychologisches Gesetz," *Wien. Sitzungsber.*, Bd. LXXII, 1875.

sidered as a very uncertain hypothesis.[1] The teleological consequences also lead astray. For example, the perception of the relation of two extensive or intensive values, $\beta$ and $\beta'$, must change if both of these change even in the same relationship. How could the mind correctly perceive the relations of the outer world if no proportion existed between the occurrences of the outer world and those of our inner world? This objection seems to be particularly striking and seems to apply well to extensive psychical values; a line twice as long as another is, as a rule, seen twice as long. Along with this Hering brought forward the still more general *a priori* objection that between physical and psychical processes there exists an immediate dependence upon each other which is at once recognized as a dependence due to cause and effect; while, on the other hand, a complicated law of these relations is very difficult to understand.

As an experimental counter-proof against Fechner's law, Hering brought forward his own experiments with weights, in which he investigated the comparing of more-than-noticeable differences.[2] If to one galvanic plate lying on the hand another plate is added, this addition appears smaller than if five plates are added to five lying on the hand. Experiments of this kind were of great importance because they tested at first hand in experience the generalization contained in Fechner's law. Their results seemed to show that more-than-noticeable differences are by no means judged as equal when they retain the same ratio to the beginning or normal stimulus, but that they are judged the same when they are absolutely and not relatively equal.

Much smaller is the number of those psychologists who accepted Fechner's formulæ without making any change or who brought forward new points of view to justify Weber's Law. To the latter belongs J. J. Müller with his

[1] *Op. cit.*, p. 38.  [2] *Op. cit.*, pp. 14 *ff.*

attempt to substantiate the usefulness of Fechner's fundamental law.[1] He started with the assumption that even with a constant stimulus there took place, because of the oscillations of the nervous excitability, a continual change in the sensation which might just as well be produced by a changing stimulus with a constant nervous excitability. In order to be able to differentiate subjectively these two kinds of changes in sensation from each other, the sensation difference caused by the variation of the stimulus must be independent of the nervous excitability and the sensation difference caused by the variation of the excitability must be independent of the stimulus. Müller, assuming that the nervous process is proportional to the intensity of the stimulus and the nervous excitability, proved that the above demand could be satisfied only if the sensation increases proportionally to the logarithm of the nervous process.

## (b) *Fechner's Reply*

Fechner answers all these objections with a counter-criticism[2] which in the most important questions retained the same point of view as laid down in the *Elemente*. Only in a few special empirical points does he admit modification or limitation, as, for example, when he says that Weber's Law taken in a generalized form can be applied with assurance only to differences in the intensity of sensations. On the other hand, the fundamental interpretation of this law, which is made firmer by being transferred from outer to inner psychophysics, remains absolutely untouched. The inner psychophysical activity is proportional to the stimulus, but the sensation depends logarithmically upon this activity. The empirical deviations, which cannot be denied,

[1] *Sitzungsber. d. Königl. Sächs. Ges. d. Wissensch.*, *math.-phys. Kl.*, 1870, pp. 328 *ff*.
[2] *In Sachen der Psychophysik*, 1877.

do not rest upon any contradiction of this logarithmic regularity but rather upon a disturbance of the ratio existing between the psychophysical activity and the stimulus. In regard to the objection first raised by Mach, which he called the *a priori* objection, he tried to prove that with a simultaneous dependence, such as exists between psychical and physical stimuli, the simple ratio possesses only a small degree of probability.[1] Body and soul are like the inner and outer modes of appearance of the same being. If, for example, we take a circle and in the middle of this or at any point inside it suppose an eye that can see in all directions, and outside of it another such eye, then, speaking generally, in looking at the circumference the same parts of this circumference will be seen at different angles and therefore appear different as to size. And these different sizes do not change by any means in a constant ratio.[2] Against this idea of proportion, Fechner brings as a special argument the fact of the threshold. According to the law of proportion, the weakest psychophysical process ought to call a sensation into existence. If the concept of the inner threshold is abandoned, the whole psychophysical interpretation of the relation between conscious and unconscious mental life must be abandoned too. Fechner's criticism of Delbœuf's "contrary sensations" was fully as keen and severe as the latter's criticism of Fechner's negative sensations. In it we see the philosophical strain that runs through all Fechner's thinking. The mediation between outer and inner psychophysics, made possible by the fundamental psychophysical formula, is the object for the sake of which Fechner adheres firmly to his original interpretation of the law.

In this storm of criticism the obvious contradictions among Fechner's opponents themselves speak strongly in Fechner's favor, so that he was able to say at the end: "The tower of

[1] *Op. cit.*, pp. 65 *ff.*   [2] *Op. cit.*, pp. 67 *f.*

Babylon was not completed because the workmen could not understand each other as to how they should build, but my psychophysical foundation must remain because the workmen could not come to any agreement as to how they should tear it down." [1]

### (c) Some Philosophical Opponents

Against Fechner's fundamental ideas some purely philosophical attacks were directed. These form merely an interlude in the real controversy over Fechner's psychophysics, for this was ultimately to be decided on the ground of psychological experience alone.

F. A. Müller[2] characterized all investigations that set out to find some functional relation between the physical and the psychical as absolutely hopeless. Now, the functional relation between the size of a sensation and the size of a stimulus, both determined by means of a certain unit of measurement, is exactly what the axiom of psychophysics is trying to represent. The supposed difference sensations of Fechner are nothing else than contrast-feelings of varying character. Müller, therefore, looked for the real interpretation of Weber's Law in the field of psychology and thereby accepted the opinion of Wundt.

The so-called "difference" opinion of sensation took the chief place in the controversy between Fechner and Ulrici. It has very often been supposed that a sensation can only arise in connection with or as a difference from another which still exists or has existed previously. In this sense Schneider[3] maintained that the sensations are not conditioned by the separate nervous excitations as such but

---

[1] *Op. cit.*, p. 215.
[2] *Das Axiom der Psychophysik und die Weberschen Versuche*, 1882.
[3] *Die Unterscheidung, Analyse, Entstehung und Entwicklung ders., u.s.f.*, 1877, p. 3.

by the differences of the nervous excitations. In favor of this "difference" opinion, Ulrici[1] pointed to the fact that very slightly saturated colors could only be recognized by a comparison with a pure gray. Later on, in connection with some criticism of Fechner's, he came to the conclusion that in addition to the psychophysical process forming the basis for a sensation there must be added a special act of differentiation.[2] But this act belongs to a mental field superior to the field of sensation, a field in which we cannot conceive of any psychophysical correlates. Now, since the real phenomena of consciousness take place in this mental field, any inner psychophysics becomes impossible.

The measurability of psychical processes upheld by Fechner was questioned by the famous historian of philosophy E. Zeller,[3] although not with a very happy argument. The latter complained of the lack of a unit of measurement applicable to all cases, in order to denote the absolute size of a sensation. The just-noticeable sensation which, according to Fechner, would serve this purpose was considered by Zeller to be of no use in this case. Now Fechner could use for such a unit of measurement any psychical value which corresponded to a stimulus which transcended its threshold value in a given ratio. Obviously, this objection of Zeller questioned nothing more than the absolute measurability of sensations, the impossibility of which Fechner had from the very beginning acknowledged.

Unquestionably, the most important of those opponents whom Fechner himself called his philosophical opponents was the physiologist J. v. Kries.[4] The measurement of a value takes for granted that determinations of equality between similar elements can be carried out, as in the phys-

[1] *Leib und Seele*, p. 294.
[2] *Zeitschr. f. Philos. u. phil. Kritik*, Bd. LXXII, p. 281.
[3] "Über die Messung psychischer Vorgänge," *Abh. d. Berl. Akad.*, 1881.
[4] *Vierteljahrsschr. f. wissensch. Philos.*, VI, 1882, pp. 257 ff.

ical universe, with space, time, and volume. The measurement number then denotes a multiple of the same thing. In the physical world intensive values are measured by reducing them by means of definite principles to spatial and temporal values. These conditions of measurability are, however, not fulfilled in the case of psychical values. Let us first of all suppose that the whole nervous system was unchangeable, so that one and the same sensation always corresponded to one and the same stimulus.[1] Let $E_1$, $E_2$, $E_3$ be the sensations corresponding to the stimuli $R_1$, $R_2$, $R_3$. In carrying out any experiment for purposes of measurement we must answer the question as to whether the contention is justifiable that the change of sensation from $E_1$ to $E_2$ is equal to any other, say, from $E_k$ to $E_l$, or, what comes to the same thing, that the sensation $E_m$ is so many times greater than the sensation $E_n$. Unprejudiced consideration will show at once that such a statement can have no sense. Intensive values are not in themselves measurable because to consider equal the different steps of an intensity series has in itself no definite meaning. The contention that the addition of sensation caused by placing a two and then a three pound weight on a certain part of the skin is equal to the placing of a ten and then a fifteen pound weight has just as much sense as if we were to say that a light vibration is equal to an auditory vibration. The apparent psychical judgment depends in reality upon our comprehension of physical values. Hering had also shown that we judge weights according to their physical measure and not according to any logarithmic principle; in the field of visual sensations the same was shown in Delbœuf's experiments and also in the astronomical determinations of stellar magnitudes.

With such considerations von Kries tried to show the im-

[1] *Op. cit.*, p. 273.

possibility of all psychophysics, and Fechner himself saw in this a fundamental objection to which one only needed to consent in order to get rid, once and for all, of the whole mass of psychophysical nonsense which had accumulated.[1] The new foundation of the theory of psychical measurement, which stands in close connection with the varying interpretations of Weber's Law, is, in any case, of more importance for the determination of the fate of Fechner's psychophysics than the settlement of those questions of principle which have not been decided up to the present.

## 4. The New Foundation of Psychical Measurement

Out of the controversy over Fechner's psychophysics, which is the principal feature of the psychology of the sixties and seventies of the last century, arose various attempts at a new foundation of psychical measurement. G. E. Müller, in his *Grundlegung der Psychophysik*, took up a position which was opposed to Fechner in its chief points, whereas Wundt took what he considered tenable in the old psychophysics of Fechner and incorporated it into his physiological psychology. The psychological interpretation of Weber's Law as formulated by Wundt has also taken on many different forms, and has in part been the starting-point for the most recent experimental investigations.

### (a) *G. E. Müller's Foundation of Psychophysics*

The investigation of Müller, appearing under the title *Grundlegung der Psychophysik*, in the year 1878, was almost entirely devoted to Weber's Law. Because of its completeness and the acuteness of its criticism it has become a landmark in the history of psychophysics. From a crit-

[1] *Revision*, p. 324.

ical survey of the facts of Weber's Law it appeared that it is valid with any degree of certainty only for the senses of vision and audition and the muscle sense, and that only within definite limits. It is, therefore, not correct to speak of upper and lower deviations, for it is rather the general rule that the relative difference sensitivity changes with the intensity of the stimulus. Within those limits where Weber's Law seems to be valid these changes are so small and occur so slowly that they can be neglected for all practical purposes.

But even within this region of validity Fechner's formula of measurement cannot be retained. Weber's Law merely says that the just-noticeable difference of two sensations $s'$ and $s''$ remains constant to the ratio of the stimuli, that is,

$$s' - s'' = f\left(\frac{r'}{r''}\right).$$

Fechner's formula of measurement, $s = \kappa \cdot \log \frac{r}{\rho}$, where $\kappa$ is a constant and $\rho$ the stimulus-threshold, does not take into account the upper and lower deviations. Now, if under the supposition of equal values of equally noticeable additions of sensation the formula $s = \phi(r)$ can be deduced from the actual behavior of the value of the difference-threshold, then there follows at once, by putting $e^{\frac{\Phi(r)}{\kappa}} = \phi(r)$, the corrected formula of measurement:

$$s = \kappa \log \phi(r),$$

and out of this, by differentiation, the corrected fundamental formula:

$$ds = \frac{\kappa \cdot \phi'(r) \cdot dr}{\phi(r)}.$$

The function $\phi(r)$ is, in accordance with the upper and lower deviations, convex toward the axis of the curve for small values of $r$; and as $r$ increases it approximates to a straight line and then becomes concave toward the axis. The turning-point lies at the maximum of the relative difference sensitivity.

For the interpretation of the validity of such a formula of measurement Müller admitted two alternatives. Either the sensation intensity $s$ is proportional to the psychophysical activity $E$, and this latter increases within certain limits almost like the logarithm of the stimulus $r$, or, conversely, there exists approximate proportionality between the two last processes, so that the sensation intensity increases in arithmetical progression, while the psychophysical activity increases in geometrical progression. According to the first view,

$$s = k''E,$$

and for the nervous excitation $E$ (psychophysical activity) we have the equation

$$E = k' \log \phi (r),$$

which Müller called the formula for the measurement of nervous excitation. According to the second view,

$$s = \kappa . \log E$$

and

$$E = \phi (r)$$

are the expressions for Fechner's psychophysical law.

The first view leads to a physiological interpretation of Weber's Law, and Müller emphatically supported such an interpretation as against the psychophysical one. First of all, a logarithmic relation between two physical states is easily thinkable. The difference, for example, in height above sea-level of two towns, where the barometer is $B$ and $b$ respectively, is equal to $C . \log \dfrac{B}{b}$, where $C$ is a constant dependent upon various circumstances. And the stimulus-threshold can easily be explained because of physiological inhibition.

Müller also directed his criticisms against the psychological interpretation of Weber's Law. According to this interpretation two sensations, in order to appear to us different in a constantly noticeable manner, must not show a constant difference to each other but rather must form a constant ratio. This leads to the equation:

$$\frac{ds}{s} = p \cdot \frac{\phi'(r)}{\phi(r)} dr,$$

where $p$ is a constant. The same equation can be deduced from $s = \kappa \cdot (\phi(r))^p$. In this manner he opposed the psychological point of view held by Plateau, Brentano, and others.

Hering's standpoint is, according to Müller, just as untenable. In his experiments with weights he ought not to have taken as his question whether two weights of 1,000 and 2,000 grammes appear to differ by the same amount of weight as two weights of 100 and 200 grammes respectively. He ought to have raised the real psychological question as to whether the two former produce an equally noticeable difference in sensation as do the two latter. We do not perceive the differences or relations of given sensations but only the noticeability of these differences and relations, and we judge these latter as to equality or difference. What difference in weight or what relation of weights we conceive as the outer cause of a difference of two weight sensations noticeable to any degree depends entirely upon our experience. And this makes invalid Hering's objection that the absence of any proportion between sensation and size of weight would make impossible the acquisition by practice of mechanical skill; this learning rests upon associations formed between weight sensations and the ideas of the amount of strength to be exerted. This substitution of the noticeability of sensations in place of the conception of their size stands the test of any further arguments of Hering. The latter might contend that if the size of a sensation corresponding to the length of a given line were to increase slower than the line, then two triangles geometrically similar but of different sizes would have to appear to us as dissimilar, since the relation of the three sides in each of the triangles would be quite different. To all of which Müller would reply that in such a case the differences in the lengths of the sides would appear equal precisely in accordance with Weber's Law.

Müller's criticism was directed against all other conceptions of psychophysics, in so far as he sought to show the untenability of the psychophysical view, as well as of all non-physiological theories. It was in the main this keen and radical attack that led Fechner to subject the principal problems of psychophysics to a revision.[1] If the criticism of Müller was valid, then psychophysics was nothing but an historical relic; and so he once more set himself to meet all attacks with the picturesque and proud statement that a post by being shaken becomes looser and looser, but a tree, if it is not torn down, will only thereby root itself more firmly in the ground.[2] Fechner outlined clearly and sharply the physiological and the psychophysical points of view between which it seemed to him a decision must be made. Out of the well-known formulæ there follows for the latter a stimulus-threshold, whereas for the former there is none. According to the psychophysical point of view Weber's Law is fundamental, but according to the physiological point of view it has no validity for inner psychophysics. If this latter is true there can be no physical principle by means of which the relation of the intensities of two physical

---

[1] *Revision der Hauptprobleme der Psychophysik*, 1882.
[2] *Op. cit.*, Vorrede, p. 5.

processes $\frac{r'}{r}$ can be translated into a difference of the succeeding dependent processes $E'-E$ in such a manner that to $n$ times $\frac{r'}{r}$ would correspond $n$ times the difference of $E'-E$. The physiological examples of Müller and others only show the dependence of end result (*e. g.*, the height of the pull of a muscle) upon the exciting stimulus but not the real dependence between two processes in motion, with which psychophysics is alone concerned. The fact of the inner threshold cannot be explained by means of resistance in the conductivity of the central substance, because the inhibition follows according to the principle of relative weakening and so can never die out. Again, the non-contradictory mathematical correlation of a whole system of formulæ supports the psychophysical view-point. And, lastly, the conception of the whole physical process of the universe as a psychophysical one necessarily presupposes a psychophysical interpretation of the formulæ of measurement.

We see again in all this how Fechner's whole thinking, rooted as it is in profound but fantastic conceptions, can never be reconciled with the demands of purely empirical thought. In the meantime, however, there sprang up a third interpretation of Weber's Law—the psychological interpretation.

## (b) *The Psychological Interpretation of Weber's Law*

The psychological interpretation of Weber's Law appears with constantly increasing clearness in the thought of Wundt. Even in 1863, in his *Lectures on Human and Animal Psychology*, he was striving toward a psychological conception of Weber's Law. He pointed to the meaning of the act of comparison and saw in our relative judgment a proof of the purely psychological nature of this law.[1] Weber's Law cannot be deduced either from the physiological peculiarities of the nervous substance or from a functional relationship between the physical and the psychical, for it is founded in the psychical processes which are at work in the comparison of sensations. It is in this sense not a law of sensation but a law of apperception. Even though in the first edition of his *Principles of Physiological Psychology* (1874) the logarithmic equation set up by Weber's Law was taken to represent the dependence of the sensation upon the physiological process, yet later this mathematical relationship was conceived as one between purely psychical factors. In this way Fechner's formula of measurement could be brought into a form in which it contained only homogeneous terms. So that now sensation and stimulus do not enter into any functional relationship, but the law only tells us how the degree of noticeability of a sensation changes with the intensity of the sensation. If we denote a constant degree of noticeability by $k$, and the change in the sensation intensity corresponding to it by $\Delta E$, then

$$k = c \cdot \frac{\Delta E}{E}$$

is the empirical expression for the observed facts. The growth of the sensation $E$ must, then, be assumed to be proportional to the stimulus. Following this interpretation, we have in Wundt's survey of the position his attempt to explain the physiological processes by means of a hypothetical apperception centre. His analysis of the inhibition processes which occur in this centre during the conduction of nervous processes is an example of a psychophysical analysis of complex cerebral functions which is intended to show that the psychological interpretation need by no

[1] *Op. cit.*, I, pp. 133 *f.* *Cf.* also above, p. 134.

means come into contradiction with our knowledge of physiological nervous conductivity.

In just as decided a manner did Theodor Lipps,[1] who at first started with a psychophysical interpretation, advance toward a psychological interpretation, in which the growth of sensations is proportional to the growth of stimuli, and the facts of Weber's Law are deduced from the universal and fundamental psychological law of the relative quantitative identity of the elements of a whole.[2] The total quantity appears reduced in proportion to its undividedness. For the manner of this reduction we can get the following formula: If component parts already present $(m)$ are increased by new homogeneous parts, then the psychical quantity of the increase undergoes such a reduction that we can put for the increase in quantity the formula $\frac{n}{m+n} \cdot C$, where $C$ is a constant. This formula expresses immediately the law of relativity, according to which a whole, in regard to its power of making an impression, appears to be increased in an equal manner if it undergoes an increase that is relatively equally large.[3] In this manner the size of the impression is determined by a purely psychomechanical process. If, however, equal and absolute differences in stimuli are found with the help of the gradation method, on the ground of a judgment of supraliminal differences, then there must occur an apperceptive division of the whole, according to which the absolute increases play their part without any reduction.

---

[1] *Grundtatsachen des Seelenlebens*, 1883, pp. 75 *f*. "Die Quantität in psychischen Gesamtvorgängen," *Sitzungsber. d. philos.-philol. u. d. hist. Kl. d. Kgl. Bayr. Akad. d. Wissensch.*, 1899, III, pp. 400 *ff*.

[2] "Das Relativitätsgesetz der psychischen Quantität und das Webersche Gesetz," *op. cit.*, 1902, I, pp. 1 *ff*. *Cf.* also W. Wirth, *Arch. f. d. ges. Psych.*, Bd. XIV, 1909, pp. 217 *ff*.

[3] *Psychologische Studien*, 2 Aufl., 1905, p. 253.

In this way Lipps approaches Wundt very closely in his assumption of a difference in the manner of judging just-noticeable and more-than-just-noticeable differences. In spite of this, the difference remains that Lipps asserts the ratio between the stimuli and the unconscious psychical processes and not between the stimuli and the sensation intensities, *i. e.*, simple contents of consciousness. In accordance with this, in explaining absolute judgment he has recourse again to the unconscious processes. A division into parts of a content of consciousness is altogether meaningless, but we can conceive of such a division in regard to unconscious real processes.

Among the other opinions that approximate to the psychological interpretation we find the one of G. Heymans,[1] in which Weber's Law is subordinated to the more general phenomenon of psychical inhibition. He observed that qualitatively similar but locally different sensations tended to crowd each other out, and this expressed itself as an inhibition in an increase of the stimulus or difference-threshold. Weak sensations are crowded out of consciousness by the stronger ones just in proportion to the intensities of the latter. An extension of this law to apply to the weak sensations of difference is all that is required to explain the general content of Weber's Law. The difference-threshold is a case of inhibition and Weber's Law is a special case, *i. e.*, a limiting case of the law of inhibition. All this assuredly calls to mind the Herbartian principles governing the mechanism of ideas. And yet what a difference between the old and imaginary statics and mechanics of ideas and this new theory of inhibition! The former included the whole of consciousness but this only a comparatively small group of psychical phenomena. In the former, brilliant mathematical speculation into the unlimited field

[1] *Ztschr. f. Psych. u. Phys.*, Bd. XXVI, 1901, pp. 305 *ff.*

of the possible challenges our admiration; in the latter, we meet the more modest results which have been laboriously gleaned from the field of experience.

These forms of the psychological interpretation seemed also, however, to be subject to the general objections which von Kries had previously directed against Fechner's psychophysics.[1] Meinong[2] renewed this argument in the following form: In general, equal differences may cause unequal sensation differences and equal sensation differences may point to unequal differences in stimulus. The disparity of two psychical contents corresponds neither with their absolute nor with their relative stimulus difference and can only be brought into a close relationship with the latter. The facts of Weber's Law allow, therefore, of no other conclusion than this, that to each definite value of sensation difference there corresponds one and only one value of the relative stimulus difference, and, conversely, one and only one value of sensation difference corresponds to each value of the relative stimulus difference. In the deduction of the formula of measurement the formation of the difference of two sensations $e_n - e$ is the point most open to attack. Sensations cannot be added or subtracted. And if the separate $e$ is conceived of as a number of degrees of noticeability we do not thereby gain any information as to the content of these degrees.

The close connection which Fechner thought to exist between the principle of psychical measurement and the psychophysical interpretation of Weber's Law has been destroyed. In spite of all the polemics against Fechner, it was once thought that psychology would achieve its object if it determined the validity of Weber's Law in every department; but at the present time we have progressed far

---

[1] *Cf.* pp. 225 *f.*, above.
[2] *Ztschr. f. Psych. u. Phys.*, Bd. XI, 1883, pp. 81 *ff.*, 230 *ff.*, 353 *ff.*

beyond this one-sided view. The inner psychophysics of Fechner, which led to a perfectly transcendental metaphysic of consciousness, has long ago been relinquished. There has been retained, however, in experimental psychology, the concept of psychical measurement and with it the task of arranging a relation based upon number between a manifoldness of correlated psychical elements and a field of outer processes.[1]

[1] *Cf.* G. F. Lipps, *Grundriss der Psychophysik*, 1903, p. 40.

# PART III

# A HISTORY OF THE MOST IMPORTANT PSYCHOLOGICAL THEORIES

## CHAPTER X

### THEORIES OF SENSATION

If psychology feels itself called upon to take the same fundamental position among the mental sciences as physics has taken among the natural sciences, it would seem pertinent to raise the question as to whether there has not occurred in the history of psychological theory a reaction similar to the one which occurred in the history of physical theories due to the so-called mechanical conception of the universe. What a gulf separates modern natural science from the Aristotelian physics dominant during the Middle Ages! Not only do changed conceptions lie at the bottom of present-day theories, but the fundamental thought, the reduction of all phenomena to the movement processes of the smallest parts, has become a new standard for all physical theories. In psychology, however, we do not notice any such radical change of position in regard to the content of consciousness; there is at most a suggestion of this,[1] and even then in a different sense, so that we see in the history of psychological theories no such thoroughgoing reaction as we do in the case of the natural sciences.

Nevertheless, we do note an analogous transformation

[1] See pp. 43 and 209.

in some departments, as, for example, in sense-perception. The more modern theories of sense-perception, which trace the rise of percepts out of elementary processes, excel early attempts at an explanation of perception as much as the mechanical theory of heat excels the earlier theory of a heat material. That modern psychology offers a more exact basis for attempts to establish a psychical mechanics, formerly undertaken in a very questionable manner, can be seen in part in the determination of psychophysical constants. Each of the more modern physical theories includes certain kinds of physical constants. The physics of Aristotle explained the fall of a body by the desire of the body to reach its natural place, the centre of the earth. The theory of Galileo about a falling body led, on the other hand, to the determination of a physical constant, *i. e.*, gravity. It is possible that the determination of psychophysical constants, such as difference-thresholds, reaction-times, scopes of consciousness, etc., has an analogous meaning for psychological theories.

Do these constants, as in physics, result in hypotheses? Without doubt there are hypotheses in psychology, as, for example, those about the physiological processes that underlie psychical phenomena; in this sense we speak of hypotheses of light sensation or of the hypothetical physiological processes underlying the feelings. The analogy between these and the real hypotheses of natural science is, however, a loose one. The ultimate physical theories, like that of the discontinuity of matter, of its kinetic-elastic or kinetic-electrical composition, contain within themselves presuppositions as to the substratum into which the phenomena are to be transformed. We do not in psychology, to continue the same examples, transform visual sensations into retinal stimulations or feelings into changes in innervation. There have been, it is true, attempts in modern psychology to transform the content of consciousness in the same empirical manner as physics has done with its phenomena.[1] But in the history of psychology any such transformation, which must necessarily have led to real psychological hypotheses, always fell within the scope of metaphysics. Such hypotheses are excluded from pure psychology because a hypothetical content of consciousness, the existence of which is only presupposed and not proved, is a concept that contradicts the phenomenological point of view. Contents of consciousness can be considered hypothetical only in the sense that we do not perceive them as separated and isolated, but that we deduce them from their effects; an example of such is the part certain difference tones of a high order play in the consonance theory of F. Krueger.[2] Such a psychological hypothesis does not, like the physical, reach over into another sphere of reality, for the hypothetical content of consciousness is lacking only in the conditions necessary for its acceptance such as the other contents of consciousness possess. And with this is closely connected the fact that the oppositions in principle, which in natural science are first met with among the hypotheses, are in psychology to be observed in the separate theories themselves.

By far the greater number of psychological theories are concerned with conscious experiences with which a so-called outer experience is connected. The processes of sensation and perception have from the very beginning challenged theoretical explanation. In the field of subjective conscious states the theories of feeling and will have been the most important. Within the theories of sensation we can further distinguish general theories and theories dealing with special sensations, *e. g.*, vision and hearing.

[1] See p. 209.
[2] *Psych. Stud.*, Bd. V, 1910, pp. 319 *ff*. *Cf.* below, 3 (*d*).

## 1. General Theories of Sensation

The distinction between sensation and perception belongs only to the most modern concepts of psychology, and accordingly in historical development theories of sensation correspond entirely with those of perception. And yet in the historical development we can recognize the material distinction between the processes of sensation and those of perception. The theories of sensation have always been dependent upon physiological knowledge; apart from isolated anticipations, any advance of the former has been dependent upon the growth of the latter. As soon as the theories of sensation became freed from metaphysical hypotheses they became closely affiliated to physiology. The theoretical utilization of the purely psychological arrangement of sensations, *e. g.*, in the modern theories of color sensations, belongs to the most modern development. In the theories of perception, on the other hand, we notice from the earliest times that they are strongly influenced by definite philosophical theories. Although such oppositions have only stood out the more clearly because of the clearer definition of terms in modern times, yet we can trace them back in their broad outlines to the earliest times.

The gradual separation between theories of sensation and theories of perception was in part prepared for by the analogous opposition in the theory of primary and secondary qualities, which is essentially connected with the name of Locke, even though it possesses a much longer preliminary history.[1] As primary differences Aristotle recognized the chief oppositions in the qualities of touch sensation, *e. g.*, warm and cold, dry and wet. In the philosophy of the Arabians these were contrasted as primary qualities (*qua-*

[1] *Cf.* Baeumker, *Arch. f. Gesch. d. Phil.*, XXI, 1908, p. 492.

*litates primæ* or *primariæ*) with the remaining derivative qualities of sensation, and this was also the case with Albertus Magnus in his division into *prima sensibilia* and *secunda sensibilia*. In the fourteenth century, as shown in Heinrich von Hessen, the expression *qualitates secundæ* gradually came to be adopted. It was, however, the mechanical theories of the universe that revived the original Aristotelian concept of common contents of perception, such as size, number, and movement. Galileo called these the first accidents in contradistinction to the purely subjective qualities of sensation; and Robert Boyle used the expression "secondary qualities" for the purely sensory qualities. And in this way the contrast was formed for which Locke used the scholastic terminology of primary and secondary qualities. Although since that time the distinction between sensation and perception has never been lost, yet even up to the present time several perceptions, *e. g.*, the spatial, have been classified as special kinds of sensations, a thing which has been due to the influence of certain theoretical points of view, as, for example, of nativistic theories. However much the psychology of the senses has proved itself to be dependent upon physical and physiological knowledge, yet a psychological interpretation and utilization of the discovery of the physiological conditions underlying sensation and perception has very often been slow in appearing. The accommodation of the eye as a purely physiological fact was discovered by Kepler; its importance for the comprehension of depth has only been appreciated in modern theories. In the same way the facts of color-mixture were known for a long time before attempts were made to explain color sensations by means of an analogous stimulation of color substances in the eye.

Among the general theories of sensation there predominated in earlier times fantastic conceptions of the origin of sensations. Modern physiology was the first to bring forward a principle which led to a general theory of sensation, namely, the principle of the specific energy of the nerves.

## (a) *The Older Theories*

Ancient ideas as to the origin of sensation were confined within the circle of thought dealing with metaphysical theories of the soul. At the beginning of his treatise on sensations, Theophrastus classifies sensation theories into two groups: in those of the first group the sensation is explained by the working of similar upon similar (τῷ ὁμοίῳ διὰ τὴν ὁμοιότητα); in the second a working of opposite upon opposite is presupposed (τῷ ἐναντίῳ διὰ τὴν ἀλλοίωσιν). The famous sensation theory of Empedocles shows the three component parts of all these theories: an emanation of small particles by the perceived objects, a special formation of canals in the sense-organs, and currents flowing through these canals to the outer movements.

In the sensation theory of Aristotle the sensation could be nothing else than the transformation of a faculty for sensation into reality. Certainly some kind of a movement, or in general some kind of a change (ἀλλοίωσις), forms the basis of a sensation; but the sensation is not, therefore, an affection of the soul. For the movement is carried along right up to the soul, but does not continue within the soul.[1] Besides this the soul does not receive the matter of the object but only the form, just as wax receives the form of a signet-ring.[2] The soul actively reproduces this form by means of the faculty of sensation. Besides the stimulus the sense-organ exerts some kind of activity in the act of sensation.[3] For the ability of the eye

[1] *De somn.*, 1.     [2] *De anima*, II, 12.     [3] *De gen. an.*, V, 1.

to produce changes in the outer world, Aristotle cites the popular belief that the look of women will at certain times produce spots on mirrors; and, in hearing, the air confined in the ear is supposed to imitate the sound movement.

The Aristotelian theory of sensation underwent transformation in two almost opposite directions. In Neo-Platonic psychology we find in Porphyry the thought that the soul in sensation merely recognizes its own content.[1] On the other hand, the Aristotelian theory was reduced to the simpler conception as typified by the picture theory. Even in the Peripatetic school there arose the theory of *species sensibiles* or *intentionales*, fine or delicate pictures, which were supposed to penetrate through the hollow nerves up to the *sensorium commune*. There existed such *species* not only for the simple sensations but also for complex ideas such as size and number, and this very questionable theory was held in great regard during the Scholastic period.

It was left for the discoveries of the modern physiology of the nerves and the opposition to the *influxus physicus* to make a change in the theories of sensation. In accordance with the ideas of his age, Descartes sought to make the origin of sensation intelligible by explaining it as a movement of the vital spirits rising from the heart, caused by the stimulation conducted along the nerves. Even though the effect of the vital spirits upon the soul remained unexplained, still the insight that sensation and its object do not need to possess any similarity was an important step for the theory of sensation.[2]

A more important modern point of view appeared later on in the Kantian distinction between the forms of perception and the matter of sensation. This distinction was

---

[1] *Cf.* a passage out of his lost work on sensation quoted by Nemesius, *De natura hominis*, chap. VI.
[2] *Princ. phil.*, I, 66; IV, 189, 197; and especially *Dioptr.*, IV, 6.

not originally used in a psychological sense, but it became almost more important for the separation of sensation and perception theories than Locke's distinction between primary and secondary qualities. To be sure, we do not look for this development among the thinkers who are classed as the direct heirs to the philosophy of Kant. It was rather the natural science of the day that appropriated this Kantian distinction and brought it into relation with physiological theories.

### (b) The Theory of Specific Energy of the Nerves

In the theories of sensation there dominated for a long time the original objective opinion that the qualities of sensation were qualities of the outer stimuli. It is customary to regard the theory of the specific energy of the nerves as a decisive turning-point. In the ancient theories of sensation all characteristics of the object were permitted to be carried over into the perceiving subject. Since the time of Descartes the similarity between sensation and object had been dropped, but the stimulus and the sensation remained unquestionably connected. This relation was eventually obscured by the theory of specific energy; the sensation effect of a given stimulation now became dependent upon the kind of nerve-fibres stimulated. With this the ultimate step away from the naïve objectification of sense-impressions has been taken.

It happened that the doctrine of the specific energy of the nerves was anticipated from purely psychological considerations. Within the circle of the so-called "fibre psychologists," the theories of Bonnet[1] are an interesting example of the fact that important insights may occasionally result from presuppositions which may later prove unten-

[1] See p. 94.

able, such as the hypothesis, in this case, of the oscillations of cerebral fibres, if they are only properly followed out. For the rise of an idea Bonnet demanded a nervous stimulation similar to the one that the corresponding sensation would cause. Now, since the mind can call into existence several separate ideas at the same time, it must be possible to stimulate at the same time several dispositions without their fusing together. Now this is possible only if each sensation depends upon the oscillation of a single fibre that belongs entirely to that sensation. In the anatomical structure of the organ of hearing Bonnet thought he saw the verification of this hypothesis. The auditory nerve branches out in the interior of the labyrinth and the cochlea, and each branch is sensitive to a particular tone, like the strings of a stringed instrument. In order to carry out this hypothesis in regard to vision, Bonnet presupposed bundles of fibres, each consisting of seven fibres corresponding to the principal colors, a simultaneous stimulation of which would cause white.

The fame of the theory of specific energy is due, however, to the great physiologist Johann Müller, who first came upon the idea in the field of visual sensation[1] and later on formulated the fundamental fact in a general manner: "Sensation is not the conduction of a quality or a state of an external body to consciousness, but it is the conduction of the quality or the state of a sensory nerve to consciousness, occasioned by some external cause, and these qualities differ in the different sensory nerves, *i. e.*, the nerves possess specific energy."[2] This idea that the difference of sense qualities depended upon the characteristics of the sensory nerves was a clear and complete expression of physiological knowledge at the time when the structure

[1] *Zur vergl. Physiol. des Gesichtssinns*, etc., 1826.
[2] *Handb. d. Physiol. d. Mensch.*, II, 1840.

of the separate sense-organs was known only in its broad outline.

Helmholtz followed on with the logical consequences of this principle and extended its validity to apply to the sensation differences within a specific field of sensation. The combination of Young's hypothesis of three nervous processes corresponding to the different principal colors along with the theory of the specific energy of the nerves led Helmholtz to the presupposition of three specifically different visual substances[1] to which there correspond in the brain just as many systems of nerve-cells. The rock upon which the Helmholtz theory foundered was the fact, discovered later, that the nerves are relatively indifferent conductors of stimuli set up in them. This forced thinkers back to the much less probable hypothesis that the specific sensation process takes place in the central organ.

Against the great authority which the principle of specific energy enjoyed among the majority of physiologists evolutionary considerations could only make slow headway. In the time of Müller the permanency of species was still maintained in the natural sciences, and the theory of originally different sensation elements was something that seemed to support this belief. Since the time of Darwin, however, several investigators, such as G. H. Lewes (1860) and A. Horwicz (1872), drew the logical consequences of the principle of evolution for the theories of sensation. Characteristic for the belief in the integrity of the separate senses is the peculiar interpretation of such physiological discoveries as could have thrown light precisely upon this point of the genetic connection of the senses. When Goltz,[2] for example, discovered that the semicircular canals took no part in acoustical stimulations but that they were an organ contributing sensations of equilibrium and of the

[1] *Cf.* below, pp. 290 *f.*   [2] *Pflüg. Arch.*, Bd. III, 1870.

movements of the body, it was looked upon as a sixth sense and placed alongside of the others. The similarity of these sensations to pressure sensations remained unnoticed, as well as its close connection with the organ of hearing from the point of view of evolution.

A successful attack against the theory of the specific energy of the nerves was made by J. Ranke in the introduction of his concept of "transition organs," which in the lower animals take care of all kinds of perceptions that in higher stages of evolution are assigned to different organs.[1] The hearing rods of many insects and the touch rods represent a slightly differentiated form of an organ of touch. In a similar manner he ascribed to the so-called organ of vision of the leech the functions both of touch and of taste. But, however forcibly the facts of comparative anatomy and physiology might demand a great limitation of the principle of the specific energy of the nerves, a great many physiologists still consider it of much importance. In the most recent times W. Nagel[2] tried to set up alongside of this principle the principle of the specific disposition of the sense-organs. Each sense-organ is specially disposed for a particular kind of stimulus through a specifically different sensitivity and receptivity, whereas for other stimuli it is absolutely or relatively insensitive.

The extraordinary importance that the principle of the specific energy of the nerves seemed originally to gain for psychology was obviously a consequence of the philosophical presuppositions suggested above. Since that time the more it became a physiological principle, the more the psychological interest turned toward theories of the special kinds of sensations.

[1] *Zeitschr. f. wissensch. Zoologie*, Bd. XXV, 1875.
[2] *Bibliotheca Zoologica*, Leuckart and Chun, Bd. XVIII, 1894.

## 2. Theories of Vision

Theories of vision take a prominent place among theories of sensation not only because it has been most common to deduce general theories of sensation out of the peculiarities of the sense of vision but also because vision was the first to be theoretically thought out. The ancient theories of light belong to the field of natural philosophy. From these sprang the problem of color vision as a physical problem, and in this form it remained dominant to the eighteenth century. It was only the distinction between physiological and physical optics that led to the more modern theories of color.

### (a) Ancient Theories of Light

The pre-Aristotelian theories of vision fall into two chief groups—the one making use of visual rays and the other of pictures.[1] In the former, objects became visible to the eye by means of the rays of light streaming out of the eye. In this form it is related to the ancient opinion that the eye is fiery—an opinion that was assented to by the Hindu physician, Suçruta, who believed that an eternal fire burned in the lens of the eye. Later on, due to the influence of Euclid, this theory became dominant among the geometer-opticians. The same theory appears again in the *Katoptrics* of Heros, and Cleomedes and Ptolemy accepted it. All the scientific optics of antiquity was founded upon this theory.

The Stoic theory of air tension is merely a modification of the visual-ray theory. According to this theory the visual pneuma or air, coming down from the central organ into the pupil, gathers together the air between the eye and the object into a cone, the point of which lies in the eye,

[1] *Cf.* A. E. Haas, *Arch. f. Gesch. d. Philos.*, Bd. XX, 1907, p. 345.

and the base coincides with the visible object. With this cone the eye, as it were, feels the objects and receives an impression of their form. We are able to see more easily by day than by night simply because the air is rarefied by light and can be more easily gathered together.

Very soon, however, the picture theory arose in opposition to the visual-ray theory. In this the movement giving rise to the impression was supposed to take place in exactly the opposite direction, from the object into the eye. In the original formulation of this theory by Democritus the pictures themselves do not penetrate into the eye, but only a copy of them produced in the air, and the clearness of this copy decreases with increasing distance. We should be able to see an ant crawling on the dome of the sky if it were not that the intervening space is filled with air. What strikes us in such an explanation is the absolute disregard to the dioptric changes of the perceptual picture. In a similarly naïve fashion our perception of distance is explained by the fact that the pupil comes into contact with the shaft of air forced upon it by the pictures. Later on Epicurus simplified this view by supposing that copies of all objects are continually being given off from their surfaces in the form of thin, film-like substances which pass through the air into the eye.

Aristotle was the first to recognize that the process of vision presupposed an impression of the object upon the eye, which was produced by the partly actually and partly potentially diaphanous intervening medium. It is also with him that the first theory of color originates. It goes beyond the beginnings made by Empedocles with his four principal colors, white, black, red, and yellow, set up as parallel to the four elements.[1] Aristotle deduced color sensations from the diaphanous medium existing between the organ of vi-

[1] Theophrastus, *de sens.*, 59.

sion and the object and presupposed that some numerical relation lay at the basis of the differences in color just as in the case of tones.[1] The treatise *On Color,* belonging to the Aristotelian school, treats of the origin of colors out of a mixture of black and white as a purely physical problem. Many of the facts of color-mixture must have been known at this time. According to Pliny the old Greek painters knew how to produce all the colors out of four color substances. One of the old paintings chemically analyzed by Davy showed only a small number of different color substances.

During the closing centuries of the ancient period there arose again the idea that the soul had a power of working at a distance without any medium—an opinion that Heraclitus had formerly held when he maintained that the soul participated in vision and considered sensation itself as a kind of volition. In such a way Plotinus explained vision as a mystical sympathy between the soul and its object, which was at most disturbed by the medium existing between the eye and its object. The seeming diminution of distant objects he explained as due to their indistinct color. And in this he reminds us of Aristotle who also tried to explain the perception of certain spatial relations by means of color. Later on in the Patristic period Lactantius and Augustine compared the eyes with windows through which the soul views the objects of the outer world. This shows that any real appreciation of the problem underlying sensation has been absolutely lost.

Alexander of Aphrodisias (about 200 A. D.), in his interesting discussion of ancient theories of light, takes issue with the pre-Aristotelian theory of the visual ray and denies that the rays of light can be material.[2] The trans-

[1] *De sensu et sensibili,* cap. 3.
[2] *Cf.* J. Zahlfleisch, *Arch. f. Gesch. d. Phil.,* Bd. VIII, 1895, p. 373.

formation of this theory by the Stoics, who compared visual perception to the touching of uneven surfaces on the ground with the help of a stick, was held by Alexander to be untenable because of the various distances of the objects. Similar objections underlie the theory that the form of contours is taken on by the air and then transplanted into the eye. Further, a visual impression is obtained only of the side of the object turned toward the eye. It is, therefore, impossible to see the whole object. Although Alexander rightly criticises the theory he is opposing for confusing sensation and judgment, yet his own conception of vision remains a very primitive one.

In regard to the other conception, that pictures of the objects affect the eye, it is argued that the continual giving off of pictures would impair the objects themselves. Neither could the distance be judged nor the geometrical form be recognized, since in spite of eye movements it remains inexplicable how a unified image could arise out of separate impressions. If, lastly, we presuppose that emanations from the object find their way to the eye, we would not be able to see near and distant objects simultaneously.

The ancients seem never to have risen much above this kind of criticism. Purely psychological considerations failed in face of that peculiar objectivism that sought in fantastic fashion to invent objective substrata for the sensations as well as for the ideational images of the sense of sight. Of all the ancient theories of light, that one lasted longest that made the greatest concessions to this objectivism, namely the picture theory. By Scholasticism this theory was transformed to the extent that only the form of objects penetrated into the sense-organ. Buridan called light, as content of sensation (*lumen*), a species of objective light (*lux*).

In the philosophy of nature of the Renaissance we again

meet with the ancient theory of colors, a knowledge of which is principally due to the translation by Simon Portius (1537) of the treatise *On Color* belonging to the Peripatetic school. Telesius[1] also was influenced by ancient thought when he tried to deduce all the colors from the principle of warmth and cold. But for the most part the traditional theories of color were swamped by the occult sciences, which were filled with enthusiastic wonder at the colors and their effects. This is the time when Paracelsus advised those afflicted with melancholia to wear chains of coral because of the stimulating effect of the red color, and when Scaliger confessed in regard to colors that they are buried in the darkest depths of human ignorance. Whatever scientific thought was achieved during this period was, in regard to color, restricted to the physical aspect of the problem.

### (b) *Separation of Physical and Physiological Optics*

The distinction between the physical and the physiological problems, which were fused together in the old theories, was prepared for by Kepler. He was the first to lay the basis for a physiological optics, inasmuch as he called attention to a number of peculiarities in visual sensation, such as irradiation and the colored fluctuation of after-images. But in his fantastic description of the colors he nevertheless proved himself a child of his age. In the same way empirical and fantastic ideas are mingled in the *Optics* (1613) of the Jesuit Franciscus Aguillonius. The quincunx of colors, white, yellow, red, blue, black, he divided according to the manner of their appearance into true, apparent, and intentional colors, and of these the apparent ones, such as those of the rainbow, he declared as inexplicable, and even as a divine secret.

[1] *De colorum generatione*, 1570.

In his historical review of the best-known theories of color, Robert Boyle[1] deals first of all with the Aristotelian and Platonic theories, in which color is taken to be a kind of flame made up of very minute particles, which are cast by the object into the eye, and the shape of which corresponds to the pores of the eye. Then he goes on to deal with some atomic theories which explain color as a mixture of light and darkness. The chemists derive it from sulphur or from salt or from mercury. And, lastly, the Cartesians explain color as resulting from the different kinds of movement made by the atoms that form light. Boyle would seem to tend toward this last hypothesis although in a very cautious, hesitating manner. The rays of light modified by reflecting or refracting bodies produce that sensation which we are accustomed to call color.[2] Nicholas Malebranche[3] revives an analogy between light and sound processes that had been previously hinted at by Aristotle. Analogous to air vibrations in the process of audition, he assumed periodical oscillations in the smallest particles of the illuminating body, and these oscillations were carried over to the eye by means of a very delicate kind of matter, which in its turn affected the eye by pressure.

Far more important than such speculative theories of color were the researches of Newton, which led to a definite separation between physiological and physical optics. By means of his proofs of the composition of white light, Newton liberated the thinking of physicists from the Aristotelian theory of color. The most important fact which this helped to establish was the arrangement of light sensations according to the common characteristic of brightness in a

---

[1] *Experimenta et considerationes de coloribus, seu initium historiæ experimentalis de coloribus a Roberto Boyle*, 1665.
[2] *Cf.* Goethe, *Geschichte der Farbenlehre.*
[3] *Réflexions sur la lumière et les couleurs et la génération du feu par le Père Malebranche*, 1669.

continuous series from black to white. This phenomenon, which forces itself upon subjective observation, had arrested the attention of the intuitive thinkers of all times; it was only later that it found its classical expression in Goethe's theory of color. Newton himself never departed from the field of physical analysis, in which he was a master; he never interested himself in the physiological problems. His physical explanation of the sensation black was that it was a mixture of all colors, like white, and only differed from white because of the absence of light.[1] This made black a physical characteristic of light, whereas in reality the objective correlate of the sensation is found in the physiological condition of the retina when not stimulated. Newton really never freed himself from the objectivism of the physicists. His famous statement that light could be divided into seven separate colors really interchanged subjective and objective. In the same way the analogies between tones and colors, which date from this time, also proved deceptive. Newton drew up a relationship between the breadth of the spectral bands and the string lengths corresponding to the tones of the Phrygian scale, and this Father Castel took as a basis for the construction of his color piano. However, with the knowledge of the varying dispersing power of refracting media, Newton's relationship was shown to be nothing but an accidental analogy dependent upon the technical conditions of producing his colors.

The old Aristotelian idea that colors are mixtures of light and shade did not entirely disappear in spite of all the advances made in physical optics. About the end of the seventeenth century, Lazarus Nuguet[2] took up this view and also sought to make a fourfold classification of

[1] *Lectiones opticæ, Opera*, t. II, p. 225.
[2] *Journal de Trévoux*, April, 1705, p. 675.

all the phenomena included under the name of color, *i. e.*, colors existing (1) in colored lights, (2) in transparent media, (3) in the organ of sight, and (4) in the soul. In this classification we must recognize the attempt to discriminate between the physical, physiological, and psychological conceptions of color, which he clearly distinguishes, according to the point of view adopted. This does not apply to his discussion of the action of colors in transparent media, which is reminiscent of Aristotle.

The most famous resuscitation of the Aristotelian theory of color is met with in Goethe's theory,[1] which has as its principal thought the notion that light and dark must be mixed together in order to produce color. Goethe thought he found in opaque media the kind of darkening necessary for the production not of gray but of colors. These attempts at a physical theory stand in contrast to Newton's theory in much the same way as his artistic thinking based on living, concrete imagery stands in contrast to the analytic thinking of the scientist. Newton's investigations had prepared the way for a physiology of light sensations and an empirical knowledge of their subjective conditions. Goethe was the one who had described so brilliantly the sense value and the ethical effect of colors, and so it was certainly the right feeling that made him oppose a theory that threatened to destroy the beautiful sense appearance of sensations.

Schopenhauer tried to approach the problem of color vision as a physiological problem from the standpoint of Goethe's theory of color. He explained color with the help of a concept borrowed from contemporary natural philosophy, *i. e.*, the concept of polarity for the qualitatively different activities of the retina. His polemic against the undulation theory during the fifties of the nineteenth cen-

[1] *Beiträge zur Optik*, 1791, 1792. *Zur Farbenlehre*, 1810.

tury stands out in the history of optics like an erratic boulder which has survived from ages long since past.

### (c) *Modern Color Theories*

However varied the lines of thought in the newer theories of color may be, they nevertheless differ from the previously discussed theories by this common characteristic, *i. e.*, of paying attention to the subjective conditions as well as to the temporal and spatial relations of light sensations. They likewise all agree in a retreat from that original objectivism which had supposed color sensations, like most other sensations, to be characteristics of outer objects. Observations about the temporal and spatial relations of light sensation reach back to a much earlier period than any theoretical use of them which goes beyond primitive attempts at explanation.[1]

In the seventeenth century the after-images of windows were described in their main outlines not as a scientific fact but as a clever conjuring feat. We are told that Bonacursius proved to the Jesuit Athanasius Kircher that one could see in the dark no less than in the light.[2] Following the instructions of Bonacursius, Kircher fixated steadily a drawing that had been put in the window opening of an otherwise totally dark room and then after the room had been darkened saw it actually reappear on a clean sheet of white paper. Kircher's explanation that the eye gives out again light that it has absorbed reminds us distinctly of ancient theories of sensation. The opinion closely related to this, viz., that objective light is actually developed in the eye, as proved by the light caused by mechanical pressure on the eye, has continued down to modern times.

[1] *Cf.* Helmholtz, *Physiol. Optik*, 2 Aufl., p. 536.
[2] A. Kircher, *Ars magna*, 1646, p. 162.

Appeal was made to the cases of men who were said to be able to see in the dark, like Tiberius Cæsar, Cardanus, Kaspar Hauser. Newton considered after-images as purely psychical phenomena, since one could recall them some time after their disappearance by means of a special direction of the attention, as in the case of the sun.

To arrive at a physiological theory of these phenomena, Jurin[1] presupposed a continuance of the stimulus and partly the appearance of the opposite excitation due to the cessation of a strong sensation. The opposite opinion to this, *i. e.*, that after-images arise because of a decreased sensibility of the fatigued retina, was later opposed by Father Scherffer,[2] who based his arguments chiefly upon the material gathered by the naturalist Buffon. Prieur de la Côte-d'Or[3] set up the relationship, so often used later on, between after-images and the phenomena of contrast. This was again modified by Brewster,[4] who showed that there is developed with each color a complementary color tending to dull the original color.

Theories of this kind were brought to a provisional termination by the investigations of Plateau[5] and Fechner.[6] The former gave consistent expression to the theories that presuppose contrasting activities in the retina; the latter explained negative after-images by the principle of fatigue. According to the judgment of Helmholtz these two investigations indicated the status of science during the fifth decade of the nineteenth century—a decade that was so important for optical research.

[1] Jurin, "Essay on Distinct and Indistinct Vision," p. 170 in Smith's *Optics*.
[2] Scherffer, *Abhandlung von den zufälligen Farben*, 1765.
[3] *Ann. de Chim.*, Bd. LIV, 1804, p. 1.
[4] *Phil. Mag.*, 1833, II, p. 89; IV, p. 354.
[5] *Essai d'une Théorie générale comprenant l'Ensemble des apparences visuelles qui succèdent à la contemplation des objets colorés*, Bruxelles, 1834.
[6] *Pogg. Ann.*, 1838, Bd. XLIV, pp. 221, 513; Bd. XLV, p. 227.

In the field of color contrast Leonardo da Vinci[1] was one of the first to point out that colors of equal perfection produced the most beautiful effect when placed next to their opposites, *e. g.*, white with black, red with green, yellow with blue. The coloring of shadows in the light of the rising and setting sun was considered objective because shadows caused by the light of the blue sky are really blue. It was left for Rumford[2] to prove the subjective nature of the coloring by observing the shadows through a tube and thereby noting how the colors disappeared. After this Plateau[3] incorporated the phenomena of contrast in his theory of after-images. Not only in time are opposing states of the retina arranged alongside of each other, but also in regard to the spatial extent of the excitation, in such a manner that around the stimulated area there is first of all a zone of a certain nature which is shown in the phenomena of irradiation, and then adjacent to it but farther away is the opposite zone which produces the contrast.

Our knowledge of the temporal relations of light sensation received its most important addition in the discovery of the differences between daylight and twilight vision and our knowledge of the spatial relations in the discovery of the differences between peripheral and central vision. And with this we have arrived at the standpoint of the most modern theories of color. The differences between them would seem to be due in great part to their various points of departure, *i. e.*, in the group of facts in physiological optics which is regarded as fundamental. The hypotheses that start with the facts of color-mixture, *i. e.*, the objective conditions of visual sensation, can be grouped together as the three-color theories; opposed to this we have the

---

[1] Leonardo da Vinci, *Trattato della pittura*, 1651, cap. CC.
[2] *Philos. Transact.*, LXXXIV, p. 107.
[3] *Ann. de Chim. et de Phys.*, 1834, LVIII, p. 339.

four-color theory, which starts with the subjective arrangement of visual sensations. Out of the critical discussions of these theories there have grown the opinions that reflect the present status of these theoretical problems.

### (1) THE THREE-COLOR THEORY

The deduction from the laws of color-mixture that three sensation processes independent of one another are called into being by the external stimulus was first of all made by Thomas Young.[1] The basic outline of his theory was determined by the fact that he ascribed to the sensory nerves only those characteristics that had been discovered for the motor nerves of man and the animals, *i. e.*, the change between rest and activity. The former corresponds to the sensation of black and the latter to that of white or colored light. The simple color sensations, from the mixture of which all others arise, must be arranged at the three corners of the color-triangle. Corresponding to this, Young presupposed three kinds of nerve-fibres in the eye, which, if stimulated separately, would give the sensations of red, green, and violet respectively. Homogeneous light excites these three species of fibres in varied degree according to the length of its waves. Of course, the facts of color-mixture forming the basis of Young's theory had long been known. Before Newton's time the trinity of principal colors, red, yellow, and blue, had been mentioned by Waller as a scientifically acknowledged fact, in an attempt at a classification of the colors. The new part of Young's theory was the hypothesis of the three physiological processes.

This most important part of the theory was introduced into modern optics by Helmholtz. The application of the principle of specific sensations to the separate nerve-fibres

[1] Th. Young, *Lectures on Natural Philosophy*, 1807.

led him to the hypothesis of special fibres for red, green, and violet sensations.[1] The effect of different kinds of light upon these elements singly could remain undetermined if only each species of fibres was dependent in a different manner upon the wave-length. If the relation between the physiological effect and the wave-length were represented by a curve, then the curves for the red, green, and violet components would have to differ in a characteristic manner.

In Helmholtz's theory of color, which later became so famous, we can separate the principal thought, *i. e.*, that changes in the state of the organ of vision are possible in three directions, from the physiological interpretation, which presupposes in the nerve substance only single changes, *i. e.*, changes that deviate from the state of repose in one single direction.[2] These special hypotheses as to the immediate effect of light were later dropped, and the expression "component" was introduced for the different parts of the color-sensation process. With this Helmholtz's theory became a three-component theory, and it is in this form that it is still under discussion at the present day.

We must also bear in mind that at that time the concept of an elementary sensation was not recognized in the sense in which it is used in modern psychology. If at the present time an elementary sensation is defined as one which cannot be further split up into parts even after the most careful subjective analysis, then it would, of course, be a contradiction in Helmholtz's color theory to say that red, green, and violet are basic sensations and that white is a mixed sensation. It is clear, however, that this contradiction has crept into the theory because of the subsequent shift of meaning of the concept "basic sensation."

[1] *Cf.* p. 277.
[2] *Cf.* von Kries, "Die Gesichtsempfindungen," in *Nagels Handbuch d. Physiol.*, III, 1905, pp. 129 *ff.* and 266 *ff.*

Not a psychological but a physiological meaning is attached to this concept by Helmholtz. In spite of occasional remarks that the three basic sensations, and especially red and violet, differ from the others in a purely subjective manner due to the greater glow of their color saturation, nevertheless the chief meaning of the concept "basic sensation" is its physiological meaning.

### (2) THE FOUR-COLOR THEORY: OPPOSITION AND DEVELOPMENT

Red, yellow, green, and blue have been recognized as the four chief colors since the time of Leonardo da Vinci, and it was Aubert who was the first to declare them the principal sensations in the physiological sense. The principles by means of which a theory of color could be arrived at were to be sought partly in general philosophical opinions, as, for example, in Mach's axiom that each psychic entity corresponds to a physical one.[1] But such a conclusion leading back from the sensations and their arrangement to the physiological processes could arrive at a special theory of color only when special presuppositions as to the nature of the physiological processes themselves had been reached.

In this way it was E. Hering[2] who gave the four-color theory its authoritative form, by making it a theory of contrast-colors. By calling the totality of color sensations variegated (*bunt*), he tried to avoid the original double meaning of the word color (*Farbe*), which even in Goethe's time, following the old meaning, was used to denote all qualities of light. The special presuppositions which Hering postulated consist in supposing that processes of an

---

[1] Mach, *Arch. f. Anat. u. Phys.*, 1865, pp. 634 *f*.
[2] *Sitzungsber. d. Wien. Akad., Math.-Naturw. Kl.*, 1874, 69 (3).

opposite nature take place in the nerves, *i. e.*, the decomposition and recomposition of highly complex substances. Let the processes of the first group be called dissimilating or D processes and those of the second assimilating or A processes, then the contrasting pairs in the black-white sensation and in the principal color sensations can be looked upon as D and A processes in a special visual substance. The organ of vision is thus made up of three visual substances to some extent independent of each other, *i. e.*, white-black, red-green, and yellow-blue substances.

It has been regarded as a special advantage of this theory that it gives us a concrete picture of the psychological arrangement of our sensations. But we must not forget that in two important points it is lacking in this direct correspondence with the subjective system of sensations. First of all, the neutral sensation between white and black stands in a relationship to the two end sensations of the white-black series different from that in which the neutral sensation gray stands to a pair of contrast colors. Secondly, there arises a whole series of difficulties by making light stimulation dependent upon six variables, whereas in the psychological system of light sensations the single sensation can be fully accounted for by three variables.[1]

The theories of Hering and Helmholtz, differing as they do in many important points, were brought into harmony in a very unexpected manner by J. von Kries, in the sense that the relative truth of each could be recognized by the other. This union was brought about in part by the discovery that a differentiation of function in the retina corresponds to the differences of daylight and twilight vision dependent upon the adaptation of the organ of vision. This division of function among the end-organs in the retina was interpreted by many investigators in this

[1] *Cf.* J. von Kries, *op. cit.*, pp. 147 *f.*

way, namely, that the cones, occurring chiefly in the centre, were responsible for phenomena seen in daylight, whereas the rods were supposed to function chiefly in dark adaptation. This functional division of the rods and cones of the retina was first made by Max Schultze.[1] The cones were assumed to furnish all kinds of light sensations but the rods only sensations of brightness. To this Parinaud[2] added the suggestion that this function of the rods depended upon the visual purple, the fluorescence of which gave off the substratum for brightness sensations. Deficient production of visual purple causes hemeralopia and the composition of our organ of vision out of rods and cones causes the Purkinje phenomenon.

Von Kries[3] also recognized the rods as the bearers of pure brightness sensations. In regard to daylight vision he presupposed that the peripheral processes of the retina worked according to the three-color component theory. This zone theory of von Kries is supposed to unite the theories of Helmholtz and of Hering. It does not attempt, however, to give a unified principle embracing the totality of optical facts nor yet a detailed conception of the nerve processes underlying those facts.

The principle generally recognized in these newer theories, according to which the psychological arrangement of the sensations forms the point of departure, is also the basis of Wundt's gradation theory. Wundt had at first[4] accepted the ideas involved in Young's theory, but even in the *Grundzüge der physiologischen Psychologie*, published in 1874, he commenced his criticism, especially because of

---

[1] *Archiv f. mikroskop. Anatomie*, 1866, 2, pp. 247 ff. Cf. G. E. Müller, in *Zeitschr. f. Psych. u. Physiol. d. Sinnesorg.*, 1897, Bd. XIV, pp. 161 ff.

[2] *Compt. rend.*, XCIII, 1881, pp. 286 f.

[3] *Die Lehre von den Gesichtsempfindungen*, 1882.

[4] *Vorlesungen über die Menschen- und Tierseele*, 1863, pp. 133 f.

the close connection of the theory with the principle of the specific energy of the nerves, and he attempted to get back to the peculiarities contained in the arrangement of visual sensations in the color-circle. It was chiefly through Hering's work that he arrived at the conviction that brightness and color stimulation were to be looked upon as different processes. Later on any correspondence between the primary physical colors and the fundamental physiological processes is unhesitatingly denied and in its place there is set up the principle that to each qualitative or quantitative difference in visual sensation there corresponds a qualitative or quantitative difference in the visual process.[1] From this there arises—to borrow an expression coined by von Kries in the study of tones—a gradation theory for light sensations which can also be distinguished from the component theories as a periodicity theory. Inasmuch as this theory denies a special place to the principal colors in the psychological color series, it is an example of the varied interpretation a principle may lead to, which at first sight would seem to imply absolute uniformity, *i. e.*, the principle of the subjective arrangement of the visual sensations.

Of the later modifications of the four-color theory the Ladd Franklin[2] theory has risen to great prominence especially in the United States. Of more interest to us than the hypothetical conception of the differences in the chemical disintegration in the rods and cones is the change in the evaluation of the principal colors. Yellow and blue are the two colors that correspond to a division of the white process; red and green, on the other hand, arise out of another division of the yellow process, since a mixture of pure green and pure red does not result in a colorless sen-

---

[1] W. Wundt, *Philos. Stud.*, 1888, Bd. IV, pp. 310 *ff.*
[2] *Zeitschr. f. Psych.*, etc., 1893, Bd. IV, pp. 211 *ff.* [*Mind*, N. S., vol. XI, p. 672. Trs.]

sation but in a yellow. Unfortunately, this theory too is lacking in any empirical determination of the presupposed pure colors.

The theory of G. E. Müller[1] represents the cleverest attempt at a further development of the four-color theory. This theory changes the concept of antagonism so that the sensations are not, as with Hering, made to be absolutely dependent upon the relation of the opposite psychophysical processes. Further, light is not supposed to affect directly the substratum of sensation but must first go through a white substance, a red, a yellow, etc. To this is added the idea of indirect values; the red material has, for example, an indirect yellow value. By means of this co-operation of the different kinds of color material we can explain in a perfect manner the finer differences in color-blindness. Inasmuch as Müller's theory divides the organ of vision unequally into different parts arranged behind each other, it can be classed as one of the zone theories.[2]

From the discussions of the last two decades one can see with some certainty that the principle at first emphatically laid down, which used the subjective peculiarities of visual sensation in order to go back to definite conclusions as to the underlying physiological processes, has not fulfilled the promises which it at first held out. Rather there seems to have arisen out of the numerous failures a demand, always growing more imperative, to separate the problems of the physiology of the organ of vision from those of a psychology of visual sensations.[3]

[1] *Zeitschr. f. Psych.*, etc., Bd. X, 1896, pp. 1, 32; Bd. XIV, 1897, pp. 1, 161.
[2] Von Kries, *op. cit.*, p. 276.
[3] *Cf.* the treatment of the present position of the theoretical problems in von Kries, *op. cit.*, pp. 279 *ff.*

### 3. Theories of Audition

In no other department of psychology has the work of a single investigator led to such unification of theoretical opinions as Helmholtz's theory of tone sensations has accomplished in the department of tone psychology. The older attempts at a theory of audition are nothing more or less than a preliminary history of the resonance theory. Further developments of the resonance theory dominate all psychological acoustics since the time of Helmholtz, except for a few isolated attempts to find an insight into the origin of auditory sensations on other principles. We must also cast a glance at theories of consonance, which are themselves of much more ancient origin than the real theories of audition and were only connected up with the latter in recent times. Here again it was not the elementary phenomena, the simple tone sensations, that caused a necessity for an explanation to be felt, but rather the more striking phenomena, the combinations of tones.

#### (a) *Preliminary History of the Resonance Theory*

The main thought of the resonance theory belongs to the eighteenth century. For the simultaneous direct perception of difference-tones Condillac[1] thought that different perceiving parts in the organ of hearing were a necessary requirement. To prove the subjectivity of auditory sensations, Lossius pointed to the sympathetic sounding of a string when its tone is being sung and suggested that the process in the ear might be analogous; "but whether there are as many fibres in the ear as there are fundamental tones, or, further still, so many as to allow of shades of difference

[1] *Traité des sensations*, I, VIII, § 4.

between these fundamentals, cannot be determined."[1] From the anatomical examination of the end-organ, Cotugno arrived at his comparison between the cochlea and a lute attuned to different tones ranging from the cupola to the base.[2]

To these beginnings of a resonance theory there were added purely psychological discussions as to the possibility of simultaneous sensations. From the very beginning the favorite example was taken from tone sensations, ever since Aristotle answered the question as to whether a multiplicity of sensations of the same sense could exist at one and the same time by pointing out that this could happen only if they mixed together like a high and low tone in a consonance. From the possibility of the separate perception of simultaneous tones, Herbart[3] came to the conclusion that each musical tone must have its distinct place in the organ of hearing. At first the anatomical discoveries did not give much encouragement to this theory. Since the nerve endings in the cochlea were surrounded by water, there was no support whatever for this would-be analogy between nerve-fibres and stretched elastic fibres. But purely psychological doubts were also raised. From the supposition of a specific excitability of the fibres there would follow as a conclusion that there must exist an infinite number of fibres; and, besides this, simultaneous excitations would be separated in space in different parts of the organ. This was a succinct expression of that nativism which had been dominant since the time of Müller.[4] The arguments of the physiologist Harless[5] rest upon a very insecure physiolog-

---

[1] *Physische Ursachen des Wahren*, 1774, p. 109.
[2] *De aquæductibus auris humanæ internæ*, Naples, 1760.
[3] *Lehrbuch zur Psychologie*, § 72.
[4] *Cf.* pp. 326 *f.* See also the article "Hören," by Harless, in Wagner's *Handwörterbuch der Physiologie*, IV, 1853, p. 311.
[5] *Op. cit.*, p. 435.

ical foundation. He questions the ability of the ear to perceive several tones separately and simultaneously. The ear is not able to recognize two simultaneous tones as separate individual sensations except in the same sense as the artist may recognize the principal colors in a mixture in spite of the fact that the impressions coming from it may be perfectly fused together. This line of thought is a capital example to show how often there may remain hidden for a long time something that we take for granted as an immediate result of introspection. The difference between hearing a certain tone in a combination of tones and of analyzing a color-mixture into its component parts is for us so striking that the analogy used by Harless appears extremely strange.

A change was made in the direction taken by the theories of audition as soon as the results of anatomical investigation came to the aid of the results already obtained by mathematical analysis. Seebeck proved that a laminar elastic body only took up out of a complex vibration those partial vibrations which came near to its own vibration frequency. Anatomical investigation then discovered a special appendage to the nerve terminals, the so-called organ of Corti, which could easily be supposed to be equipped with special elastic properties.

### (b)  The Theory of Resonance

Following along these lines Helmholtz arrived at a mechanical theory of hearing in his *Lehre von den Tonempfindungen* (1862).[1] He started with the presupposition that the ear is able to analyze complex vibrations into simple pendular vibrations. The combination out of many sepa-

[1] [English translation, by A. J. Ellis, *Sensations of Tone*, 3d ed., London, 1895. Trs.]

rate vibrations of a clang produced by a musical instrument comes to our perception as a clang by means of the ear. In reality the movement of the particles of air is always simple, brought about by a single cause. The only analogy found in nature for such an analysis of periodic movements into simple ones is in the phenomenon of sympathetic vibration. Under the influence of a powerful clang only those strings of a piano, with its damper raised, vibrate sympathetically which correspond to the simple tones contained in the clang. If, now, each string of the piano were connected with a nerve-fibre, then each clang, precisely as it happens in the ear, would produce a whole series of sensations corresponding to simple pendular vibrations.

Some such arrangement as this Helmholtz really believed he had found in the inner ear. The ends of the auditory nerve are everywhere connected with a special auxiliary apparatus which, vibrating sympathetically with the outside vibrations, very probably shakes and stimulates the nerve mass.

After the problem of audition had thus been transformed into a mechanical one there arose the opportunity for the use of mathematical assistance which Helmholtz could manage with a master-hand. The mechanics of resonance show, first of all, that bodies which sound for a long time, *e. g.*, tuning-forks, resonate strongly, because they sum up for a long time the really weak thrusts and pulls of the sound-waves. But there must exist the greatest possible correspondence between the fundamental tone of the body in question and the stimulus tone. If, however, we take bodies in which the sound dies down rapidly, *e. g.*, tightly stretched membranes or thin, light strings, then we find that their resonance is not so restricted to a definite periodic vibration of the stimulus tone. For if a sounding body comes to rest after, say, ten vibrations, it is not so important that new shocks which it receives after this period should correspond perfectly with the period of the former shocks.

For this relationship Helmholtz brought forward a mathematical theory which does not depend upon the nature of the resonating body. Let $x$ be the distance of a body $m$ from its position of equilibrium, and $-a^2x$ the elastic force. Now, let a periodic force, $A\ sin\ nt$, act, and also a force checking the vibrations, the intensity of which is proportional to the velocity, *i. e.*, $-b^2 \dfrac{dx}{dt}$. Then the equation for the movement is:

$$m\frac{d^2x}{dt^2} = -a^2x - b^2\frac{dx}{dt} + A\ sin\ nt.$$

From the integral of this equation Helmholtz was able to draw up a table which would show after how many vibrations the intensity of a freely vibrating body would be reduced to a tenth for determined differences between the specific tones of a stimulating and a resonating body, by means of which the intensity of perfect resonance would be reduced to a tenth. For example, a body the resonance vibration of which is reduced to a tenth by a difference of an eighth of a tone reaches, when freely vibrating, a tenth of its vibration intensity after 38 vibrations; whereas for a body that requires a difference of two tones in order to resonate as much less, the second phenomenon will occur already after 2.37 vibrations. These figures become of some importance when considering the so-called trill threshold. Trills of about eight beats per second can be obtained at almost every part of the scale. They are, however, not everywhere equally plain, for in the bass they become indistinct by running together. If now the upper threshold of the velocity of the trills is conditioned by the after vibration of the receiving fibres, then in the light of Helmholtz's theory this fact would be a proof that it must be different parts of the ear that are made to vibrate by different tones. For if the ear were to vibrate as a whole and be capable of a noticeable after vibration, it would do the latter in its own specific vibration period, which would be absolutely independent of the period of vibration of the primary exciting tone. In such a case not only would the trill threshold be everywhere equally high, but there would also be mixed with the two tones a third tone which belonged to the ear. The result, therefore, would be quite different from what is actually observed.

What parts in the ear actually vibrate in sympathy with the separate tones cannot be definitely stated. At first Helmholtz supposed that the varying firmness and elasticity of the rods of Corti were the reason for the varying pitch. After Hensen's[1] measurements of the dimensions of the basilar membrane, and the observations of C. Hasse that the bow of Corti is wanting in birds and amphibia, it became more natural to suppose that the pitch depended upon the varying breadth of the basilar membrane. The number of outer fibres in the cochlea amounts, according to Waldeyer, to about 4,500. With a medium difference-threshold of 0.5 vibrations which increases decidedly as it approaches the limits of the musical scale, this number of fibres would be fully sufficient to account for distinguishable differences in pitch. Any number of other differences in pitch could also be perceived by this theoretical arrangement. For a tone lying between two neighboring rods of Corti would set them both vibrating sympathetically, but that rod would vibrate more strongly which was more perfectly attuned to the tone in question. The least perceptible difference in pitch would then be dependent upon the delicacy with which the degree of excitation of these two

[1] *Zeitschr. f. wissensch. Zool.*, Bd. XIII, p. 492.

nerve-fibres could be compared. This theory also explains the fact that our sensation increases continuously with a continuous increase in pitch, as, of course, must be the case if only one rod of Corti is set into sympathetic vibration at a time.

The sensation of tones of different pitch is thus a sensation in different nerve-fibres. From this there also follows directly an explanation of timbre which depends upon the fact that a clang, besides setting into vibration the particular rod of Corti corresponding to its fundamental, causes vibration in a number of others, *i. e.*, stimulates sensations in many different groups of nerve-fibres. The resonance theory also explained in general the phenomenon of clang analysis as long as the vibrating movements of the air and other elastic bodies arising out of several simultaneous sources of sound are the sum of the separate movements which the separate sources of sound produce. This law, however, has exact validity only for infinitely small vibrations. The totality of phenomena, which arise from the fact that the real vibrations are very small but still not infinitely small, was arrived at by Helmholtz[1] by means of mathematics. One set of such phenomena are the combination-tones, which Sorge had called attention to as far back as 1740 in his *Vorgemach musikalischer Komposition*. Of these combination-tones the objective ones that are known to take place as vibrations in the air outside the ear come under the ordinary interpretation. The subjective combination-tones, however, must arise somewhere in the outer parts of the ear between the tympanum and the resonance apparatus. In the asymmetrical setting of the tympanum and in the loose connection of the malleus and incus at the joint Helmholtz saw more than sufficient cause for such deviations from the simple laws of vibration.

[1] " Über Kombinationstöne," *Poggendorfs Annalen*, Bd. XCIX, p. 497.

### (c) Further Development of the Resonance Hypothesis

Since the days of Helmholtz several investigators, although acknowledging the mechanical processes of sympathetic vibration as giving the best all-round picture of the hearing process, nevertheless show great hesitation in accepting it as final and comprehensive. Hensen[1] pointed out that it would be the business of future investigations to search for a series of nerve processes which were tuned down with a kind of damper to the series of tones that we are able to hear. Besides that it might also be necessary to search for another apparatus which would bring to perception such phenomena as beats.

L. Hermann[2] arrived at a considerable modification of the resonance hypothesis by starting with the idea that each kind of period, including that of the rise and fall of a tone intensity, would be sensed as a tone as long as its frequency came within the range of our tone sensations.[3] R. Koenig[4] had already made fairly accurate observations on the phenomena appearing during the simultaneous sounding of two or more tones. He traced these back to the beats of the primary tones, and by doing this returned to the explanation that had been first given by Lagrange[5] for difference-tones, independent of any theory of hearing. Such an explanation of difference-tones, which is quite similar to Young's, contradicts, however, the principles of the Helmholtz theory of resonance; for two simultaneous simple tones affect only the resonators corresponding to their vibration period. A third resonator, whose vibration period might correspond

---

[1] Hermann's *Handbuch der Physiologie*, III, 2, 1880, p. 99.
[2] *Pflüg. Arch.*, Bd. XLIX, 1891, p. 499.
[3] *Pflüg. Arch.*, Bd. LVI, 1895, p. 467.
[4] *Poggend. Ann.*, Bd. CLVII, 1876, p. 177.
[5] *Misc. Soc. Taur.*, 1795.

to the beat period of the two primary tones, could not possibly be affected by these.

Besides this, the fact was also brought forward against Helmholtz's conception of combination-tones that they appear very clearly with a moderate intensity of the primary tones, *e. g.*, during the dying down of tuning-forks. The extent of their audibility was also restricted. Koenig could testify with certainty only to the existence of difference-tones if the difference between the primary tones was within half an octave.[1] Besides this, Voigt[2] formulated the mathematical theory for the phenomena that arise out of the sounding together of two tones, without having to presuppose, with Helmholtz, a deviation from the linear laws of sound. In the periodic maxima of the resulting vibration, which, in conformity with the older beat-tone theory, are bound to cause a tone sensation, he was able to represent not only Helmholtz's but also Koenig's tones. This proof of Voigt's also increased in importance because Hermann emphasized the special conditions of the deductions of Helmholtz. For he not only neglected the higher powers of the amplitude of the difference-tones, but also made the elastic force of the reaction dependent upon the elongation $x$ and $x^2$, and thereby introduced an asymmetrical elasticity. With the physically simpler hypothesis of a non-linear but still a symmetrical elasticity the velocity must be an uneven function of the elongation. Then we get the ternary, quinary, etc., combination-tones, and not the binary, which correspond to the difference-tones.[3]

For such reasons Hermann returned to an explanation of difference-tones out of beats. He set resonators sounding by means of air vibrations. Now, these resonators affect

---

[1] *Quelques expériences d'acoustique*, 1882, pp. 87 *ff*.
[2] *Nachr. v. d. Göttinger Gesellsch. d. Wiss.*, 1890, No. 5, p. 159.
[3] *Op. cit.*, p. 507.

the nerve-fibres through the mediation of nerve-cells, which are, as it were, attuned to their own specific period, and which, because of their elective excitability for a specific frequency of stimulations, were called by him counting-cells. The decisive point in Hermann's theory is the supposition that these counting-cells stand in functional relationship to all resonators. Now, if the tone $n$ is interrupted $\nu$ times, it will stimulate the counting-cell $\nu$, and this will be heard as an interruption-tone. Difference-tones arise from the fact that the vibration resulting from two primary tones is a vibration which approaches the arithmetical mean of the vibration periods, which rises and falls in amplitude, and which, therefore, immediately changes the phase. Such a middle or mean tone can, according to Hermann, be heard, and the difference-tone is nothing else than the interruption-tone of a middle tone. By this means Hermann avoided the Wundtian hypothesis of direct stimulation of the auditory nerve. With Helmholtz the mechanical analogy of sympathetic vibration was the determining factor. Hermann, on the other hand, in order to picture the processes in the counting-cells, drew an analogy with electrical processes, which may likewise take place according to the laws of linear elasticity. If the state of a nervous organ oscillates between varying grades of dissimilation and assimilation, we can put the $D$ force proportional to the extent of the deviation from the $A$ side, and conversely. The organ then oscillates isochronically about the state of equilibrium with a decrease in amplitude determined by the degree of damping.

Among the theories that attempt to give a mechanical account of sound excitation without using the facts of resonance, the most noteworthy besides Meyer's[1] is the theory of

---

[1] [Max Meyer, *The Mechanics of the Inner Ear*, University of Missouri Studies, 1907. *Arch. f. d. gesamt. Physiol.*, Bd. CLIII. The following is a brief and simple statement of his theory: "Another theory

R. Ewald,[1] which represents a specifically modern way of thinking. Ewald agrees with Mach's statement that there exists a relation between the problems of technology and those of physiology, inasmuch as the former has the task of attaining certain ends with a free choice of the means, whereas the latter has to search for the means that have really been used for a definite purpose. According to Helmholtz's theory, the perception of a single tone would be impossible, because in every case the higher resonators must be affected by a fundamental tone. Besides this, it does not give an explanation of interruption and difference tones, of the difference between tone and noise, or of consonance and dissonance. A purely psychological difficulty also arises from the impossibility of explaining the serial arrangement of tones, and a phylogenetic difficulty from the uselessness of the adaptation of the resonance apparatus to specific sources of sound, since these change during development. Ewald, therefore, returned to the older view-point that the apparatus receiving the sound always vibrates as a whole. On the basilar membrane, in the form of static waves, sound pictures were supposed to arise which differed according to pitch and affected the end-organs of audition in

---

avoids these difficulties by merely assuming that the ribbon-like partition of the tube (cochlea), when pushed by the fluid, moves out of its normal position only to a slight extent and then resists, and that, therefore, the displacement of the partition must proceed along the tube. If successive waves of greater and lesser amplitude, as we find them in every compound sound, act upon the tympanum and indirectly upon the fluid in the tube, the displacement of the partition must proceed along the tube, now farther, now less far, now again to another distance, and so on. Accordingly one section of the partition is displaced more frequently, another less frequently, others with still less frequencies in the same unit of time. This theory then makes the hypothesis that the frequency with which each section of the partition is jerked back and forth determines the pitch of a tone heard, and explains thus the analyzing power of the ear." Ebbinghaus's *Psychology*, translated and edited by Max Meyer, 1908, p. 77. Trs.]

[1] *Pflüg. Arch.*, Bd. LXXVI, 1899, p. 147.

accordance with their spatial arrangement. Differences in pitch were determined by the distance between the nodal lines and by the lengths of the separate wave valleys. In his experiments with elastic membranes stretched across wooden frames Ewald believed he had obtained an experimental foundation for his hypothesis.

In spite of all this, the point of view established by Helmholtz still remains the dominant one in physiological and psychological acoustics at the present time. Even his theory of combination-tones, which seemed to be the most insecure, has quite recently been supported by the investigations of K. L. Schaefer and Waetzmann.[1] These investigations deal with the intensity of difference-tones, which, according to Helmholtz's theory, should be proportional to the product of the amplitudes of the primary tones. No other psychological theory can compare with the resonance theory in regard to the fortunate position it has maintained in spite of all hostile attacks.

### (d) Consonance Theories

About twenty-five hundred years ago Pythagoras gave science this riddle to solve: In what relation does consonance stand to the relations between small whole numbers?[2] But it was not until Fourier formulated his theorem and applied it to the analysis of tones made by the ear that the fundamental question was made clear. This theorem showed how any periodically changing value, however constituted, could be expressed as the sum of simple periodic values, *i. e.*, by means of the sine and cosine of the variable quantities. The Pythagoreans expected to find the number re-

---

[1] *Cf. Ann. d. Phys.*, 1909, Bd. XLVIII, p. 1067, and literature cited there.
[2] *Cf.* Helmholtz, *Lehre von den Tonempfindungen*, 4 Aufl., 1877, p. 374.

lations, which exist between the seven tones of the diatonic scale, in the distances of the planets from the cosmic fire. The speculations of the Chinese also stretch back to the earliest period. Tso-kiu-ming, the friend of Confucius, set up an analogy between the five tones of the old Chinese scale and the five elements—water, fire, wood, metal, and earth. Later on the twelve half tones of the octave were supposed to correspond to the twelve months of the year. The musical literature of the Arabs is rich in analogies between the consonant intervals and the elements, the temperaments and the constellations. In the Middle Ages the harmony of the spheres played a great part. Athanasius Kircher conceived of a music produced by the macrocosm and the microcosm.

In contradistinction to such fantastic analogies there arose gradually the idea that it was the duty of a real theory of consonance to explain the affective characteristics of specific tone combinations in psychological or physiological terms. The usual designation of consonance as an agreeable and of dissonance as a disagreeable tone combination cannot in this sense be called a theory. Besides this it is easy to show that the affective impression of isolated intervals has changed considerably even within the course of history. The ancients called the octave the most beautiful consonance; the monks of the ninth century praised the fifth as the sweetest of all combinations; whereas at the present day we are inclined to give the first place to the major third.

The psychological problem implicit in the relation of consonance to whole numbers was first treated by the mathematician L. Euler.[1] From contemporary æsthetics he borrowed the principle that an object is pleasing if it shows some definite rule as regards its arrangement. A combination of tones will please us the more the easier we are able

[1] *Tentamen novæ theoriæ Musicæ*, 1739.

to find the law of its arrangement, which is expressed as regards time in its rhythm and as regards pitch in its intervals. Just as we easily notice the regularity of a rhythmical period in which two, three, or four like notes of the one voice are apportioned to one, two, or three notes of the other, in the same way we can easily comprehend it when two, three, or four vibrations of a tone correspond to one, two, or three of another. And this is more pleasing than if the relation of the vibrations can be expressed only by large numbers. As to the psychological processes, however, by which the number relation of the two tones sounded together was comprehended, Euler was unable to give any explanation. The psychological facts appeared unrelated alongside of the physical, and the metaphysical soul force functioned as a go-between in just as unsatisfactory a manner as it did with Leibniz, who supposed the soul to carry out an unconscious calculation of the number of vibrations.[1]

The empirical missing links were found in the nineteenth century in the unconscious perception of the vibration rhythm.[2] This theory has in modern times found its best expression in Th. Lipps.[3] Although tone sensations make up a continuous undifferentiated series, yet they are in origin discontinuous phenomena, the rhythm of which is carried over to the soul and to its excitations. The rhythms of these psychic excitations, which underlie our conscious tone sensations, are friendly or support each other if they fit into each other in a simple manner, but they are antagonistic if they do not fit together but cross and oppose each other. Now, this fitting together or support of one psychic content by another gives rise to pleasure and the opposi-

---

[1] *Principes de la nature et de la grâce*, 1718, 17.
[2] F. W. Opelt, *Allgemeine Theorie der Musik auf den Rhythmus der Klangwellenimpulse gegründet*, 1852.
[3] *Psychologische Studien*, 1885, pp. 92 ff.

tion or inhibition gives rise to displeasure. This principle explains the affective states of consonance and of dissonance.

Attempts to find the missing link between the physical and the psychological conditions in certain concomitant sense phenomena date back to the eighteenth century. As far back as 1700 the deaf Sauveur explained dissonance by means of the overtones which he had discovered. And Estève in 1751 derived consonance from coinciding partial tones. In a similar way Tartini's considerations regarding the reason of consonance[1] were based upon the difference-tones discovered by himself and Romieu in 1753. According to the criticism of his contemporaries, Tartini's book was so obscure that no one could really form an opinion of this matter. Later on overtones were again used by Rameau and D'Alembert.[2] Since each sounding body produces besides the fundamental (*générateur*) also the twelfth and the next higher third as overtones (*harmoniques*), it follows that the major chord is the most natural of all. The minor triad arises if we seek three tones which have the same overtone, namely, the fifth of the first tone. This is, however, not so perfect and natural. In the way in which it is taken for granted that the natural corresponds absolutely with the pleasing is mirrored the whole disposition of the age, which was characterized by the desire for a return to nature. The historical importance of all these attempts lies in the fact that they gradually shifted the problem of consonance from the field of metaphysics to that of the natural sciences.

It was Helmholtz who first developed these beginnings into a real phonetic theory. He had analyzed the single clang into its component parts and had noted the special phenomena arising in combinations of clangs; *i. e.*, beats and combination-tones. Then he explained dissonance by

[1] *Traité de l'Harmonie*, 1754.
[2] *Eléments de Musique suivant les principes de M. Rameau par M. d'Alembert*, 1762.

means of the beats arising from all these component parts. The psychological content of Helmholtz's principle of consonance is surprisingly simple. Those clangs are consonant which continue alongside of each other in an undisturbed, even flow; if, however, a part of the clang total falls apart into uneven tone beats and the compound clang becomes rough, there arises a dissonance. The decisive characteristic is positive for the dissonance. Consonances are those intervals in which such disturbances of sensation are wanting. This union of the feeling of unpleasantness with the roughness of the dissonance has first of all a physiological basis, since any intermittent excitation exerts a greater strain upon the nervous system than an even, continuous stimulation. Along with this we have also the psychological peculiarity that the separate tone beats of a dissonant compound clang form a confused tone mass which we are unable to analyze clearly into its separate elements.[1] This psychological motive is clearly of an intellectualistic character. The analysis of a tone mass into its component parts, the counting of vibrations, obviously presupposes processes that are very nearly allied to intellectual ones.

To this Helmholtz joined a second principle that is obtained out of the phenomena of the relation of clangs.[2] The degree of the direct relationship of tones is determined by the number and the intensity of the partial tones common to two fundamental clangs. This relationship is not apprehended by means of conscious analysis, but rather is it immediately perceived as a similarity of the clangs, so that consonance can be called similarity produced by common partial tones and dissonance as a want of similarity or the presence of a relatively small amount of similarity.[3] The first principle of consonance applied to simultaneous tones,

[1] *Lehre v. d. Tonempf.*, 4th ed., p. 369.     [2] *Op. cit.*, pp. 423, 584.
[3] After Stumpf, *Beiträge zur Akustik und Musikwissenschaft*, H. 1, 1889, p. 3.

whereas the second principle is of significance only in regard to successive tones. For in the first case a common partial tone would be only a third weaker tone, which could not be heard as common to the two strong tones. It is strange that Helmholtz nowhere calls attention to this duplicity in his theory of consonance.

In lieu of all these theories of consonance C. Stumpf formulated the so-called theory of fusion. Since the difference between consonant and dissonant tones can lie neither in unconscious functions nor yet in the feelings, we must with Helmholtz seek this difference in the region of tone sensations, not, however, in the accompanying overtones or beats but rather in the two tones themselves. As the only characteristic that presented itself in this connection, Stumpf[1] thought he must take the fusion of simultaneous tones. This definition returns to the original definitions of the words consonance ($\sigma\nu\mu\phi\omega\nu\iota\alpha$ = sounding together) and dissonance ($\delta\iota\alpha\phi\omega\nu\iota\alpha$ = sounding apart), and thereby corresponds with the peculiarity of consonance almost universally emphasized in the ancient theories of consonance, *i. e.*, that in it there takes place a mixture of simultaneous tones.[2] In contrast to the striking affective impression of consonance this characteristic of fusion has gradually been forgotten during succeeding ages. In modern times it has been occasionally mentioned, as, for example, by L. Bendavid,[3] the writer on æsthetics, who understood by consonances such tones "in which the ear imagines it hears only one tone when they are sounded simultaneously."

An understanding of Stumpf's definition of consonance

[1] This principle was first formulated from his own observations on the piano, 1883; for a full description, see "Konsonanz und Dissonanz," *Beitr. z. Akust. u. Musikwiss.*, 1898.

[2] *Cf.* Stumpf, "Geschichte des Konsonanzbegriffs," I. Teil, *Abh. d. Münch. Akad., phil.-hist. Kl.*, 1897.

[3] *Versuch einer Geschmackslehre*, 1799, p. 435.

depends upon a correct comprehension of his concept of fusion. This is not the same as the old concept of the unity of consciousness nor does it correspond with not differentiating the tones in question; for in this latter case at the very moment in which we differentiate the tones of a consonant interval this interval itself must of necessity become a dissonance. Fusion can be better described as the joining together of two contents of sensation into one whole, or as unity, or as the approach of the complex clang to unison. The psychological conditions can be supposed to lie in the similarity of the tones, a fact that is, however, mentioned much later than fusion.[1] Such a similarity is universally agreed upon only in the case of the octave. In the case of the fifth most authors are even inclined to assume just the opposite relationship. In contradistinction to that similarity the degree of which is measured by the difference of pitch between the tones, the similarity of consonant tones must denote a new characteristic. Stumpf eventually decided the question in this manner by supposing that there exist two independent and fundamental relations between tones—similarity, which depends upon the difference between the number of vibrations, and fusion, which depends upon the relations between the number of vibrations. Fusion can be explained only by reference to physiological conditions. At the simultaneous sounding of two tones having a simple relation between their vibration periods, there take place in the brain processes more nearly allied to each other than would be the case with vibration periods not making such simple proportion. These simple relations are supposed to form a special kind of union which Stumpf called specific synergy.

In more recent times F. Krueger, from his observations on

[1] *Cf.* Stumpf, " Die pseudo-aristotelischen Probleme der Musik," *Abh. d. Berl. Akad.*, 1897, pp. 12 *f.*

chords, came to the conclusion that the coinciding of difference-tones differentiates consonant from dissonant intervals purely as a matter of sensation.[1] In the discussion with Lipps and Stumpf[2] that followed, Krueger emphasized the series of gradations between consonance and dissonance, in the middle of which series he placed the neutral sonance. The discussion also brought into particular prominence certain principles of method which carry us quite beyond the immediate field of consonance problems, no matter what is thought of the explanation by difference-tones.

[1] Krueger, "Differenztöne und Konsonanz," *Arch. f. d. ges. Psych.*, Bd. I, 1903, pp. 205 *ff.*; Bd. II, pp. 1 *ff.*

[2] *Psych. Stud.*, Bd. I, pp. 305 *ff.*; Bd. II, pp. 205 *ff.*; Bd. IV, pp. 201 *ff.*; Bd. V, pp. 294 *ff.*

# CHAPTER XI

## THEORIES OF SPATIAL PERCEPTION

If we make a division into simple sensations, on the one hand, and sense-perceptions as complex psychical phenomena, on the other, we find that among the latter spatial perceptions would only form one group along with many others; *e. g.*, musical perception of clangs mentioned above. In the historical development, however, attempts to clear up the nature of the formation of ideas by the help of spatial perceptions are considerably in the majority. Certainly temporal ideas have from the very beginning attracted attention to themselves, but the real nature of the problem of time has only been recognized in more recent times. In those early attempts at explanation we rarely pass the stage of wonder at the mysterious nature of time, which no one could describe so emphatically as Augustine.[1] In contradistinction to this, psychological attempts at a theory of space stretch back to a much earlier period. Theories of spatial perception are, indeed, the typical examples of perception theories, which have been contrasted to theories of sensation ever since the concepts of sensation and perception began to be distinguished from each other.[2]

As long as the distinction between sensation and perception had not been drawn, the only question which received consideration was the question as to how contents of the outer world were able to reach the subject. This was the standpoint of the early Greek natural philosophers. The

[1] *Confessiones*, l. XI, c. XXVIII.  [2] See p. 271.

division began to appear in Plato, who in the *Theætetus* denied to the soul the perception of the object and of the color itself; for the idea of the object arises only out of a judgment passed upon the colored content of perception. Aristotle touched a new side of the problem when he found that certain qualities, such as motion, size, form, and number, were common to the content of all or of most sense-perception. After this conceptual division the problems of spatial perception lay in the hands of natural scientists. Even though the very marked oppositions between nativism and empiricism arose only within modern times, yet they show themselves in some special problems of spatial perception at a very early period. The sense preferred by the older theories is generally the visual sense. By means of the changing relationship into which spatial ideas of the visual and tactual senses are brought, the above-mentioned oppositions become more and more explicit.

## 1. The Natural Scientists of the Middle Ages

The most important contribution of the Middle Ages to the theory of vision is without doubt the *Optics* of Alhacen, which Witelo translated from the Arabic in 1269.[1] It is true that the physiological conditions of vision are presented by Alhacen in the traditional manner. When, however, we come to his discussion of the content of vision we are surprised at his psychological insight. He first of all draws the distinction between superficial and definite seeing or comprehension (*comprehensio superficialis et certificata*), which corresponds to our distinction between direct and indirect vision. Movements about the axis of vision are required in order to make objects perfectly perceptible. Since under changing conditions the same characteristic

[1] *Cf.* Siebeck, *Arch. f. Gesch. d. Phil.*, II, 1889, p. 414.

may return, the visual sense is able to recognize the simplest characteristics of objects; *i. e.*, brightness, color, and position, to which may be added distance, form, similarity, etc. But similarity, for example, cannot alone be the content of sensation, since, although the form of each object reaches the organ of vision, a particular form of similarity is never to be found there. It is much more likely that the idea of similarity arises only out of the comparison of different forms. In a corresponding manner thinking (*ratiocinatio*) is taken up with the recognition (*cognitio*) of an object, which process is pictured as an assimilation of the form of the seen with the memory image. By an analogous assimilation of an object with like objects arises the knowledge of kinds or species. In this manner sensation is supplemented, so that in the repeated perception of an object a complete act of perception is made up of sensation, recognition, and discrimination.

This demonstration of special psychological processes in perception is certainly remarkable. Alhacen considered the processes of perception as unconscious processes. He considered them as paralleled by the unconscious links in the process of cognition and thought them to be unconscious because of their rapidity. By doing this he anticipated some of the most important lines of thought in modern empirical theories. The same empirical point of view was also taken by Alhacen in a series of special problems dealing with vision. An immediate perception of depth is possible only if the latter is not too great and if the eye can follow some boundary all the way. Judgment as to the size of an object is based upon the distance and the angle of vision.

In his explanation of the perception of place Alhacen abandons his empirical standpoint and goes over to a point of view which, in modern terminology, we would designate as nativistic. Not only would the form of a thing be perceived in the eye but also the place of the organ upon which the form lies. Such a change in view-point can be observed right into modern times. The outer superficial differences between localization on the flat field of vision and the apprehension of depth impressed themselves upon psychological thought sooner than the more hidden common characteristics, which occur in the sense-perception of both these phenomena equally.

Alhacen also made observations on the temporal peculiarities of visual perception. Only in the case of known impressions does the perception take place instantly; in the case of strange or indistinct impressions a noticeable period of time elapses before their recognition. That a definite time is always necessary is clear to us from the phenomena of color-mixture with the rotating color-wheel. This temporal course is due, according to Alhacen, partly to peripheral causes, as we should say to-day; *i. e.*, the conduction of the impression in the nervous system. But besides this he points to psychological conditions to account for the varying degrees of rapidity with which impressions come into consciousness, and he tries to group these under certain general laws. Among various objects, that one will be recognized the soonest whose form shows the least similarity to that of the other figures. In a garden we notice the rose more quickly than the myrtle. Furthermore, the simple is more quickly apprehended than the complex. We see, first of all, the surrounding circle and then the many-sided figure drawn within it. With this Alhacen is touching upon questions dealing with the theory of apperception, which carry us far beyond the theory of the formation of sense percepts. Last of all, he tells us that sense illusions depend upon sensation, upon an act of knowledge, or upon an act of judgment. To the last class belong the real illusions of perception, such as the illusive movement of the moon, in which case the unperceived movement of the clouds is transferred to the moon because of the lack of some stationary object for the purpose of comparison. In spite of all imperfections Alhacen has given us a remarkable sketch of a theory of visual perception, and its attempt to give an explanation of psychical processes distinguishes it favorably from the conception of vision as a purely physical problem, a conception which at the beginning of the new era of the natural sciences was the dominant one.

The newer observations seem at first to confirm the old theories.[1] J. B. Porta[2] had described the camera obscura, and although it was only much later that Scheiner[3] made the observation that the picture on the retina arose according to the same principle, yet it provided the obvious analogy of a similar picture being produced in the eye and so appeared to prove the validity of the old picture theory. These new views were carried over by Kepler[4] into physiological optics. Brightness and color are emanations from bodies possessing light or color, and they cast a reverse picture on the retina just in the same way as in the camera obscura. By his geometrical proof that almost parallel rays of light falling upon the pupil are brought to a focus upon the retina, Kepler disposed of the old opinion that the picture is produced upon the choroid or upon the crystalline lens. The change in accommodation is caused by the changes in distance between the crystalline lens and the retina. Besides this Kepler recognized that in the judgment of the distance of an object the distance between the two eyes, the so-called basal distance, serves as a base-line, and

[1] *Cf.* W. Wundt, *Beiträge zur Theorie der Sinneswahrnehmung*, 1862, pp. 75 *ff.*, from which some of the following material has been taken.
[2] *Magia naturalis, sive de miraculis rerum naturalium*, Antwerp, 1590.
[3] *Oculus, sive fundamentum opticum*, London, 1652, p. 176.
[4] *Astronomiæ pars optica*, 1604, c. V; *Dioptrice*, 1611.

therefore the most important factors in the recognition of depth, apart from the binocular parallel axis, were known to him. In a most remarkable manner do his philosophical opinions come to the surface in the problem of upright vision, which naturally arose after his discovery of the inverted position of the retinal image. The inversion of the image, which is projected in the direction of the reaction, is supposed to correspond to a distinction that he draws between passive sight and active light emanation.[1]

Kepler's most important physiological discovery, namely, that the picture projected through the lens comes into existence upon the retina, was called in question after later observations. In 1668 Mariotte[2] discovered the blind-spot, sometimes named after himself. This discovery caused such excitement that it had to be demonstrated even to the King of England. Since no visual sensation occurs at the point where the optic nerve enters the retina, Mariotte concluded that it was not the retina but rather the choroid that formed the sensitive sheath of the eye. It was almost a hundred years later before this dispute between the physiologists was finally settled by Haller,[3] by pointing out that the structure of the retina at the blind-spot differed from that of the rest of the retina. To solve the psychological difficulties that still seemed to exist, Bernoulli[4] brought forward the observation that our attention is generally concentrated upon objects seen in direct vision. He also hinted that the space in the field of vision corresponding to the part projected onto the blind-spot would be filled out by our imagination.

Descartes's famous *Dioptrik*, which explains localization on a plane surface of vision in a nativistic manner, can be

[1] *Paralip. ad Vitellionem*, 1604, p. 169.
[2] *Philos. Transact.*, 1668, t. II, p. 668; t. IV, p. 1023.
[3] *Element. Phys.*, t. V, p. 477.
[4] *Comment. Academ. Petrop.*, t. I, p. 314.

looked upon as a fusion of the physiological knowledge of the seventeenth century with general philosophical opinions. The recognition of the position of objects is dependent upon the position of the parts of the brain at the point where the sensory nerves arise, for the soul at any given moment apprehends the position of all the things which lie along straight lines stretching from the sensory parts of the body to infinity. The optical inversion of the retinal image is counteracted by a corresponding inversion of the fibres of the optic nerve in the brain, so as to make objects appear upright.

To explain perception of depth Descartes made use of the most important empirical factors. The changes in the form of the eye which take place in near and distant vision for dioptric reasons are accompanied by changes in certain parts of the brain by the help of which the soul perceives distance. Further, from the angle of convergence of the eyes we draw conclusions as to the distance of objects with the help of a kind of natural geometry. In a very clever manner he applied his theories to the explanation of optical illusions. We see an object in a false position because of confusion of the position of the nerves. We judge bright objects to be near because the contraction of the pupil caused by the intensity of the light is connected with the movement made in the adaptation of the eye to near vision. In spite of all these valuable observations the peculiarly psychological processes seem to have eluded him, for he remained too much bound up in his materialistic conception of the soul and the old introspection psychology.

## 2. Some Special Problems

The opinions which in modern times have developed into the sharp contrasts of nativistic and empirical theories showed themselves in the earlier days not only in the attempts to explain the phenomena of vision in general but also in the treatment of certain special problems. The general peculiarities of the organ of vision had long been known before a theoretical interpretation of them was thought of. Kepler was the first to arrive at a correct general knowledge of the refractive qualities of the eye. And yet we have reports as to the use of spectacles long before his time. Pliny[1] notes the fact that there are concave emeralds that possess the quality of gathering the sight together, and probably a use of this quality was made by the short-sighted Nero in his custom of watching the gladiatorial combats through an emerald.[2] At the beginning of the fourteenth century spectacles were described as the invention of a Florentine nobleman, Salvinus Armatus, who died in 1317. In something like the form of eye-glasses their use soon became quite common. The canon Van der Paele, in Jan van Eyck's triptych at Bruges, is holding such a pair of eye-glasses in his right hand.

Among the first purely psychological problems of visual perception to be discussed is the fusion of the images arising in the two eyes. The anatomical hypothesis that the optic nerve-fibres join together in the required manner in the chiasma is traceable to Galen. In principle Johann Müller seems to have agreed with this hypothesis, inasmuch as he also demanded an anatomical foundation for single vision. There is a much greater variety of attempts to come to a psychological understanding of single vision. Very striking is Porta's[3] presupposition that we always see alternately with one eye at a time. This idea was supported later in the eighteenth century by Du Tour[4] because of the analogy with the phenomenon of rivalry between the two

[1] Plinius, l. XXXVII, c. V.  [2] Plinius, l, II, c. XXXIV.
[3] *De refractione*, 1593.  [4] *Acta Paris.*, 1743.

halves of the field of vision. In the relationship of this hypothesis to the contention that only one single content of consciousness is present at any given moment,[1] it is not so strange as it appears at first sight.

Much greater popularity was enjoyed by the intellectualistic explanation that the single percept arose out of the two retinal images by means of a special act of the understanding. Kepler[2] seems to have leaned toward this explanation, although he dismissed the problem of single vision very simply by supposing that we have a single image if the two retinæ are stimulated in the same manner and a double image if they are stimulated in different ways. His contemporary, Aguillonius,[3] modified the theory by supposing that visual impressions were always projected onto a certain plane cutting through the fixation-point, the so-called horopter. After all these attempts at explanation we come to the formulation of a law for such phenomena. Johann Müller maintained that single and double vision were dependent upon the question as to whether the images fell upon the same or upon different portions of the two retinæ.[4]

The oldest attempts at an explanation of depth seem to arise from the question as to the apparent size of the moon at the horizon and at the zenith. This question can be followed through centuries of human thought.[5] Aristotle's[6] explanation that the humid vapors in the atmosphere produced an enlargement of the image is one that was frequently repeated. Ptolemy[7] (about 150 B. C.) also conceived the refraction of the light rays in the vapors of the atmosphere as a reason for an objective enlargement. But besides this he also pointed to the influence which the

---

[1] See p. 182.
[2] *Dioptrice*, Prop. 62.
[3] *Opticorum libri* VI, Antwerp, 1613.
[4] See below, p. 327.
[5] *Cf.* E. Reimann, *Zeitschr. f. Psych.*, Bd. 30, 1902, pp. 1 *ff.*
[6] *Problemata*, sect. XXVI, Probl. 55.
[7] *Almagest*, l. III, c. 3.

filling out of the distance would have upon our perception of that distance and therewith upon the apparent size. The Aristotelian idea was refuted in the Middle Ages by Alhacen. Then Vitellio (1270) pointed out the changes that the apparent form of the celestial vault undergoes, and since that time psychological explanations have been dominant. Later on, however, Gassendi maintained that the moon appears larger when near the horizon, since in this position the pupils become enlarged because of the weaker light.[1] Father Gouye,[2] Molyneux,[3] and Samuel Dunn[4] brought forward their observations against the explanation of the phenomenon which held that the greater apparent distance of the stars on the horizon was caused by the illusion of filled space, and pointed out that the illusion in regard to the moon still remained even if the other objects were absent. A good orientation as to the status of the question in the eighteenth century can be obtained in Smith's *Optics* (1738). In this book he attacks Berkeley and returns to the old explanation by the apparent form of the celestial vault, the horizontal measurement of which, according to his own investigations, is three or four times greater than the vertical. In contradistinction to the varied series of such attempts at explanation, the fundamental fact of ordinary binocular perception of depth, *i. e.*, the difference of the image in the two eyes, a fact which was known since the time of Euclid by many of the ancient opticians, only came to be fully recognized in the nineteenth century. In addition to the older cursory observations of Smith in regard to stereoscopic fusion, it was, above all, Wheatstone's discovery of the stereoscope (1833) that led to a fuller knowledge of such phenomena.

[1] *Opera*, vol. II, p. 225.
[2] *Mémoires de l'académie de Paris*, 1700, p. 11.
[3] *Philos. Transact.*, vol. I, p. 221.
[4] *Philos. Transact.*, vol. LII, p. 462.

Last of all, the development of visual images after operations on the born-blind played an important part. This was mostly interpreted to support the empirical point of view. Molyneux declared that in such a case the previous differentiation arrived at by the sense of touch between a ball and a cube could not be immediately transferred, an opinion that we also find clearly stated in Locke. The description given by Jurin[1] (1738) of the origin of a differentiation on the ground of a change in the images according to the angle from which they were seen was a common one down to the time of Johannes Müller, after which nativism successfully opposed these empirical lines of thought.

### 3. Nativism

Although nativistic elements are to be found in many of the older theories, yet it remained for the nineteenth century to work out coherent nativistic theories. In the theory of sense-perception we see very clearly the dependence of the positive sciences upon philosophy during the first half of the nineteenth century. The influence of Kant affected not only the philosophers, for we see Kantian ideas finding their way into the natural sciences. The nativism of Johannes Müller, which he applied only to his theory of vision, was very soon applied also to the tactual sense, and the theory, with many modifications, still has influence at the present day.

#### (a) The Founding of the Theory by Johannes Müller

Kant's theory of the *a priori* character of space was transferred by Johannes Müller to the problems of sense-perception,[2] and he thereby gave modern nativism its au-

[1] *Cf.* Smith, *Optics*, Remarks, p. 27.
[2] *Zur vergleichenden Physiologie des Gesichtssinns des Menschen und der Tiere*, 1826.

thoritative form. He firmly maintained that the retina senses itself as spread out and that the images upon its surface arrange themselves in two dimensions. The third dimension, depth, is added by reason of the experiences we have from looking at objects from different points of view. Since the latter depends upon some act of judgment, Müller called it an idea in contrast to the sensation which we derive from a plane surface. From the study of double images he formulated the important theory of identical retinal parts. Only impressions that fall on certain points in both eyes are referred to the same point in space. The crossing of the optic nerves makes it possible for a single divided nerve-fibre to lead to such corresponding parts of the retinæ. In the sensorium two such parts correspond to only one single part. The problem of upright vision could give this theory no difficulties. If we see everything inverted then the arrangement of the whole remains exactly the same and the tactual sense makes its localizations agree with the visual sense.

A remarkable consequence for natural science that grew out of this theory is the conception of an absolute physiological size of the extent of the field of vision determined by the sensitive part of our retina. An object lying immediately upon our retina would be seen in its absolute size, as, for example, in the entoptic perception of the choroid.

### (b)  *Its Transference to the Sense of Touch*

The different kinds of theories of space can also be differentiated in a characteristic manner by considering how far the view-point of a certain theory is made to cover spatial ideas arising from both touch and vision. Nativistic theories are, as a rule, more consistent. If spatial perception is once thought to be innate, then this is shared equally by the visual and by the tactual sense. Empirical theories tend, on the whole, to give the primacy to touch in the sense that its localizations precede those of the visual sense. If our perception of space is derived from experience, then it is easy for the experiences of one sense to influence those of another. There has scarcely been an absolutely empirical theory of tactual perception. The attempts to make the spatial images of the sense of touch comprehensible without nativistic presuppositions really always go over to the lines of thought involved in the genetic theories.

Since John Locke pointed out that the sense of touch, because of the peculiar insistence of its sensations, gave us an immediate idea of the outer world, empirical theories immediately took advantage of this wonderful power. The immediate localizations of the sense of touch served as a support to the sense of sight in Berkeley's theory of perception, and Condillac promoted the sense of touch to the only original localizing sense.

The turning-point in the theory of tactual perception is characterized by the fact that E. H. Weber transferred the modern concept of nativism into the department which his own experimental investigations had illuminated so much. In 1829 he made the discovery that two impressions on the skin will be clearly perceived as different only if they are separated from each other by a sufficiently large intervening space.[1] Strikingly different values were found for this spatial threshold on different parts of the body; on the cheek, for example, it was considerably larger than on the lips. This difference can be brought immediately to perception by touching the cheek just in front of the lobe of the ear with the two points of a pair of compasses and then by drawing them rapidly along the skin across the cheek

[1] *Ann. anat. et physiol. de subtilitate tactus*, 1834, p. 46.

until one point rests on the upper and one on the lower lip. In this case the ends of the compass do not seem to be drawing two parallel lines, for they seem to move apart as the lips are approached. As an explanation of this striking phenomenon Weber presupposed that only one sensation arises if two similar impressions stimulate the same elementary nerve-fibre. Since, however, the total diameter of all the nerve-fibres is much smaller than the total surface of the skin, each elementary nerve-fibre must make sensitive a much greater part of the skin than the part corresponding only to its own diameter.[1]

The skin would seem to be divided up into small, sensitive circles each of which receives its sensitivity from one elementary nerve-fibre. Two simultaneous impressions of the same kind fuse together whenever they fall within the same circle of sensitivity. In order to be spatially differentiated, not only must they fall into two different circles of sensitivity but there must also lie between them one or more other circles of sensitivity. With this last statement Weber avoided the objection later unjustly brought against him by Kölliker and Lotze; *i. e.*, that each circle of sensitivity was enclosed within a narrow line possessing a high power of differentiation from all the adjoining parts. So far, then, the idea of a circle of sensitivity was determined in a purely anatomical manner. Tactual perceptions themselves could become possible only through experience. The perception of supraliminal distances was supposed to depend upon the number of circles of sensitivity lying between any two points. The finer the spatial threshold the greater does the distance appear to be, a postulate which Weber thought to be proved by the above-mentioned experiment with the compasses. In spite of some concessions to experience, the distance of two circles of sensitivity re-

[1] *Über den Tastsinn und das Gemeingefühl*, pp. 526 *ff*.

mains an absolute measure for our sense-perception of the world. We must add in conclusion that Weber in a later revision of his theory explained the idea of a break or space between two impressions to the want of sensation, otherwise generally occurring, on the intermediate circles of sensitivity. He also abandoned the search for a special organ for the so-called spatial sense. His theory, therefore, sums up perfectly the position reached by the investigations of his day.

### (c) *The Later Nativistic Theories*

A more exact knowledge of different phenomena of binocular vision from the middle of last century onward made a revision of Müller's opinions absolutely necessary. The fact that single vision is really possible on non-identical points of the retina had always caused difficulties and had required special auxiliary hypotheses, as, for example, the one of E. Brücke[1] that fusion arose through the wandering of the fixation-point.

These attempts at explanation lead us back to a form of nativism which ascribes to the retina the innate capacity of projecting visual impressions in the direction of their entrance and is, therefore, customarily called the projection theory. In its principles this theory takes us back to fairly old theories of sense-perception, and the statement of it by Porterfield[2] helps to counterbalance the empiricism of the eighteenth century.

In recent times this was modified by A. Nagel,[3] who made both retinæ project independently upon two different spherical surfaces, the intersecting line of which runs through the fixation-point. In this way many of the characteristics of

---

[1] *Müller's Archiv*, 1841, p. 459.
[2] *On the Eye*, vol. II, 1759, p. 285.
[3] *Das Sehen mit zwei Augen*, 1861.

double images can be explained. Schleiden[1] also supported the projection theory inasmuch as he presupposed an immediate perception of direction. The concept of productive imagination used by him leads one, however, far beyond nativistic theories.

In the endeavor to do justice to the phenomena of fusion of double images and the perception of depth from the standpoint of a subjective identity hypothesis, Panum[2] was the investigator who went furthest. The perception of height and breadth depends upon an innate and specific kind of sensation of the relation between the separate points of the retina and their projection lines, which sensation arises out of the specific arrangement and quality of the nerve elements of the central optical region. Each point on the one retina has corresponding to it an identical point on the other and besides that a corresponding circle of sensitivity. With such corresponding points single or double vision arises according to the relations existing between them. The perception of depth is based upon a sensation of the binocular parallel axes and is supposed to arise from the reciprocal action of the central stimulations produced by the contours of both the retinal images.[3]

The logical conclusions of the principles laid down by Panum are met with in the theory of Ewald Hering.[4] From the stimulation of a point on the retina there arise, in addition to the visual sensation, three kinds of spatial feelings. The first two kinds are dependent upon the height and breadth of the given part of the retina; they join together for the common field of vision into a feeling of direction and coincide exactly for corresponding points of the retina. The

---

[1] *Zur Theorie des Erkennens durch den Gesichtssinn*, 1861.
[2] *Physiologische Untersuchung über das Sehen mit zwei Augen*, 1858.
[3] *Op. cit.*, pp. 52, 85 *ff*.
[4] *Beiträge zur Physiologie*, 1861–4, and Hermann's *Handbuch d. Physiol.*, III, 1, 1879, pp. 343 *ff*.

third spatial feeling is a feeling of depth, which for each two identical retinal points takes on equal but contrary values and for symmetrically placed positions equal and similar values. Up to this point the presuppositions answer the requirements which every theory of spatial perception is bound to meet. If instead of spatial feelings we substitute the expression "local signs," this theory can readily be transformed into one of the theories that we shall have to consider later. The further contention that those stimuli which fall upon corresponding points always give rise to only one simple sensation is, to be sure, exclusively the prerogative of the identity hypothesis. For single vision with disparate parts of the retina Hering gives the purely psychological reason that in such a case the practice and training of the attention necessary for the separation of complex sensations is wanting. In the binocular fusion of two impressions the total resulting sensation receives the middle value of the feeling of direction and of the feeling of depth. In this way the feelings of depth of identical parts which have equal but opposite values are reduced to zero. All points whose depth values have in this way been reduced to zero appear to our immediate experience to lie upon a plane surface.

In later theories these basic principles of a nativistic theory so masterfully sketched by Hering are all lost in a mesh of wondrous hypotheses. An example of such an one is the theory of Hasner,[1] which characteristically terminates in an extreme rationalism. Perception and sensation both stand on the same level, but the activity of the senses themselves is conceived of as a sort of mathematical calculus. The concept of red is supposed to arise out of four hundred and fifty-two billions of time intervals per second, including certain wave-lengths and duration of oscillation. In its ap-

[1] *Beiträge zur Physiologie und Pathologie des Auges*, 1873.

plication to visual perception this questionable principle leads to a statement such as this: the number of stimulated sensitive elements in the retina drawn upon the horizontal and vertical lines of vision, which are used as the two axes, yields the concept of a surface according to definite mathematical laws.[1] In contrast to this we find a very cautious formulation of a nativistic theory by C. Stumpf.[2] Starting from the standpoint inherent in the principles of Panum and Hering, he contented himself with bringing forward the possibilities of sense development, among which the sensational nature of perception is conceived to be the most probable. In this respect his standpoint is characteristic of modern times, seen in the cautiousness practised in the decision of the ultimate problems of sense-perception.

We note in this development of the nativistic theories a gradual retreat of the really nativistic elements to the farthest outposts of sense-perception. The inevitable concessions to the influence of experience have made it necessary to tear down the rigid scaffolding of the conventional nativism of Johann Müller and to restrict nativistic presuppositions to the always hypothetical foundations. In contrast to this we see in the empirical theories a continually increasing emphasis and value placed upon empirical lines of thought.

### 4. Empiricism

Empirical theories of space originally accompanied sensational theories of knowledge. Corresponding to the various motives that led up to philosophical sensationalism we find that the rise of empirical theories of space was dependent upon very varied conditions. The classical form of such a theory is to be found in the formulation by Helmholtz in the nineteenth century.

[1] *Op. cit.*, p. 11.
[2] *Über den psychologischen Ursprung der Raumvorstellung*, 1873.

### (a) The Origin of Empirical Theories of Space

There are no systematically empirical theories of space to speak of until the time of Locke, whose doctrine of knowledge forms the philosophical background for these theories. Of course, we can trace back some beginnings to a much earlier period.[1] Even Locke's famous comparison of consciousness, which has not as yet received any impressions from experience with "white paper void of all characters" (*tabula rasa*), has an ancient original in the πίναξ ἄγραφος of Alexander of Aphrodisias.[2] In mediæval philosophy the term *tabula rasa* became common, and with it Albertus Magnus describes the attitude of receptive intelligence, which, like a polished and smooth slate, stands ready for the reception of impressions. In his emphasis upon the sense of touch Locke introduced a thought that became characteristic for nearly all modern empirical theories. Formerly Democritus had credited the sense of touch with a knowledge of the true being of all things. With Locke it is the sense that recognizes the primary qualities as differentiated from the others. Many empirical characteristics are to be found in the theory of Malebranche, who anticipated some of the thoughts of the more influential Berkeley by trying to determine different "signs" for the perception of distance, and who characterized this sensation in contradistinction to the simple sensations as a complex sensation (*sensation composée*).[3]

Berkeley,[4] however, was the first to formulate a complete empirical theory in which all localization by the visual sense was derived from the sense of touch. The child

---

[1] See above, p. 318.
[2] *Cf.* Baeumker, *Arch. f. Gesch. d. Phil.*, Bd. XXI, 1908, p. 296.
[3] *Recherche*, l. I, c. VIII, § 4.    [4] *Theory of Vision*, 1709.

learns first of all to differentiate between the movements of its own hands and feet. Simultaneously with these movements there takes place a visual sensation in the eye, and from that time on the tactual perceptions remain associated with definite visual sensations. If, now, a visual sensation stimulates a particular part of the retina without any accompanying tactual impression the child comes to the conclusion that the object occupies the same place that previously, say, its finger occupied. In this way the separate visual impressions are given a position in space; by means of the continual connection with tactual impressions perceptions of extent, form, and the other spatial ideas come into being.

In such a theory there are recognized definite psychical processes in vision. Berkeley himself did not know what to make of them. All he did was to describe them in the terms of the old introspection psychology as processes of inference that take place so quickly that we are not aware of them unless we pay special attention to them. From this time onward this empirical theory remained securely established in British psychology as a true companion of that philosophical empiricism which through the two Mills and Alexander Bain had forced an entrance into modern psychology.

### (b) *Helmholtz's Theory of Space*

The typical supporter of empiricism in the theory of spatial perception in Germany is Helmholtz. According to his empirical view our sensations are signs for our consciousness, the significance of which our reason has to learn. The signs received by the visual sense are not only different as regards intensity and quality, *i. e.*, as regards brightness and color, but there also exists a difference dependent upon the position on the stimulated retina, a so-called "local sign." Besides this, we feel the degree of innervation that takes place in the nerves moving the ocular muscles, and we learn from experience what changes take place in the visual image of an object in accordance with the change in movement. The psychical functions which build up out of these signs our spatially arranged world were originally considered by Helmholtz as intellectual processes. Later, however, he reduced the much-disputed unconscious inference to associative processes.

The mass of details on which Helmholtz used this auxiliary hypothesis is controlled by a few theoretical considerations which stand out with remarkable clearness. Helmholtz started out from a differentiation between what in the perceptions received by the visual sense is conditioned directly by sensation and what, on the contrary, is conditioned by experience and practice. The memory images of past experiences combine with present sensations and produce a perceptual image in which consciousness does not draw any distinction between what has been contributed by memory and what by present sensation. In order to carry out this distinction, which is fundamental to his theory, he starts with this empirical postulate, "that no undoubtedly present experience can be put aside or avoided by an act of the intellect or reason." From this he concludes "that nothing in our sense-perceptions can be recognized as sensation which can in the perceptual image be avoided or turned into its opposite by means of elements which can be proved to arise from experience."[1] These view-points are of some importance, even though the cogency of the empirical explanations might singly be called in question.

[1] Helmholtz, *Physiol. Opt.*, 2d ed., p. 611.

## 5. The Genetic Theories

The genetic theories developed out of the endeavor to avoid the anticipations of nativism and to dispense with the inductive conclusions of empiricism. A welcome means for this purpose was found in the concept of association along with the addition of the ideational mechanics of Herbart. However unsatisfactory an extension of this concept to the totality of psychical processes may be, it certainly showed itself to be of prime importance in the theory of the origin of sense-perception. To Herbart can be traced a whole series of fusion theories, among which the oldest are generally those that imagine they can dispense with any physiological aid. These purely psychological theories tried to deduce the necessity for spatial arrangement from the nature of the soul itself and the stream of ideas and thereby to make comprehensible that decisive transition from the sphere of purely intensive states into the spread-out, extensive manifoldness. Out of these theories there gradually developed those that accepted certain physiological preconditions and which we shall therefore group together under the name of "Local Sign Theories."

### (a) *Herbart's Fusion Theory*

From the application of his principles of psychical mechanism to the origin of spatial perception there arose for Herbart the general outlines of a fusion theory. His chief argument against nativism is still of metaphysical origin. The impressions received through the medium of the eye cannot be from the very beginning spatially arranged, because in the unity of the soul the sensations produced on separate parts of the retina must necessarily at first coincide. As soon, however, as the eye is moved there occur series of sensations which are joined together with some regularity. Movement in a given direction causes associations which become active again in movement in the opposite direction. In these series of complexes no one member can be put into another place, but any change of direction is possible.[1] Such an arrangement of sensations appears to us as a spatial arrangement, and it obtains its natural middle point because of the fact that the percept of that which is in the centre of the field of vision is always characterized by the greatest strength, and it therefore tends to inhibit the percepts of the outlying points. Spatial perception, therefore, consists in a graded fusion of one percept with a series of other percepts, which fusion because of its unnoticeably short duration produces the impression of a simultaneously given manifold.

In this theory one of the most important elements for later theories would appear to be the emphasis laid upon the movements of the eye. But we must note the fact that Herbart used this idea quite differently from the way in which it was used in the later theories of fusion. The movement of the eye of which Herbart speaks could be perfectly supplanted by a movement of the outer objects if this would be sure to produce the same succession of percepts. He is concerned only with the relative shift in position and not with the sensations that accompany real movements of the eye.

### (b) *Purely Psychological Theories*

Herbart's fusion theory was converted into a purely psychological theory by Waitz.[2] He started with the prin-

[1] *Psychologie als Wissenschaft*, II, 1, ch. 3, and *Lehrbuch z. Psych.*, II, ch. 3.
[2] *Lehrbuch d. Psychologie als Naturwissenschaft*, 1849, §§ 20-27.

ciple that in the soul, because it was an undivided entity, two sensations differing merely in intensity could not exist at the same time. They would tend rather to come into opposition with each other, an opposition that could not be appeased by successive perception. This last method does not agree with the way in which sensations actually occur, and therefore another solution is necessary. The soul is constrained to perceive the simultaneously given manifold spread out part next to part, and in this constraint lies the origin of our spatial percepts. Similarly, there arises the impossibility of comprehending these states existing next to each other as purely intensive qualities. The soul has to oppose them to itself as foreign objects in extended form. This thought seemed to be given a concrete form in certain optical phenomena of rivalry. If two colors are placed in the field of vision, at first both appear confused. Then one or the other seems to stand out more prominently; *i. e.*, the sensations come into opposition with each other until eventually they both take their proper place side by side.

This standpoint was transcended by making use of the eye movements themselves. The idea was anticipated in the little-known work of the physiologist Steinbuch.[1] But more influential than this were the theories of George,[2] who gave to the very movement of the organ a part in the production of spatial perception. It is only when tactual sensations of the skin are combined with those of movement that we are able to have, in the reflection based upon this, a spatial disposition of sensations. To carry this thought further it was absolutely necessary to have an exact analysis of the sensations arising through movement. George spoke simply of movement in general and approached empiricism

[1] *Beitrag zur Physiologie der Sinne*, 1811.
[2] *Lehrb. d. Psychol.*, 1854. *Die fünf Sinne*, 1846, p. 235.

very closely in his presupposition of a logical elaboration of the experiences obtained from movement. The analysis of the complex of experiences occurring during a movement led investigators to recognize a series of sensations of strain graded as to intensity which are accompanied by temporal percepts. The way in which spatial perception separates itself out of this complex was shown in the theory of Alexander Bain,[1] the most perfect of the purely psychological theories. The spatial percept can separate itself from the temporal because the same differences in the percept which are necessary to measure a spatial distance may be experienced within different periods of time according to the velocity of the movement. Beside this the arrangement of spatially indicated impressions becomes independent of the order of their succession, inasmuch as we may comprehend successively a series of objects at varying velocities.

### (c) *The Local Sign Theories*

A new way to the localization of sensations was opened by Lotze with his concept of the "local sign." Later on his theory developed partly in a physiological and partly in a psychological direction. All these later forms of the theory of local signs have a common point of contrast to the purely psychological theories, inasmuch as they supply physiological aids to the psychical mechanism, which alone in the latter theories is supposed to explain our separation of objects in space.

#### (1) LOTZE'S THEORY

The doubtful contention of Lotze that the soul as a non-spatial entity is only capable of intensive states is reminiscent of his spiritualistic conception of the soul.[2] He places

---

[1] *The Senses and the Intellect*, 2d ed., 1864, pp. 197 ff.
[2] See p. 30.

himself at once beyond all the older attempts to conjure spatial perception out of intensive states by simply conceding that spatial perception is an original and *a priori* possession of the soul which is not produced by outer impressions but merely turned by them to special uses.[1] The perception of the actual position of outer objects is therefore not really a perception or apperception but rather a re-creation of space. The older attempts to find in the sensation as such characteristics which would force one to a spatial arrangement are inconclusive for this reason alone, that they, strictly speaking, attempt to prove much more than is really present in experience. For those lines of thought are not restricted to a certain field of sensation but are valid for sensations altogether. Now, just as truly as a tone can never appear as a point of sensation, so can a color never reach a purely spatial determination.

Therefore, with two sensations that are going to be separated in space there must be combined auxiliary determinants that will represent their local character. This local sign is a physical nervous process which for each part of the nervous system has a constant association with that varying nervous process which supplies purely intensive excitation. In order, however, for the local signs not only to separate sensations spatially but also to lead to a constant co-ordination, they must themselves form members of a regular series. In the tactual sense they consist of sympathetic sensations that spread over a circle of irradiation. In the formation of local signs for the sense of vision Lotze for the first time uses to their full extent the movements of the eye. Each stimulation of the retina causes a reflex movement which attempts to bring the stimulus on to the point of clearest vision. After such movements have been often made certain sensations of movement become associated

[1] *Medic. Psych.*, 1852, II, chaps. I and IV.

with each impression. Localization with the eye at rest becomes possible owing to the fact that in this case the different impulses to movement compensate each other and call up by means of association the corresponding sensations of movement.

### (2) ITS PHYSIOLOGICAL DEVELOPMENT

The concept of the local sign, the crucial point of Lotze's theory, challenged a closer investigation of its physiological basis. In the tactual sense Meissner[1] explained the physiological substratum of the hypothetical circles of irradiation by supposing that each stimulus affects several sensitive points in varying degrees. The hypotheses of Czermak[2] made use of a combination of Weber's circles of sensitivity and Lotze's local signs. His original interpretation of Weber's experiments depended upon the manner in which the nerve-fibres spread out. Later on he abandoned these anatomical presuppositions[3] and approached nearer to the standpoint of Lotze and Meissner, inasmuch as he supposed that each point of the skin had a local sign of the sensation itself and also one conditioned by the extent of the excitation. From these he arbitrarily distinguishes a third local sign, one that is immediately accessible to observation, namely, that of the circle of sensitivity. This last clearly shows the inner contradiction between the theory of local signs and the theory of circles of sensitivity.

The discovery of the cold, warm, and pressure spots of the skin by Blix[4] in 1882 marked a decided advance. After it had been shown that with successive stimulation there could be discrimination between two neighboring pressure

[1] *Beiträge zur Anatomie u. Physiologie d. Haut*, 1852.
[2] *Müller's Archiv*, 1849, p. 252.
[3] *Wiener Sitzungsber.*, Bd. XV, 1855, p. 466; Bd. XVII, 1855, p. 577.
[4] *Upsala Läkareförenings förh.*, Bd. XVIII, 1882–3.

spots the theory of circles of sensitivity had to be finally abandoned.[1]

### (3) ITS PSYCHOLOGICAL DEVELOPMENT

The motive for a deeper psychological interpretation of the theory of local signs lay in the fact that it really remained unexplained how purely qualitative characteristics found in sensations because of a special nervous process could lead to an extensive or spatial differentiation. In this sense Wundt[2] was the first to investigate the psychological significance of local signs. Each point of the surface of our skin contributes to the sensation a definite local characteristic which, because of experience, is differentiated from the different qualities of the impressions. This special quality of a sensation, as soon as it appears as a partial content of a perception, arouses a visual image of the place corresponding to it. For one born blind the muscle sensations caused by touching objects form a similar means of assistance.

In a similar manner visual percepts are interpreted as a common product of retinal image and kinæsthetic image. From the empirical fact that in percepts of the perfected visual sense sensation qualities of the retina and kinæsthetic sensations of the eyeball are known to be at work we can draw the conclusion that both factors have contributed to the origin of visual percepts.[3] With the original qualitative differences of the retinal sensations which are dependent upon the place of stimulation there are combined the different degrees of intensity of the sensations of strain accompanying movements and positions of the eye. All localization is therefore dependent upon a system of com-

---

[1] *Cf.* M. von Frey and R. Metzner, *Zeitschr. f. Psychol.*, Bd. XXIX, 1902, pp. 161 *ff.*
[2] *Beiträge zur Theorie der Sinneswahrnehmung*, 1862.
[3] "Über das Sehen mit einem Auge," *op. cit.*, pp. 105 *ff.*

plex local signs. A closer insight into the process of the formation of ideas proves the latter to be a kind of assimilative fusion. Now, since each position of the eye has corresponding to it a complex of pressure sensations in the eyeball and of local signs of the retina, the fusion products form a qualitative local sign system of two dimensions. This system controls the flat visual field of monocular vision, and in binocular vision a local sign system of the second order is added, the members of which are the local signs for depth.[1]

The concept of the local sign has been retained in all later genetic theories. It has, however, occasionally relapsed into its simple primitive meaning; i. e., as depending no longer upon movement reflexes as with Lotze but upon purely qualitative differences in sensation, which also occur with the eye at rest. From this point of view T. Lipps[2] formulated a theory of visual space presupposing that sensations on different points of the retina are somehow different and become bound to each other or opposed to each other according as they are near to or far from each other. These arrangements, innate in the individual, arise in the species from the fact that impressions from different retinal points more often correspond the nearer they are. Now, similarity of impressions occasions their fusion, dissimilarity their separation. The same thing is true for the sense of touch. Whereas with Wundt the local signs of the skin achieved a spatial significance only through the mediation of another sense, Lipps, on the other hand, thought he could explain separation in space by means of sensation signs differing merely in quality, with this proviso, however, that the tactual image in general corresponds to the spatial arrangement of the stimulated points. Different points of the skin will be

[1] W. Wundt, *Grundz. d. physiol. Psychol.*, II, 6th ed., 1910, pp. 716 *ff.*
[2] *Grundtatsachen d. Seelenlebens*, 1883, pp. 515 *ff.*

the more often simultaneously stimulated the nearer to each other they are and, conversely, more seldom the farther apart from each other they lie. Simultaneous stimulation gives rise to a tendency to fuse, non-simultaneous to a tendency to separate the impressions. Lipps regards this tendency as valid not only for stimuli of the same sense, but as a law of the spatial complication for disparate stimuli it becomes also a secondary principle which binds together the independent spatial percepts of the sense of vision with those of the sense of touch.

# CHAPTER XII

**THEORIES OF FEELING AND VOLITION**

In the history of psychological thought we can separate easily two chief lines along which theoretical opinions as to the subjective side of the conscious life have moved, namely, theories of feeling and theories of volition. We shall limit ourselves to these elementary phenomena. The opinions about the higher processes of consciousness are partly dependent upon these and partly show themselves in the hypotheses which have been treated in discussing the general trend of psychological thought (Chapters I–III).

## 1. Theories of Feeling

Characteristic phenomenological presuppositions serve as preliminaries to the several theories. The differences among these influence in a peculiar manner the attempts at a theoretical explanation. Theories of feeling can in general be differentiated according to the relation in which the affective experiences are supposed to stand to the other contents of consciousness. At first feelings were considered as modifications of another psychical activity, and thereby the primitive need for unification was most easily satisfied. Corresponding to the intellectualism of all beginnings of psychological thought, cognition or, in general, ideational activity takes the place of a supraordinated function. Then there appear theories which indeed recognize the psychological peculiarities of the feelings but try to deduce them from other foreign conditions. These attempts in part try to deduce them from other psychical contents, such as ideas and their interrelations, and so lead to psychomechanic theories of feelings and again bring forward physiological connecting-links, admitting heterogeneity between feelings and the intellectual contents of consciousness. In contradistinction to all these there stands the group of theories which preserves the psychological nature of feelings and, as with other processes of consciousness, attempts to explain them as psychophysical processes.

### (a) *Phenomenological Presuppositions*

The best orientation for theories of feelings can be obtained from the classification of the contents of consciousness.[1] The dependent position of the feelings contrasts plainly with that of the sensations and sense-perceptions, which from the very beginning secured a sure place in psychological classifications. On the other hand, the feelings have wandered restlessly from one group of the contents of consciousness to another. As often as the phenomenological presuppositions changed, the attempts to explain the nature of the feelings changed also.

The alternative reaching furthest back is the one that asks the question whether feelings are, like ideas, psychical acts that refer to a special object or whether they refer only to the ways in which the other real acts of perception and ideation come to consciousness.

In spite of all other differences in the question of feelings, the second of the two possibilities has almost unanimously been accepted. From Aristotle onward descriptions of feelings have generally taken this direction. It is, however, only in connection with his *Ethics*[2] that he speaks of pleasure as connected with certain psychical activities, and as

[1] *Cf.* p. 190, above.   [2] *Ethic. Nic.*, X, chs. IV and V.

completion of the act it may change in accordance with the kind of act. The later English psychologists agreed with James Mill[1] in teaching that the feeling accompanying the perception is contained in the act itself. And Bain went so far in his description of the relation of feeling to sense-perception as to maintain that each sensation has a double characteristic, an intellectual and an emotional side.

In German psychology Domrich[2] called feeling the way in which consciousness was excited by perception. This explanation has been retained by many even to the present day. Nahlowsky[3] differentiated feeling proper from the pleasure and pain immediately connected with sensation, *i. e.*, the so-called feeling tone. This was taken up by the Herbartians Waitz and Volkmann, since it gave them the possibility of saving the Herbartian theory from the notion that all feelings arose from some relation between ideas.

There is less consensus of opinion in deciding the opposite question whether every psychical act must be necessarily accompanied by a feeling. This problem really belongs to modern psychology, inasmuch as it discovered the contradictions in the traditional theories. We do, however, find that Aristotle in his *Ethics*[4] says that not only all kinds of sensations but also all psychical activities are accompanied by feelings, although in his psychology[5] he speaks of indifferent sensations, *i. e.*, without feelings. In the nineteenth century we find both points of view. James Mill[6] emphatically upholds indifferent sensations. Just as emphatically do A. Bain and J. S. Mill maintain that each sensation has an accompanying feeling. These latter are joined by so many psychologists that Horwicz takes it as

[1] *Anal. of the Phen. of the Hum. Mind*, II, ch. XVII.
[2] *Die psychischen Zustände, ihre organische Vermittlung und ihre Wirkung in Erzeugung körperlicher Krankheiten*, 1849.
[3] *Das Gefühlsleben*, 1862, Einleitung. [4] *Ethic. Nic.*, X, ch. IV.
[5] *De An.*, III, 7. [6] *Op. cit.*, II, ch. XVII.

## THEORIES OF FEELING AND VOLITION

an almost universally recognized fact that all sensations are accompanied by differing degrees of pleasantness and unpleasantness.

Lastly, it would seem as if these two diametrically opposed view-points could be brought into unison. The Wundtian theory of feeling acknowledged indifferent psychological processes in spite of the fact that feelings in general were defined as reactions of apperception to the separate contents of consciousness. Each sensation of a moderate intensity is accompanied by a feeling of pleasure, of a greater intensity by a feeling of displeasure. Since, however, the feeling character changes constantly with the intensity of the sensation, an indifference point must lie somewhere between the two opposites. Against this theory Brentano[1] has urged the following objection, that the displeasure arising with a great intensity of sensation is not really connected with the quality of the sensation but rather with the sensation of pain accompanying the increased intensity of the sensation.

The most convincing proof, however, of the ambiguity of the phenomena in question is the dispute as to whether feelings can be arranged in one or more than one dimension. The pleasure-pain theory, which arranges all feelings between these two opposites, has from the very beginning been favored by ethical and æsthetic motives. In principle it is still held by many prominent psychologists of the present day, e. g., Jodl and Külpe. By others it is just as emphatically rejected as insufficient on introspective evidence. Above all, Wundt[2] showed its insufficiency for the description of the effects of colors and clangs. T. Lipps[3] also expressed his conviction that there exists a number of elementary feelings. The most modern revision of this

[1] *Op. cit.*, pp. 197 *ff.*
[2] *Grundzüge d. phys. Psych.*, 1st ed., 1874, pp. 436 *ff.*
[3] *Selbstbewusstsein, Empfindung und Gefühl,* 1901.

question stands in close connection with the postulation of new classes of states of consciousness, as in the so-called states of awareness.[1] The definite acceptance and the possible range of these new concepts seem to many psychologists to be necessary factors in the ultimate decision as to the place of the feelings.

### (b) Intellectualistic Theories of Feeling

Under the protection of intellectualism, theories of this kind, although really at the uttermost limit of proper psychological analysis, can be traced through the whole history of psychology. The Aristotelian comparison of pleasure with assent and pain with negation contains the elements of a theory which recognizes feeling as a mode of the activity of cognition. His theory of the emotions falls under the same point of view, for it is intimately associated with ethical considerations. Aristotle's famous description of the emotions, with its ethically significant differentiation between the emotions and the passions, has been a model for centuries. He crowned his ethics with the statement that the highest pleasure is occasioned by the activity of the highest faculty of the soul, the νοῦς. The experience of the valuable, which theoretical knowledge brings, spreads to other experiences. This theory shows only a few new points of view during succeeding ages. Spinoza went to the support of the old differentiation between activity and passion with all the means furnished by the more modern theory of knowledge. The affection is an activity or passion according to the clearness or unclearness of the motivating idea. Locke[2] was content with the neutral designation of pleasure and pain as simple ideas which are related to different states of the soul.

[1] See pp. 136 and 211.   [2] *Human Understanding*, II, ch. XI.

The association psychology gave impetus to new viewpoints. Hume considered the feelings as impressions of self-perception by means of the ideas and brought about a connection between these two by means of association. On the other hand, the attempt was made to explain how it was and in what way the affective experiences could arise out of a special kind of cognition. With such an intention Leibniz[1] brought the feelings into connection with confused or unclear ideas. He was joined in the nineteenth century by Hegel with his well-known explanation of the feelings as an obscure kind of knowledge. Contradicting his master on this point, Ch. Wolff described feeling precisely as an intuitive knowledge of the state of the body and pleasure or pain as arising according to the perfection or imperfection of this knowledge. The concept of perfection, the ethical and æsthetic ideal of the eighteenth century, thus became dominant in the theory of feelings as well.[2] Echoes of the old ways of thinking are still heard in the post-Kantian psychology, although the recognition of feelings as a special class of psychical processes was hardly denied after Kant. Such trains of thought were apt to arise in the interpretation of the so-called common or organic feelings, which seemed to give direct information as to the well-being of the body. Some interpreted the organic feelings as a consciousness of the state of health of the body,[3] others described them as a struggle of the weaker sensations from different organs of the body trying to rise into consciousness.[4] At this point the intellectual theory of feelings goes over into a sensational theory.[5]

[1] *Nouveaux Essays*, II, ch. XX, § 6.
[2] For the relation of psychology and æsthetics, *cf.* R. Sommer, *Grundzüge einer Geschichte der deutschen Psychologie und Ästhetik von Wolff-Baumgarten bis Kant-Schiller*, 1892.
[3] George, *Die fünf Sinne*, 1846, pp. 44 *ff.*
[4] Waitz, *Grundlegung d. Psych.*, 1846, p. 64.   [5] *Cf.* p. 355.

### (c) Psychomechanical Theories of Feeling

The theory that all feelings depend upon the reciprocal action of ideas goes back to the observation that several æsthetic feelings are dependent upon the relations of simple impressions. The earliest to be recognized were the feelings arising from musical intervals in regard to their dependence upon the relations of tone sensations. We have the old story of Pythagoras in the blacksmith's shop hearing different consonant intervals in the clang of the hammers. In the weight of the different hammers he traced the relations of the fifth, the fourth, etc. In the field of æsthetics this correlation of the feelings with the relations between ideas was pursued further. Aristotle tried to put upon a sure foundation the Platonic specifications of the beautiful by adding a series of psychological characteristics.[1] Unity, inner connection, the golden mean between extremes, similarity of parts or their relations characterize the æsthetically valuable. The corresponding relations between ideas form the subjective correlates of these objective facts.

These purely psychological beginnings of a theory of feelings based upon the relations of ideas to each other soon received support from the presuppositions of materialistic psychology. According to this latter the real harmony or the conflict of the bodily processes that underlie all ideational activity is the decisive factor for pleasure or pain. The older interpretations of this kind did not start with the simple feelings but rather with the more intense affections, such as the emotions. In ancient times Zeno the Stoic gave the famous definition of an emotion as a movement in opposition to the nature of the soul, which we can picture

[1] *Cf.* O. Külpe in *Philos. Abh., M. Heinze zum* 70. *Geburtstage*, 1906, pp. 101 *ff.*

concretely as a twisting of the soul pneuma. In modern psychology the same standpoint is seen in Descartes' theory of the emotions.[1] Its definition of the emotions as excitations of the soul due to the movement of the animal spirits upholds the old opinion that the emotions, as affections of the soul, require a physical basis. The more such attempts keep to the lines of thought of materialistic psychology the more do they depart from a real theory of feeling.

On the dividing line between metaphysical myths and empirical theories there stands in the eighteenth century the theory of C. Bonnet. He is to be credited with the empirical differentiation between feeling and sensation, as we should say in our modern terminology. In the impression which an object produces we must differentiate that which characterizes the object from that which determines the reaction of the soul. The latter is the feeling which appears in two chief kinds, as pleasure and pain. The real cause of pleasure is supposed to be due to a moderate excitation of the fibres of the brain. Besides this there is a relative pleasure arising from the excitation of different kinds of fibres; in this class belongs the harmonious effect of combinations of certain tones or colors which arise out of a certain succession or combination of movements in the sensory fibres. It was Herbart, however, who finally and decisively separated the psychological part of these theories from their materialistic presuppositions and thereby formulated a purely psychomechanical theory of feeling. Herbart's theory was also not without forerunners. We can trace it back to Scholasticism, and find Buridan[2] making the peculiar attempt to describe the feelings from the standpoint of a psychical mechanism, certainly a very primitive one. The soul strives to prolong a pleasant experience and

[1] *De pass. an.*, I, 27.
[2] *Ethic.*, VII, 25 f., 202 a; 26 f., 203 a (ed. 1489).

to terminate an unpleasant one; as long as it is occupied by one single feeling it cannot bring another into consciousness to the same degree. If feelings of the same kind occur simultaneously, they serve mutually to strengthen each other, just as pleasure at the sight of a flower is increased by the pleasure arising from its scent. Opposite feelings, on the other hand, tend to weaken each other.[1]

These influences were certainly not without effect during the following centuries. The most decisive thing in Herbart's theory was the surprising combination of a psychical mechanism with an extreme intellectualism. For Herbart feelings are ideas which oppose or hinder each other. The state of ideation itself is a strain, since ideation as an activity strives to maintain itself and is nevertheless continually subjected to inhibition. In particular, feelings are differentiated into those that are determined by the content to which they refer and those that are dependent upon the general affective-conative state. To the first group belong the æsthetic and sense feelings, both of which are made up of partial ideas; to the second group belong the emotions.

The most important change that the Herbartian school made in the theory of feelings handed down to them by their master consisted in the separation of sense-feelings as "the tone of a sensation" from feelings proper.[2] They candidly admitted that difference in experiences which Herbart had only with difficulty been able to overcome by means of his artificial theory of partial ideas. The question as to the tone of sensations has remained a matter of dispute down to the present time. In recent times affective sensations are spoken of and they are supposed to belong to the class of sensations.[3] This is, of course, purely

[1] *Cf.* p. 91.
[2] *Cf.*, *e. g.*, Volkmann, *Lehrb. d. Psychol.*, 1875, p. 236.
[3] See p. 206.

a question of classification and has directly nothing to do with definite theories of feeling. If, however, such ambiguity reigns in mere descriptions of our affective experiences, then the attempts at theoretical interpretation are very likely to diverge to a much greater degree.

### (d) Physiological Theories of Feeling

Attempts to build up a theory of feelings on physiological characteristics lead first of all to the hypothesis that feelings have as their substratum nerve processes which are similar to those that condition the rise of a sensation. Under the influence of modern brain physiology this opinion soon merged into the theory that it was a question of central nervous processes.

Because of their psychological presuppositions and conclusions the hypotheses of the first kind represent sensational hypotheses of feeling. Feelings are classified as a special quality of sensation along with the other sensations, from which they are differentiated only by the fact that they can, in their capacity as a general sensation, accompany any other sensation. The nerves of the skin and of the inner organs that have to do with organic sensations are supposed to be the bearers of that special sensation quality. This point of view was upheld about the middle of the nineteenth century by Domrich[1] and Hagen[2], and it found a welcome support because of the customary confusion between the concepts of sensation and feeling.

Besides this the older opinions common among physiologists as to the nature of the organic feelings seem to have influenced psychology. In physiology, from time immemorial, organic feeling (cœnæsthesis) has been contrasted with

[1] *Die psychischen Zustände*, 1849.
[2] *Psychologische Untersuchungen*, 1842.

the sensations of the outer senses as an apprehension of the state of the inner organs, and this was brought about by the sensory nerves of those organs. This unsatisfactory distinction was abandoned by J. Müller from psychological motives. Because of the similarity of those sensations classed together as organic sensations with those of the tactual or "feeling" sense, he put them all into the same group. E. H. Weber went a step further, inasmuch as he presupposed a double method of sensation of those parts supplied with sensory nerves, namely, sensations proper and organic feelings, which latter give us a consciousness of our bodily condition. In order to round this out to a general theory of feeling it was only necessary to extend this same thought to all feelings. This was done by Lotze[1] when he sacrificed his older intellectualistic conception of feeling as an unconscious judgment of the harmony or lack of harmony among the vital functions of the body[2] and considered feeling to arise by means of a specific nerve process that changes with the intensity and quality of the sensory stimulation.

An important set of facts had up till now been insufficiently noticed in the majority of these theories, *i. e.*, the relation of feelings to the movements of expression. From the standpoint of the physiological theories these could be explained by the co-operation of the central physiological processes. The feelings themselves were then, following the explanation of Ribot,[3] generally transformed into phenomena of the central nervous system accompanying the bodily processes. They were, however, at the same time supposed to express the general state of the body. This is Meynert's[4] view, who explained the feeling of joy as due to functional hyper-

---

[1] *Medic. Psychol.*, p. 233.
[2] See article, "Seele," in Wagner's *Handwörterbuch*, Bd. III, 1, p. 191.
[3] *La psychologie des sentiments*, 1897.
[4] *Klinische Voerlsungen über Psychiatrie*, 1897.

æmia of the brain, whereas anæmia caused by the contraction of the arteries gives rise to sadness. The most influential of the varieties of this theory has been the one that has emphatically degraded feelings to mere secondary states. According to James and Lange, a stimulus calls forth as a reflex the movement of expression. The sensations arising from this movement are then the real basis for our affective experiences. As James's oft-quoted sentence has it: "We do not weep because we are sad, but we are sad because we weep."[1] With Lange[2] this view is extended to a general relationship between physical and psychical states—a relationship that can be criticised from the standpoint of theory of knowledge. As long as we consider the psychical state as the cause and the physical state as the effect, it remains incomprehensible why it should give rise to these special physical symptoms. If, however, we reverse this relationship the state of the soul becomes readily comprehensible since it is simply the sensation of all bodily disturbances. This theory found favorable ground in the discussion of the emotions. Lange described these as sensations of organic disturbances produced by the changes in innervation of the sympathetic nerves. In support of his theory he pointed to the great extent of the movements of expression and to the reinforcing reaction they have upon the emotions.[3] The fundamental truth in this theory, which is seen in the facts of sympathetic movements and in the peripheral irradiation of the motor excitation accompanying every feeling, has gained for it much sympathy.

[1] *Mind*, O. S. IX, 1884, pp. 189 *f.*
[2] *Über Gemütsbewegungen*, 1887.
[3] For some anticipations of this theory, see Titchener, *A Text-Book of Psychology*, II, 1910, p. 479.

### (e) Psychophysical Theories of Feeling

With the recognition of feelings as independent kinds of contents of consciousness the problem of psychophysical theories of feeling becomes slightly different from what it formerly was. It is no longer a question of a dissolution of feeling into the other contents of consciousness but rather a psychophysical interpretation of the affective processes. This can, of course, lead to quite different results according to differences in collateral points of view. The recognition of feelings as belonging to the general classes of psychical processes was the first step toward theories of this kind. But the interpretation of feelings as states into which the soul is placed by means of its sensations and ideas allowed, on the one hand, the thought to arise that the feeling contains within itself a dim knowledge of the real state of the soul, and by allowing this the theory at once became an intellectualistic one. And, on the other hand, this interpretation, by its presupposition of a metaphysical concept of the soul, went far beyond the immediate knowledge derived from self-observation. It remained for the psychology of the nineteenth century to get rid of those intellectualistic and metaphysical motives. Since the time Wundt[1] emphasized feeling as that side of self-consciousness which relates to the real state of the perceiving subject, there was started a more exact analysis which ultimately made this relation to self-consciousness untenable. For, in contradistinction to self-consciousness, which is a much later development, feeling represents an original content of consciousness. The direction in which Wundt himself later interpreted the feelings as psychophysical processes was determined for him by the supposition of a very close con-

[1] *Vorles. üb. d. Menschen- u. Tierseele*, 1863.

nection between the great variety of affective states and the physiological symptoms of expression.[1]

Of the theories that fall within the group we are discussing there remains to be mentioned the one that departs furthest from the immediate experience of consciousness, inasmuch as it sees in the affective states the evolutional starting-point for all kinds of contents of consciousness. A. Horwicz in this sense regarded feelings as the most original independent psychical states, out of which sensations and ideas had developed.[2] His theory has lasted in some form or other down to the present time because of the favor with which any line of thought connected with evolution is regarded. We meet it also in some American text-books of psychology in which at times a cautious adherence to experience is combined with the most audacious biogenetic hypotheses.[3]

## 2. Theories of Volition

Whereas the feelings, in spite of their ceaseless change, can easily be grasped as unitary processes the characteristics of which are independent of the flow of time, volitional experiences, on the other hand, group themselves so characteristically into different stages that the separate theories of volition can be differentiated according to the stage in the course of the volitional process that they have chosen as their starting-point. In doing this the will has traversed the whole ladder of psychical functions from an absolutely transcendental faculty down to the idea accompanying a reflex movement. And the analysis has met with greater difficulties the more the problems of ethics have been allowed to come to the front. In this confusion with purely

[1] *Cf. Grundz. d. phys. Psych.*, II, 6th ed., pp. 368 *ff.*
[2] *Psychologische Analysen*, Bd. II, 1878.
[3] *Cf., e. g.*, E. B. Titchener, *A Text-Book of Psychology*, I, 1909, § 74.

philosophical questions the history of volitional theories shows clearly again that change in view-point that has determined the fate of so many psychological theories.

The theory of volition was naturally influenced by the original intellectualism of all psychological theories. Obviously, here has been chosen as a starting-point that stage in the developed volitional act that seems to be experienced as a choice between possibilities and which seems to show most clearly its dependence upon intellectual processes. In contradistinction to these intellectualistic theories we have the absolute ones which, emphasizing the experience of decision or resolution, regard the will as a transcendental power or faculty. Common to both these volitional theories is the fact that they are nourished by the ethical problem of the freedom of the will. Among the theories that consider the psychological constitution of volitional experiences we have, first of all, a group of heterogenetic theories which attempt to deduce the will from other psychical processes. When more emphasis is laid upon the feelings that accompany every act of will we are led gradually from the latter theories to the emotional theories of volition.

Even though all these theories of volition have to do with the same problem, yet we are scarcely justified in judging the older theories by the same standards by which we judge the modern theories. For modern psychology has found in the reaction experiment a help toward an extraordinarily refined quantitative and qualitative analysis.[1] The old struggle about the problem of the freedom of the will is entirely different from the careful description of simple volitional processes which modern psychology attempts to give.

[1] *Cf., e. g.*, N. Ach, *Über die Willenstätigkeit und das Denken*, 1905.

## (a) *Intellectualistic Theories of Volition*

The compelling motive in the intellectualistic theories which made volition dependent upon cognition has been the problem of the freedom of the will. The latter has itself gone through many changes. The conception of freedom, a product of ancient thought, was superseded in the Middle Ages by the unfathomable controversies as to the primacy of the will or the intellect, until in modern philosophy the classical period of the problem of the freedom of the will, with its metaphysical conception of freedom, prepared the way for the transition to the absolute theories of volition.

### (1) THE ANCIENT CONCEPT OF FREEDOM

The concept of freedom arrived at in ethics led up to the question of the motivation of actions. Socrates had connected freedom of action with correct knowledge or insight. Plato at first maintained a purely psychological freedom but at the same time adhered to the Socratic contention that the bad man, wanting in right knowledge, does not act with freedom. Aristotle arrived at a provisional conclusion inasmuch as within the larger psychological division of willing and desiring he set aside voluntary actions as the subject-matter for ethics, although these actions themselves arise from a decision deep-rooted in the man himself. The deeper underlying problem was disclosed when the recognition of the unity of all natural phenomena demanded by logic came into opposition with the freedom of the will demanded by ethics. This happened in the philosophy of the Stoics. In spite of all attempts to save the freedom of the will by means of artificial differentiation, as, for example, that of Chrysippus into chief and secondary causes, the Stoics generally ended in an unequivocal determinism.

One thing must not be forgotten in this survey of the ancient theories of volition, namely, that the concept of freedom of choice in the sense of arbitrary choice was quite foreign to them. Absolute freedom of choice, which baffles all philosophical comprehension, points clearly to that period during which most of such irrational elements found their way into philosophy, namely, the Patristic period. The dogmas of original sin, of divine grace, and of predestination demanded kinds of freedom different from that bequeathed by antiquity, the unequivocal determination of the will by the idea of the good. If the latter contains a *non posse peccare*, then mankind must also have a *posse non peccare* or the *possibilitas boni et mali*. These are the dogmatic problems of the famous theory of freedom of Augustine, the unavoidable ambiguities of which gave rise to those endless disputes which the history of the church has recorded for us.

### (2) THE PRIMACY OF WILL OR INTELLECT

The two boundaries between which Scholastic theories of will moved are laid down, on the one hand, by the description of the will as a *syllogismus practicus*, which explains will as an activity of the intellect, and, on the other hand, by the concept of the *actus purus*, which recognizes the will as an absolute faculty. In the important discussion as to the primacy of the will or the intellect between Thomas Aquinas and Duns Scotus, besides metaphysical and dialectical appeals, psychological ones were also introduced, the most important of the former being that of intentional relationship.[1] Under this view-point the ranking of the psychical

[1] *Cf.* above, pp. 74 *f.*

functions was determined by the objects to which they referred. The will aims at the *bonum*, the intellect at the *verum*. The Thomists placed the *verum* above the *bonum* and from that deduced the primacy of the intellect over the reason. The Scotists followed the converse line of reasoning. Or, again, the Thomists maintained that the intellect seeks the general *verum*, whereas the will only desires the special *bonum*. The Scotists then put the general *bonum* as the object of the will and in this way retained their original order of values. The common presuppositions of these arguments, viz., that the real effectiveness of the functions themselves corresponds to the relative value of the psychical functions and these again to the order in rank of the objects to which they refer, is a striking example of the reaction of the constitution of the outside object upon the conception of the psychical processes, a reaction that we have noticed in several other places.[1]

The contrast between the two parties is seen again in the problem of the freedom of the will. The Thomists declared that the will must necessarily strive for that which is recognized as good by the intellect. Of psychological free choice there remained only the fact that the will decides upon the best of the possibilities shown to it by the intellect. This theory logically ended in intellectual determinism in Thomas Aquinas. Against this the criticism of his opponents was naturally directed. They unanimously declared that with a will dependent in this manner upon its ideas the possibility of acting otherwise, and therewith all responsibility, came to an end. Therefore, Duns Scotus reserved for the will the freedom of choice in contradistinction to the impulses or desires arising from pleasure or pain which must necessarily follow their motives.[2] Ideas

[1] *Cf.* p. 144.
[2] *Cf.* Siebeck, *Ztschr. f. Phil. u. phil. Krit.*, Bd. CXII, p. 179.

are reduced to the rank of occasional causes. In the more or less confused mass of ideas only those are clearly perceived upon which the will spontaneously directs its attention and by so doing increases their intensity. This combination of will and attention was a far-reaching idea which was not logically followed out and which only arose again in modern theories of volition, where the elementary phenomenon of volition is transferred to the impulsive apperception of an idea of movement.[1]

Several of the pupils of Duns Scotus tried by a slight approach to the Thomistic standpoint to tone down the blunt autocracy of the will, which with their master had really made impossible any genuine motivation. Petrus Aureolus supplied the will, which still retained the capacity of arousing itself, with an intellectual activity dependent upon the will but yet knowing the aim of the will. The resulting relationship he expressed by the comparison that the sailor at first moves the ship and this having become the means of movement in its turn accidentally moves the sailor. These attempts at agreement were ruined by the accentuation of indeterminism by William of Occam. He gave the problem of the will a new view-point inasmuch as he brought the affective side of our life into connection with the volitional processes. To the will itself he ascribed perfect freedom in the sense of arbitrary choice. The acme, however, is reached in Buridan's theory of freedom, which inaugurated a new epoch in the treatment of the problem of the will.

(3) THE CLASSICAL PERIOD OF THE PROBLEM OF THE FREEDOM OF THE WILL

In his investigations on the will Buridan brought the traditional theory of freedom into connection with the be-

[1] See below, p. 370.

ginnings of a psychical mechanism.[1] The will is not a special power in addition to the intellect but rather an activity of the soul proceeding in another direction. After a judgment as to the acceptability of an object there necessarily follows pleasure or displeasure, which stimulates the will. To the latter Buridan gives the power of *liberum arbitrium*. It is free to decide when the motives are of exactly equal intensity. There is no such thing as choice if the will decides for the good. Now, since it is supposed to do this by necessity, there is a contradiction in Buridan's theory of the will which is to some extent smoothed over by the fact that true freedom lies in the power of the will to keep the motives before the intellect long enough for true insight to be reached.

At any rate, Buridan abandoned the idea that the will could decide without any motives. The freedom of man in comparison to the non-freedom of animals was illustrated by the famous picture, ascribed to him, of the donkey that was bound to die of hunger if placed between two bundles of hay of exactly the same size.

The age of Buridan and his immediate successors has been called the classical period of psychological thought for the theory of the will from the time of Augustine to Leibniz. Occam's conception of freedom as the undivided, that is, not affected by more or less, occurs again in Descartes' *Méditations*. His indeterminism is just as much an anticipation of Kant's doctrine of the intelligible character as Buridan's opinion of freedom as the *libertas finalis ordinationis* is an anticipation of the Herbartian conception of "inner freedom" as a harmony between insight and will. In the period from Descartes to Kant the problem of the freedom of the will remains the central problem in the

[1] *Cf.* Siebeck, *Beiträge zur Entstehungsgeschichte der neueren Psychologie*, 1871.

field of volitional theory. From the mass of attempted solutions not much of importance has resulted for psychology. Descartes' theory of the will did not advance beyond the intellectualistic standpoint of Scholasticism. True freedom consists herein: with imperfect knowledge to restrain from willing and with perfect knowledge to allow that knowledge to work as the decisive motive. The attempt to explain psychologically this notion of freedom came to grief in the theory that imperfect knowledge was connected with the movement of the nerve spirits.[1] All this resulted in the dominance of an intellectualistic ethics and a spiritualistic metaphysics. Locke, with his unpretentious remark that freedom as a faculty cannot possibly be attributed to the will, itself a faculty, did not add anything to the psychology of the problem. He came nearer to psychological experience when he allowed uneasiness, a feeling, to function as a motive for the will. The more insistent the metaphysical side of the problem of the will became the less the traditional intellectualistic theory sufficed to give a satisfactory solution.

### (b) *The Absolute Theory of the Will*

All the difficulties which were bound to overtake an intellectualistic theory of volition were solved at one stroke by the absolute theory inasmuch as it transformed the will into a transcendental faculty. When Kant raised this pure will to the rank of the intelligible character of man he not only crowned his own solution of the problem of the freedom of the will but he also pointed the way for future metaphysics of volition; namely, that metaphysic suggested by Maine de Biran which triumphed in the philosophy of Schopenhauer and which in Hartmann was fused with the

[1] *Les passions de l'âme*, I, arts. 47–50.

results of modern science. In Schopenhauer's theory of the will, which follows from his metaphysical presuppositions, every true act of will must also of necessity be a movement of the body. This shuts out the inner acts of will to which there corresponds no visible movement of the body. Through an obvious misunderstanding of their psychological peculiarities, these were grouped along with the intellectual processes.

The invasion of the field of empirical psychology by a conception of the will partly derived from logic and metaphysics is already seen in Beneke, who relegated the tendencies of the original faculties to the sphere of the unconscious.[1] Later on Fortlage saw in the elementary impulse the solution of the riddle as to how consciousness arises out of unconscious psychical phenomena.[2] The impulse anticipates a subsequent perception. Its immediate satisfaction would not rise to consciousness. But as soon as this is postponed there arises an intermediate state of doubt or of straining of the attention, *i. e.*, consciousness.

A peculiar use of the absolute theory of the will is met with in several physiologists dealing with the senses. Hand in hand with the nativistic explanation of spatial perception there goes the belief in the influence of pure will to carry out movements of the eye, and this is supposed to be an important addition to the contents of the sensations.[3] In their mixture of physiological and transcendental motives theories of this kind reflect the many-sided nature of the problems of sense-perception.

[1] *Cf.* O. Külpe, *Wundts Phil. Stud.*, Bd. V, 1889, pp. 179, 381.
[2] *System der Psychologie*, 1855, I, pp. 53 *ff*.
[3] See, for example, E. Mach, *Beiträge zur Analyse der Empfindungen*, 1886, p. 57.

### (c) Heterogenetic Theories of the Will

The heterogenetic theories of volition arose through the influence of the assistance given by association psychology. A unified form was given to them by Herbart,[1] for whom each idea below the threshold of consciousness changed itself into a striving toward an idea. The experience of desire is occasioned when the rising into consciousness of an idea is hindered. Suppose, for example, an idea $a$ is associated with $a$; now if during the time that an idea $\beta$ opposed to $a$ is dominant in consciousness $a$ is reproduced by a new perception, then $a$ is at one and the same time propelled and repelled, and in so far as it is surmounting the resistance it is desire or impulse. If to this desire fulfilment is added, it passes over into volition proper. Voluntary movements arise by means of the associations of feelings with perceived movements.

More modern attempts to derive volitional processes from such psychical components as do not yet contain the peculiar quality of striving or conation can be grouped partly under the purely genetic and partly under the physiological standpoint. In the former case the will is pictured as a combination of idea and feeling, as, for example, in Th. Waitz.[2] Desire, for example, is the unpleasant feeling that arises when some pleasant idea is at the same time recognized as not present to the senses. In H. Spencer the simple act of will is pushed still further back to the mental representation of the act, which follows the actual accomplishment of the act. The complex volitional act is preceded by a reproduction of the nervous excitation which actually occurred during a former action. Since, however,

---

[1] *Lehrbuch der Psychologie, Werke,* Hartenstein ed., vol. V.
[2] *Lehrb. d. Psych.*, 1849, § 40, pp. 417 *ff.*

this itself consisted in the idea of a movement combined with feeling, the will itself consists in a reproduction of this idea.

The opposite line of thought, according to which will is a development of feeling, is represented in the standpoint of Horwicz.[1] For him feeling is the elementary psychical process out of which both idea and will have been developed. The whole development of the will is traced back to impulse, and this, according to Horwicz, consists of a feeling of pleasure and displeasure which shows itself in movements.[2]

Among those who from the physiological standpoint have refused to admit volitional processes as elementary psychical functions, Münsterberg[3] has been one of the most influential. The totality of physiological processes which lead up to an act of volition forms an unbroken chain of cause and effect, and there is nowhere any room for the introduction of a psychical factor. According to his fundamental principle that sensations are the most elementary, unanalyzable parts of consciousness,[4] he reduces this problem to the question as to what quality, intensity, and feeling tone characterize the sensations making up our will. Following the first hypothesis, he comes to the same conclusion as Hobbes and considers all volitional processes as complicated reflexes and attempts biogenetically to trace the evolution of voluntary acts out of useful reflexes. His second hypothesis leads him to take the decisive step of analyzing the outer volitional action into its psychological parts, which he finds to be sensations of innervation. If, before a real movement, certain muscle sensations are anticipated, they produce the conscious state called willing.

[1] *Zur Entwicklungsgeschichte des Willens*, 1876.
[3] *Die Willenshandlung*, 1888.
[2] *Cf.* p. 359.
[4] *Cf.* p. 209.

### (d) The Emotional Theory of the Will

The starting-point of those modern theories of the will which take into account the affective side accompanying every volitional process is to be found in the eighteenth century in David Hume. Very probably stimulated by Shaftesbury's theory of the emotions, he based his theory of volition upon his theory of the emotions in the clear knowledge that the will never comes into being without a characteristic affective accompaniment.[1] In the nineteenth century Bain moved along similar lines of thought, for he discovered the elements of volition in a spontaneous activity which is guided by feelings. Every pleasure is connected with an increase and every pain with a decrease of the general vital functions. The connection with the feelings of certain outer activities calling forth pleasure and avoiding pain is then explained from the standpoint of association psychology.

The further development of the emotional theory of volition was partly determined by the general classification of the contents of consciousness. If only two kinds of psychical elements are supposed to exist—feelings and sensations—then it is necessary to show the affective elements contained in our volitional experiences. Along these lines lies Wundt's theory of volition, in which feeling, emotion, and will form progressive stages of processes that belong together, and in which the apperception of a psychical content is held to be the elementary form of a volitional process. The outer volitional act, regarded as a phenomenon of consciousness, becomes nothing else than an impulsive apperception of an idea of movement.

T. Lipps arrived at another form of emotional theory of

[1] *A Treatise of Human Nature*, bk. II, part III, sect. III.

volition. According to the requirement[1] made by him of adding to every content of consciousness the real psychical process appearing in it, we postulate, on the basis of the experienced feeling of effort, a real psychical process of effort or striving which represents a psychical activity that is hindered or overcomes hindrances in its natural progress. The result of such a hindrance is pictured as a blocking, which results in an increase of the psychical activity. Here Lipps is following precisely in the spirit of Herbart's psychical mechanics. His endeavor at first had been to transplant the Herbartian ideas from the realm of metaphysics to the region of experience,[2] but this was abandoned after an insight into the insolubility of such problems. Now Lipps recognizes it as incomprehensible how it happens that we experience in outer volitional action the bodily activity as our own activity; we have no insight into the manner in which the bodily sensations might arise out of such an activity. Instead of the influence of the soul upon the body, we must postulate a real psychical process which corresponds to an unknown bodily process, and thus the psychology of Lipps ends again in metaphysics.

In contrast to these emotional theories we find in most recent times an attempt to reduce the phenomena of volition to the facts of reproduction and association, and chiefly to the so-called persevering and determining tendencies. This opinion is held by Külpe and the psychologists of his school, and has been investigated experimentally. The discovery of the determining tendencies seems to point to a new concept that will be of the greatest importance in this branch of psychology.[3] A similar line of thought is found in the volitional theory of Meumann, who

[1] See p. 43.
[2] *Grundtatsachen des Seelenlebens*, pp. 19 *ff*., 594 *ff*.
[3] *Cf.* N. Ach, *Über den Willensakt und das Temperament*, 1910; on the introduction of the term "determination," see p. 286.

considers the chief part of the volitional process to be the phenomenon of selection that is occasioned by approved ideas directed toward a certain end.[1]

[1] E. Meumann, *Intelligenz und Wille*, 1908, p. 191.

# INDEX OF NAMES

Ach, N., 136, 137, 211, 360, 371.
Agrippa of Nettesheym, 56.
Aguillonius, F²., 283, 324.
Albert von Bollstädt, 172.
Albertus Magnus, 272, 334.
Alcuin, 21.
d'Alembert, 149, 158, 311.
Alexander of Aphrodisias, 73, 168, 281, 282, 334.
Alexander of Hales, 54.
Alhacen, 7, 317, 318, 319, 320, 325.
Amerbach, 75.
Ampère, 65.
Anaxagoras, 16, 17, 26.
Angell, 165.
Anselm of Canterbury, 75.
Aquinas, 9, 22, 54, 74, 75, 169, 179, 194, 362, 363.
Arago, 132, 238.
Aresas of Croton, 47.
Aristotle, 5, 7, 8, 18, 19, 21, 26, 27, 48, 50, 54, 56, 60, 68, 72, 73, 74, 89, 90, 149, 167, 169, 179, 180, 182, 193, 200, 269, 271, 273, 274, 280, 281, 284, 285, 286, 298, 317, 324, 347, 348, 350, 352, 361.
Armatus, Salvinus, 323.
Arnobius of Sicca, 35.
Aubert, 292.
Augustine, 20, 50, 74, 168, 193, 281, 316, 362, 365.
Augustus, 91.
Aureolus, 364.
Avenarius, 163.
Averroës, 21.
Avicenna, 53, 54, 74, 91.

Bacon, Francis, 3, 36, 148, 149.
Bacon, Roger, 55.
Baeumker, 271, 334.
Bain, Alex., 102, 161, 175, 180, 204, 335, 340, 348, 370.

Baldwin, J. M., 10, 11, 139.
Barach, 52.
Bastian, 41.
Baumgarten, 78, 99.
Becker, J. J., 147.
Bell, C., 229.
Bendavid, L., 313.
Bendixen, 230.
Beneke, 67, 81, 156, 178, 180, 367.
Bergemann, 88.
Berkeley, 27, 28, 76, 77, 161, 199, 325, 328, 334, 335.
Bernouilli, 224, 225, 240, 321.
Bernstein, 246, 247.
Bessel, 131.
Biunde, 80.
Blix, 342.
Boerhave, 120.
Boethius, 72.
Bonacursius, 287.
Bonatelli, 128.
Bonnet, 62, 77, 94, 96, 120, 183, 184, 186, 275, 276, 353.
Bouguer, 237, 238.
Boyle, 272, 284.
Brentano, 82, 84, 85, 154, 159, 160, 161, 163, 175, 178, 179, 180, 200, 201, 202, 205, 248, 260, 349.
Brett, 10.
Brewster, 288.
Broca, 122.
Brown, 100, 196.
Brücke, 125, 330.
Büchner, 40.
Buffon, 61, 288.
Burdach, 30.
Buridan, 91, 182, 236, 282, 353, 364, 365.
Burnet, 15.

Cabanis, 28.
Cardanus, 288.

## INDEX OF NAMES

Carus, C. G., 30, 67, 114.
Carus, F. A., 8.
Casmann, 22, 57, 75.
Castel, 285.
Chrysippus, 361.
Chun, 278.
Cicero, 91.
Clauberg, 58.
Cleomedes, 279.
Cohen, 159.
Comte, 81, 82, 154, 215, 217.
Condillac, 28, 77, 113, 114, 186, 199, 297, 328.
Confucius, 309.
Constantine of Carthage, 52.
Cornelius, 102, 163.
Cotes, 224.
Cotugno, 298.
Cousin, 51, 53.
v. Craanen, 93.
Creighton, 115.
Crusius, 61.
Czermak, 342.
Czolbe, 40.

Damascenus, 52.
Darwin, 115, 116, 229, 277.
Davy, 281.
Delbœuf, 248, 249, 250, 253, 256.
Delezenne, 241.
Democritus, 5, 33, 34, 37, 47, 145, 280, 334.
Descartes, 7, 22, 23, 36, 51, 58, 60, 76, 93, 113, 120, 154, 161, 169, 170, 274, 275, 321, 322, 353, 365, 366.
Dessoir, 9, 10, 57, 98.
Dicæarchus, 34, 49.
Diderot, 38, 39, 99, 149, 150.
Digby, 120.
Dilthey, 210.
Diodorus of Tyre, 49.
Diogenes of Apollonia, 33, 88, 181.
Dionysos, 16.
Domrich, 348, 355.
Donders, 125, 133.
Drobisch, 107.
Dunn, 325.

Duns Scotus, 31, 55, 194, 362, 363, 364.
Dürr, 157.

Ebbinghaus, 2, 207, 213, 219.
Eberhard, 234.
Eckhart, 8, 194.
Edwards, 139.
Ellis, 299.
Empedocles, 15, 273, 280.
Epicurus, 34, 35, 36, 280.
Erdmann, 68, 156.
Eschenmayer, 235.
Estève, 311.
Euclid, 279, 325.
Euler, 309, 310.
Ewald, 307, 308.
Exner, 68.
v. Eyck, 323.

Fechner, 99, 110, 125, 129, 130, 133, 138, 175, 178, 218, 219, 220, 221, 222, 223, 226, 227, 228, 232, 234, 239, 240, 242, 243, 244, 245, 246, 249, 252, 253, 254, 255, 257, 259, 261, 262, 263, 266, 267, 288.
Feder, 117.
Féré, 229, 230.
Fichte, J. G., 104, 114, 170, 171, 174.
Fichte, J. H., 30.
Fischer, 30.
Fischer, K., 9, 30.
Fisher, 10.
Flammarion, 3.
Flourens, 121.
Fortlage, 81, 367.
Fortuninus Licetus, 36.
Fouillé, 185.
Fourier, 308.
v. Frey, 343.
Fries, 64, 104.
Fritsch, 123.

Galen, 48, 52, 57, 74, 168, 323.
Galileo, 2, 269, 272.
Galin, 241.
Gall, 121, 154, 215.
Galuppi, 235.

## INDEX OF NAMES

Gasparin, 3.
Gassendi, 36, 37, 325.
Gauss, 225, 226.
Geiger, 115.
George, 199, 339, 351.
Gerhard, 173.
Gerhardt, 233.
Gladstone, 115.
Gockel, 22, 147.
Goethe, 284, 285, 286, 292.
Goltz, 277.
Gouye, 325.
Gregory of Nyssa, 20, 50.
Gruithuisen, 143.

Haas, 279.
Haeckel, 41.
Hagen, 355.
Haller, 117, 120, 321.
Hamann, 153.
Hamilton, 83, 101, 156, 173, 176, 184, 187, 188, 197, 200, 201, 215.
Harless, 298, 299.
Hartenstein, 104, 368.
Hartley, 38, 92, 93, 94, 95, 103, 161, 199.
v. Hartmann, 9, 114, 132, 174, 176, 366.
Hasner, 332.
Hasse, 302.
Hauser, 288.
Hegel, 67, 68, 351.
Heinrich von Hessen, 272.
Heinroth, 30.
Helmholtz, 124, 125, 126, 127, 132, 133, 174, 176, 177, 245, 277, 287, 288, 290, 291, 292, 293, 294, 297, 299, 300, 301, 302, 303, 304, 305, 306, 307, 308, 311, 312, 313, 333, 335, 336.
van Helmont, 57.
Hensen, 302, 304.
Heraclitus, 14, 15, 17, 281.
Herbart, 29, 30, 65, 66, 67, 80, 90, 103, 104, 105, 106, 107, 108, 110, 111, 122, 124, 151, 153, 161, 174, 179, 182, 185, 197, 199, 201, 208, 210, 214, 298, 337, 338, 353, 354, 368, 371.

Herder, 99, 117, 153.
Hering, 117, 249, 250, 251, 256, 260, 261, 292, 293, 294, 295, 296, 331, 332, 333.
Hermann, 304, 305, 306, 331.
Herophilus, 48.
Heros, 279.
Herschel, 238.
Herz, 97, 153.
Heymans, 265.
Hickok, 139.
Hilary of Poitiers, 35.
Hipparchus, 238.
Hirsch, 132.
Hissmann, 62, 95.
Hitzig, 123.
Hobbes, 36, 37, 76, 92, 214, 369.
Hoffbauer, 97.
Höffding, 102, 137, 169.
Holbach, 38.
Home, 99.
Horwicz, 216, 217, 277, 348, 359, 369.
Huarte, 57.
Hugo of St. Victor, 21.
Hume, 31, 76, 77, 92, 170, 186, 196, 199, 214, 351, 370.
Husserl, 85, 157, 189, 205, 206.

Irwing, 62, 96.
Isaac of Stella, 21.
Itelson, 233.

de Jaager, 133.
Jäger, 41, 116.
Jakob, 97.
James, 229, 357.
Jesus, 18.
Jodl, 206, 349.
John of Salisbury, 53.
Jouffroy, 65.
Judd, 13.
Jurin, 288, 326.

Kant, 9, 28, 31, 39, 40, 63, 64, 79, 97, 100, 104, 124, 150, 151, 152, 153, 156, 161, 170, 196, 200, 203, 234, 275, 326, 351, 365, 366.
Kepler, 272, 283, 320, 321, 323, 324.

## INDEX OF NAMES

Kinnebrook, 131.
Kircher, 287, 309.
Kirnberger, 241.
Knutzen, 151.
Koenig, 304, 305.
Kölliker, 329.
Krause, 23.
von Kries, 255, 256, 266, 291, 293, 294, 295, 296.
Krueger, F., 270, 314, 315.
Krug, 63, 197.
Külpe, 108, 349, 352, 367, 371.
Kurella, 229.

Lacaille, 237.
Lactantius, 281.
Ladd Franklin, 295.
Lagrange, 224, 304.
Lamarck, 114.
Lambert, 117, 224. 226, 236, 237.
Lamettrie, 38.
Lancisi, 120.
Lange, C., 229, 230, 357.
Lange, F. A., 33, 81, 82, 176.
Langer, 250.
Laplace, 226, 240.
Laromiguière, 186.
Lazarus, 111.
Lehmann, 102, 230.
Leibniz, 9, 27, 28, 29, 59, 60, 77, 104, 117, 139, 147, 171, 172, 173, 177, 185, 199, 214, 233, 234, 310, 351, 365.
Lelut, 80.
Leuckart, 278.
Lewes, 174, 176, 203, 277.
Liebig, 126.
Linné, 61.
Lipps, G. F., 224, 228, 267.
Lipps, T., 31, 43, 100, 110, 175, 205, 264, 265, 310, 315, 344, 345, 349, 370, 371.
Listing, 125.
Locke, 7, 27, 58, 59, 60, 72, 76, 77, 83, 92, 160, 169, 173, 182, 184, 186, 195, 196, 198, 203, 271, 272, 275, 326, 328, 334, 350, 366.
Loeb, 42, 115.
Lossius, 62, 95, 96, 187, 297.

Lotze, 30, 100, 108, 110, 175, 180, 197, 198, 200, 201, 329, 340, 341, 342, 344, 356.
Lubbock, 112.
Lullus, 147, 148.

Maass, 98.
Mach, 134, 163, 246, 253, 292, 307, 367.
Magendie, 121.
Magnus, 116.
Maine de Biran, 28, 29, 366.
Malebranche, 92, 93, 173, 233, 284, 334.
Mantegazza, 41.
Marbe, 137.
Mariotte, 321.
Marpurg, 241.
Martineau, 154.
Maskelyne, 131.
Masson, 238.
Maudsley, 82, 174, 176, 215, 216.
Maupertuis, 39.
Maximus of Tyre, 90.
Maxwell, 3.
Meiners, 78.
Meinong, 266.
Meissner, 342.
Melanchthon, 147.
Mendelssohn, 151, 196.
Merkel, 222.
Methodius of Tyre, 35.
Metzner, 343.
Meumann, 371, 372.
Meyer, J. B., 150.
Meyer, M., 306.
Meynert, 94, 122, 356.
Michalski, 3.
Michelet, 68.
Mill, J., 101, 173, 335, 348.
Mill, J. S., 82, 96, 101, 126, 127, 156, 160, 175, 180, 215, 335, 348.
Mittenzwey, 185.
Moleschott, 40.
Molyneux, 325, 326.
Montaigne, 57.
Moritz, 118.
Mosso, 229, 230.

## INDEX OF NAMES

Müller, F. A., 254.
Müller, G. E., 219, 227, 228, 232, 257, 259, 260, 261, 262, 296.
Müller, J., 124, 125, 126, 132, 276, 277, 298, 323, 324, 326, 327, 330, 333, 356.
Müller, J. J., 251, 252.
Munk, 122,
Münsterberg, 162, 208, 209, 369.

Nagel, A., 330.
Nagel, W., 278.
Nahlowsky, 348.
Natorp, 158, 189.
Nemesius, 20, 274.
Nero, 323.
Newton, 214, 284, 285, 286, 288, 290.
Notker, 72.
Nuguet, 285.

Occam, 55, 364, 365.
Opelt, 310.
Origen, 19.

van der Paele, 323.
Panum, 125, 331, 333.
Paracelsus, 56, 57, 283.
Parinaud, 294.
Parmenides, 88.
Paulsen, 31.
Philo, 18, 50, 75.
Plateau, 222, 248, 249, 260, 288, 289.
Plato, 14, 17, 18, 20, 23, 47, 48, 56, 69, 72, 89, 144, 145, 167, 193, 214, 317, 361.
Plattner, 96, 120, 161.
Pliny, 281, 323.
Plotinus, 19, 20, 91, 168, 281.
Ploucquet, 117, 233.
Poincaré, 10.
Poisson, 240.
Porphyry, 20, 274.
Porro, 3.
Porta, 320, 323.
Porter, 139.
Porterfield, 330.

Preyer, 117.
Priestley, 38.
Prieur de la Côte-d'Or, 288.
Ptolemy, 279, 324.
Purkinje, 124.
Pythagoras, 308, 352.
Pythagoreans, 15, 308.

Rádl, 41, 113.
Rameau, 311.
Ranke, 278.
Rehmke, 163, 210.
Reid, 196.
Reimann, 324.
Reimarus, 113, 115, 151.
Reinhold, 64.
Renz, 223.
Rhode, 17.
Ribot, 9, 11, 356.
Rickert, 162.
Riehl, 157.
Romieu, 311.
Rosenkranz, 40, 68.
Rumford, 289.

Sauveur, 311.
Scaliger, 283.
Schaefer, 308.
Scheiner, 320.
Schelling, 7, 30, 67, 114, 124, 127, 174.
Scherffer, 288.
Scheuchzer, 98.
Schleicher, 116.
Schleiden, 331.
Schmucker, 139.
Schneider, 254.
Schopenhauer, 31, 114, 286, 366, 367.
v. Schubert, 30, 68.
Schultze, 294.
Schulze-Ænesidemus, 65, 80.
Schütz, 234.
Scotus Erigena, 74.
Seebeck, 299.
von Selpert, 121.
Seneca, 171.
Sennert, 35.
Shaftesbury, 370.

# INDEX OF NAMES

Siebeck, 8, 9, 21, 51, 52, 53, 54, 55, 90, 168, 193, 317, 363, 365.
Sigwart, 157.
Simon Portius, 283.
Simonides, 91.
Simpson, 224.
Smith, 288, 325, 326.
Socrates, 18, 361.
Sommer, 351.
Sophia Charlotte, 38.
Sorge, 303.
Speck, 94.
Spencer, 41, 103, 112, 140, 154, 161, 175, 199, 204, 368.
Spinoza, 25, 38, 124, 161, 214.
Steinbuch, 339.
Steinheil, 223, 239.
Steinthal, 111.
Stern, 118.
Stoics, 34, 35, 49, 171, 282, 361, 362.
Strato, 34, 73.
Strunz, 57.
Stumpf, 124, 206, 312, 313, 314, 315, 333.
Suçruta, 279.
Sulzer, 241.

Tartini, 311.
Telesius, 283.
Tertullian, 35, 50.
Tetens, 62, 78, 153, 196.
Theophrastus, 273, 280.
Thomas, 33.
Thury, 3.
Tiberius, 288.
Titchener, 115, 194, 357, 359.
Toland, 37.
du Tour, 323.
Tso-kiu-ming, 309.
Tumarkin, 99.
Tylor, 112.

Überhorst, 248.
Überweg, 82.
Ulrici, 80, 175, 177, 180, 254, 255.

Valentin, 143.
Vico, 112.
Vierordt, 134, 135, 223.

da Vinci, 289, 292.
Virchow, 41.
Vitellio, 325.
Vives, 7, 56, 92, 169.
Vogt, 41.
Voigt, 305.
Volkelt, 137.
Volkmann, A. W., 125.
Volkmann, W. F., 9, 108, 200, 348.

Waetzmann, 308.
Wagner, 41.
Waitz, 107, 338, 348, 351, 368.
Waldeyer, 302.
Waller, 290.
Wasmann, 115.
Watson, 165.
Weber, E. H., 127, 130, 220, 221, 239, 240, 242, 244, 328, 329, 330, 342, 356.
Weber, W., 129.
Weigel, 72.
Weininger, 118.
Weiss, 104.
Wheatstone, 325.
William of Conches, 52.
Willmann, 192.
Willy, 163.
Windelband, 135, 157.
Wirth, 131, 181, 188, 264.
Witelo, 317.
Wolf, 223.
Wolff, 7, 59, 60, 61, 78, 147, 150, 196, 203, 217, 233, 234, 351.
de Wulf, 6.
Wundt, 4, 9, 13, 31, 32, 44, 102, 111, 112, 115, 123, 133, 134, 135, 153, 157, 162, 163, 175, 180, 185, 207, 210, 217, 218, 219, 232, 250, 254, 257, 262, 263, 265, 294, 295, 320, 343, 344, 349, 358, 370.

Young, 277, 290, 294, 304.

Zahlfleisch, 281.
Zeller, 255.
Zeno, 352.
Ziehen, 94.
Zöllner, 174, 176.

# INDEX OF SUBJECTS

Analysis, principle of, 202–5.
Association, doctrine of, 87–103; beginnings of association psychology, 88–92; dominance of doctrine of, 92–103.
Attention, 184–9.
Audition, theories of, 297–315.

Classification of contents of consciousness, principles of, 191–205; modern forms of, 205–7.
Color theories, modern, 287–296; three-color theory, 290–2; four-color theory, 292–6.
Consciousness, 166–189; history of the concept of, 166–172; early development of the concept of, 166–9; modern concept of, 169–172; range of, 181–4; graduation of, 184–9; classification of contents of, 190–211.
Consonance theories, 308–315.
Contents of consciousness, classification of, 190–211.

Darwinism, influence of, 115–117.
Dualism, 14–24.

Empiricism, 333–6.
Error, theory of, 222–9; Gauss's Law of, 225.

Faculties, doctrine of mental, 44–69; newer psychology of, 58–69.
Feeling, theories of, 346–359; intellectualistic, 350–1; physiological, 355–7; psychomechanical, 352–5; psychophysical, 358–9.
Freedom, ancient conception of, 361–2; of the will, 364–6.
Fusion theory, Herbart's, 337–8.

Ideas, mechanics of, 103–111.
Inner sense, doctrine of, 69–86; older doctrine of, 5, 72–76; as an independent source of experience, 76–82; relation of, to theory of knowledge, 82–86.
Intentional relationship, principle of, 200–2.
Introspection, 212–215.

Light, ancient theories of, 279–283.
Local sign theories, 340–5.

Materialism, 32–42; atomistic, 33–36; mechanistic, 36–38; psychophysical, 38–40.
Measurement, psychical, 232–267; development of methods of, 218–231; early history of, 232–242; earliest suggestions of, 242–4; founding of, by Fechner, 242–4; new foundation of, 257–267.
Methods, psychophysical, 212–231; older forms of, 220–2; expression, 229–231.
Monism, 25–42.

Nativism, 326–333.
Nativistic theories, 330–3.
Non-derivability, principle of, 194–200.

Observation, 212–215.
Occult, relation to modern psychology, 3.
Optics, physical and physiological, 283–7.

Perception, spatial, theories of, 315–345; special problems of, 322–6.

Phenomena, differentiation of physical from psychical, 159–163.
Philosophy, relation to psychology, 156–9.
Phrenology, 119–123.
Physiology, of the senses, influence of, 123–7; as basis of psychology, 215–218.
Psychical element, concept of, 210–211.
Psychologism, 156–9.
Psychology, general characteristics of the history of, 1–2; occult, relation to modern, 3; applications of, 4; beginnings of modern, 7–8; bibliography of history of, 8–11; dualism in, 14–24; metaphysical and empirical tendencies in, 12–14; monism in, 25–42; descriptive, 43–86; explanatory, 87–140; as a mechanics of ideas, 103–111; comparative, 111–118; ethnic, 111–113; animal, 113–115; individual, 117–118; experimental, 127–140; development of the fundamental concepts of, 141–267; idea of, as a science, 141–165; older conceptual formulations of, 147–150; problem of a science of, 150–5; modern concept of, 155–165; and philosophy, 156–9; and natural science, 159–165.
Psychophysics, 245–257; objections to Fechner's, 245–252; philosophical opponents of, 254–7.

Renaissance, 56–58.
Resonance, preliminary history of theory of, 297–9; theory of, 299–303; further developments of theory of, 304–8.

Scholasticism, 50–55.
Science, influence of natural, 119–140; psychology as a, 141–165; natural, and psychology, 159–165.
Sensation, theories of, 268–315; older theories of, 273–5.
Soul, conception of, 12; doctrine of the parts of, 46–50.
Space, empirical theories of, 334–5; Helmholtz's theory of, 335–6; genetic theories of, 337–345.
Specific energy of the nerves, theory of the, 275–8.
Spiritualism, 26–32.

Theories, psychological, 268–372.
Touch, in spatial perception, 327–330.

Unconscious, concept of, 172–181; representatives and opponents of the concept of the, 172–5; arguments for and against, 175–181.

Vision, theories of, 279–296.
Volition, theories of, 359–372; intellectualistic theories of, 361–6.

Weber's Law, 235–242; psychological interpretation of, 262–7.
Will, absolute theory of the, 366–7; heterogenetic theories of the, 368–9; emotional theory of the, 370–2.